LEVITATION

Please return / renew this item by the last date shown above
Dychwelwch / Adnewyddwch erbyn y dyddiad olaf y nodir yma

LEVITATION

THE SCIENCE, MYTH AND MAGIC OF SUSPENSION

PETER ADEY

For Arthur

Published by Reaktion Books Ltd
Unit 32, Waterside
44–48 Wharf Road
London N1 7UX, UK

www.reaktionbooks.co.uk

First published 2017
Copyright © Peter Adey 2017

Printed and bound in Great Britain by TJ International, Padstow, Cornwall

A catalogue record for this book is available from the British Library

ISBN 978 1 78023 737 4

Contents

1 Balance 7

2 Faking on Air 55

3 Science, Spiritualism and Scepticism 87

4 Reverie, Dreams and the Surreal 111

5 Super 147

6 Anti-gravity 185

7 Exorcize the Pentagon 217

8 Luftmenschen 243

References 265
Acknowledgements 285
Photo Acknowledgements 287
Index 289

1 Balance

> I fling myself towards scholarly pleasure measured gravitationally,
> as affecting the weight of bodies, hoping to arrive at being
> scholarly in the middle of the moment where the heavy becomes
> light, where gravity is flight.
>
> NICOLA MASCIANDARO

A FEW YEARS AGO I picked up a second-hand book really because of its cover. It was the *National Geographic Atlas of the World*. And on the front it showed a strange, abstract sort of scene. Above a green carpet of what was presumably grass were lots of figures that looked almost like chess pieces but dressed in the garb of different countries and cultures. They were positioned in the sky, hovering just above the earth. They were definitely levitating just a little bit above the ground, to the extent that their shadows could be made out. Curiously, each figure was positioned slightly differently. Some a little more to the foreground; others a little lower or higher than the rest. This was not a completely abstract scene. I think it was being used as some kind of metaphor for global and geographical difference – to suggest that we all come from different sets of conditions and circumstances that position us unevenly in relation to power, wealth and the social and political relations that could constrain or enable our lives. But what if we were to take the cover more literally? What if we believed that the little pieces playing the game of life were able to levitate, and some more so than others? What if we held on to the book's figurative sense of difference, expressed in the patterning of vertical hierarchies?

This is a book about levitation. That act of the body's lifting up, rising from the ground without mechanical aid or rocket power. Without any help or support, levitation can be miraculous and awe-inspiring, and it can be quite strange and even frightening. Today, of course, modern levity of a rather different kind has become pretty normal and routine. Flying has become a common mode of traversing the globe and even covering shorter distances, but at speed. Flight is gradually becoming made available to not only the rich in the Western world, but more disparate social groups. In Shanghai and elsewhere passengers routinely float on a cushion of magnetic force, relying upon maglev technologies, developed first in the United States and explored in early schemes in Germany, the UK and eventually in China, Japan and South Korea.

Coexisting with the contemporary joys of weightless travel and the condition of being footloose and fancy-free once reserved for the elite is, however, something quite different.[1] There are modes of flight released from the technical apparatus of the jumbo jet or the maglev and the vast infrastructures that support them. There are forms of levity that differ from accounts of the vertical omniscience from an elevated perspective frequently associated with the aerial view, or from the speed and thrust of modern powered flight.[2] Societies have almost always believed it was possible, or desirable, to float unaided in a more vulnerable or prone position, even if only for a moment. Even today magicians and stage artists often thrill and tantalize spectators with feats of levitation. This book is interested in such phenomena.

There are also common cultural encodings of the pull or push of being above, or of rising, especially in opposition to falling and downwardness, which often has highly negative associations. As Jason King shows, these meanings are not only held in common, but are experienced to a disproportionate extent. From within black political movements and culture, literature and music, rising, spiritual ascension, getting up, standing up and uprightness have been common tropes – just as much as shame and embarrassment has been levelled disproportionately at the 'downward' trajectories of black communities, subjected to continual disenfranchisement and social immobility, especially in the United States.[3] *Levitation* often reflects this unevenness.

To some extent *Levitation* could be thought of best as a pre- and parallel history of flight, but it is not really about flight of the aeronautical kind, even if they are difficult to separate. Historians of aviation have told us that the promise of flight cannot be conveniently divided from other myths of ascension. Joseph Corn identified this within *The Winged Gospel*: the messianic yearning for aerial mobility that took such a hold in the United States, launching barnstormers and a general aerial craze – an airmindedness – in all corners of the country. In the U.S., Russia, Germany, France, Britain and elsewhere, pilots and early aviators took on almost godlike properties, just as astronauts would do later. The Italian Futurists would draw similar conclusions, finding in flight a collusion of technology and religion or a new spirituality:

> Our forebears drew their inspiration from a religious atmosphere which fed their souls; in the same way we must breathe in the tangible miracles of contemporary life – the iron network of speedy communication which envelops the earth, the transatlantic liners, the dreadnoughts, those marvellous flights which furrow our skies.[4]

Many authors have articulated the centrifugal energies of flight, spinning out into literature, art, architecture, fashion and design as aviation captured so much of the early twentieth century. Flight meant romance and thrill, before it began to signal its decline into consumer-based capitalism and mundanity. Outside these cultures of flight, levitation is a much more private and stripped-back affair, moving with a logic which is more inward-looking; centripetal, perhaps. We find other energies raining in on levitation from different genres of science, art, religion, culture and politics. In this regard, the book asks what kinds of cultural, political and spiritual lives inhabit the levitator and their believers. What, moreover, can we say about the modes of science, writing, illustration, poetry, philosophy, law, technology and the wider popular, spiritual and visual imagination that has sought to know them?

Non-historical phenomena

It may be that we have always been able to do it; we have always levitated. Mircea Eliade, the historian of religion, determined that the belief and practices of levitational ascent could be found within traditional and customary societies, particularly within the performances of shamanic practice. Pre-modern accounts of elementals, levitations and dream states still persist in shamanic ascensional rites of transcendence in Inuit communities in northern Canada, central Asia and Siberia. In these belief systems, shamans hold the power for spirit flight, possession and bodily levitation. Their customs and forms of oral storytelling hint at a prior history of levity. They suggest that, in a more primordial earth, we once knew how to do this – only we seem to have somehow lost the technique or knowledge through more grounded and rational systems of thought that place their dependence on technology to take us into the air. In a primordial world, Eliade argued, we may have all had the ability to levitate away. Society's descent or degeneration has made us forget or relinquish these abilities so that levitation has had to be learned anew.[5]

For Eliade, and controversially for his critics, accounting for the primordial acceptance of ascent and levitational ecstasy meant conducting something other than straightforward historical inquiry. Levity was not necessarily subject to the structures and conditions of a historical context. The urge or yearning for levity, Eliade argues, should be thought of as a 'nonhistorical phenomenon' too. Levitation belongs as much to 'man as such, not to man as a historical being'. This 'man as such' is the phenomenological world of 'dreams, hallucinations, and images of ascent' that for Eliade can be 'found everywhere in the world, apart from any historical groundwork or other "conditions"'.[6]

Eliade's approach is instructive, but let me be clear that it is not the intention of this book to attempt to abstract levitation away from the deep roots and rhizomes of time, space and culture that make it difficult to tear the levitator from anything like the earth-ing of historical context. And yet, Eliade's approach does free us somewhat. If we might begin to apprehend levitation as an ontological condition of existence, too, then the elevations performed by levitation and its experience may well be enabled to transcend the structures of historical setting. Neither committed to man and woman 'as such' nor as 'historical', this book will spend its time hovering appropriately between the two.

Oppositional forces

What holds the levitator in suspension for a while? As we will see, levitation resembles the skilfulness of finding balance through training, habit or meditation. In early modern science an object's levitative qualities were considered the product of equalling forces working in opposite directions. Lest the levitator shoot off into the heavens or sink and crash to the earth, their floatation had to be balanced. We will come back to this notion later on, because it is worth explicating these early ideas of levity and gravity in early modern science.

Newtonian physics would augur in understandings of gravitation as a force produced by all objects of mass. But it was not always this way. To be sure, the Aristotelian universe understood by way of Plato's *Timaeus* realised that things held a relative lightness and heaviness which could be identified simply by comparing the weight of two objects. Within this school of thought the density of objects had little to do with their weight. In his *On the Heavens*, Aristotle developed the principle of *absolute* lightness and heaviness. By this he supposed that all objects had particular dispositions towards weight and levity. Some tended to want to move upwards, and others down. Some moved towards the extremities of the universe – the periphery – and therefore upwards, or as lightness. And others erred towards the centre – which therefore meant down, or as performing the qualities of weightiness and heaviness.

Neoplatonists had other cosmologies in mind when contemplating the descent (or Fall) and ascension of the soul not under gravity but spiritual attainment, through the influence of Plotinus, Proclus and others.[7] In the fourth century, Iamblichus of Chalcis, father of the rituals of theurgy – practices which closely resembled pagan rituals of purification and religious rites – saw a closer relationship between Athenian philosophy and mysticism with magic. Some of his practising followers were even supposed to have warded off an earthquake – a view which would be reflected in Enlightenment understandings of catastrophe as divine will.[8] But more interesting to us is the rumour which circulated that when Iamblichus prayed he would turn golden and begin to levitate. Eunapius' biography of Iamblichus tells the story of a question once posed by one of his pupils:

'a rumour has reached us through your slaves that when you pray to the gods you soar aloft from the earth more than ten cubits to all appearance; that your body and your garments change to a beautiful golden hue; and presently when your prayer is ended your body becomes as it was before you prayed, and then you come down to earth and associate with us.'[9]

Of course Eunapius' account is not part of a full history of Iamblichus, but instead told through his tendency to narrate by anecdote.[10] Iamblichus, known for other mystical skills of sense and apperception, was apparently not quick to mirth, but he laughed at his student's suggestion. For some, the stories of Iamblichus' levitation closely resemble Jesus' transfiguration as recounted by Mark.[11] For others, the story is revealing of wider notions of Mediterranean and Syrian ascetics and mystics as apparently adorned with special powers. In the Neoplatonic tradition, Iamblichus' levity was not necessarily the first rising in a stage of ascension to heaven or other astral spheres, but an embodiment of godliness. For Iamblichus 'saw the gods here below, hidden in our embodied and aesthetic life'.[12]

Arab physicians, attuned to the body's physiology, would promulgate these notions widely in their published health regimens for sovereigns and princely individuals. The eleventh-century philosopher Avicenna draws on 'absolute lightness' in order to understand the lightening qualities which could be taken into the body and its various chambers.[13] An element like fire was understood to have the qualities of 'absolute lightness', as opposed to air, which held more relatively light qualities compared to other elements. For Avicenna, fire overcame the insubstantiality of air and reduced the coldness of other heavy materials. In every sense fire 'brings the elementary properties into harmony'.[14] Under different conditions lightness could also be drawn into the body by intaking air, and so warming it. Otherwise heat was provided by the friction of a massage, as well as through exercise. The body's liveliness as lightness could be posed in contrast to the 'fall' of sleep.

Equilibrium

The idea that levitation is a kind of tension – balanced between opposing forces of gravity, levity or spirituality, while also walking a tense line between lightness and heaviness, laughter or sombreness, foolhardiness or safety – is a strong one in this book. Levitation is of course political. It is a pulling and pushing, a straining and releasing, that perhaps found other early expression in funambulism, or tightrope walking. Galen would call these practices 'bad art'.[15] *Le Antichità di Ercolano*, a manuscript depicting the engravings discovered in Herculaneum published in the mid-eighteenth century, illustrates an array of tightrope walkers performing various acts and skills on the rope. As the Roman courtier Petronius suggested:

> The hempen rope is extended over wooden supports, and on it the aerial voyager strides, balancing himself with outstretched arms over the abyss, lest his foot slip from the taut cable. Thus doth man's life depend on a rope and a breath of air.[16]

The funambulist was not just an ancient Roman phenomenon. In Britain a tightrope walker who visited the northern city of Durham in the thirteenth century fell to his death, supposedly from between the cathedral's towers. The cathedral vaults the Durham skyline beyond the rocky ground that elevates the city

Engraving from *Le Antichità di Ercolano* (1757–92).

between the River Wear meander, making an impregnable geography for the monks who founded the cathedral. While this may make the cathedral seem weighty and exceptionally heavy, its construction would usher in a new age of levitative Gothic architecture. Utilizing stone ribbed vaults in its construction, Romanesque Durham began to be reworked with new sets of building materials that would become common to the Gothic style – what Friedrich Heer has described as 'numbers, lines of force, and rays of light'.[17] With Durham or Chartres, the vaults of the Gothic cathedrals rose higher; they were 'visions of paradise' giving the 'illusion of floating downwards from celestial heights'. The poet Eugene Jolas described Gothic cathedrals as the geometrical or architectonic expression of the will to '"ascent", "elevation", "levitation", "angelic flight", and so on'.[18]

Our falling tightrope walker was notable because the event formed part of Henry VIII's exceptions to Thomas de Melsonby, Prior of Durham Cathedral, who was seeking election to the position of bishop. Durham's bishopric was a highly regarded seat of power, and the sovereign often sent those to Durham whom he wished to remove to an arm's length. Among other things, allowing the acrobat to walk between two of the cathedral's towers was shown as irresponsible. Henry is believed to have used the funambulist's fall as an excuse to limit the prior's powers. It was a nudge, if not a shove, to his fall from grace. Histories of the *histrio* are finely weighted: they show enthralment at the gaiety of the trickster but, like King Henry, level impropriety at the act. The tightrope-walking funambulist, strung up between two towers, could also have been seen as a mimicry or even mockery of other more spiritual forms of levity.

St Augustine would make this comparison really quite stark. He is mentioned by the poet Théodore de Banville in the context of his criticism of shows and spectacles that regularly included similar feats of levity. As Augustine argues in his expositions on

the Psalms, there is a big difference between the plucky skill of
the tightrope walker, the 'funiambulus' balanced in the air, and
the miracles of a levitator inspired by divine or holy presence:

> After much practice a man has learned to walk a tightrope, and
> as he hangs there balancing he has you hanging in suspense. But
> look at one who achieves feats worth watching. Your acrobat has
> learned to walk on a rope, but he has never made anyone walk on
> the sea, has he?

Elsewhere, Augustine would be just as sceptical of other forms
of levity, grounded as they were in the worship of other gods. In a
passage showing real cynicism at Roman polytheism in *De civitate
dei* (413–26), Augustine comments on the state of theological ideas
in the face of the Sack of Rome in AD 410. The sacking of the city
followed the Roman adoption of Christianity, which would replace
the rites and traditions that had been devoted to the worship of
pagan gods. Augustine's text is a defense of Christianity, and
something of a response to the rich religious elite, who were
contemplating their misfortune as a product of their new Christian
spiritual allegiance. In a long passage, Augustine mocks the range
and assortment of the Roman gods and their apparent commitment
to many quotidian tasks. He ridicules Jupiter for being both
everyone and anything, and thus in Augustine's view, nothing:

> Let him be Diespater, who brings the newly born forth into
> the light of day. Let him be Mena, whom they set over the
> menstruation of women; Lucina, who is invoked by women in
> childbirth; let him bring help to the newly born by receiving
> them into the bosom of the earth, and in this capacity let him be
> called Ops. Let him open their mouths to wail, and be called god
> Vaticanus; let him lift them up from the earth and be called the
> goddess Levana.

In Augustine's typically overwrought prose, he is rehearsing the figure of the goddess Levana. For Augustine, Levana illustrates the polytheism of pagan rituals; she was often invoked in the context of birth and the fatherly duty of lifting a newly born baby from the ground – to raise them up above the earth and from their mother.

Later commentators would hold the funambulist in similar disdain to Augustine. Johannes Leonhardus Schlicher, who published *De funambulis exercitatio philosophica* in 1702, suggests that the funambulist's exposure to danger was an act against God: 'Funambulists, therefore, do a wrong in their recklessness not only against themselves but against God, their creator.'[19] Schlicher's account is one of the most developed of medieval thought to discuss the moral, ethical and to some extent political import of the tightrope walker. This meant seeing the funambulist as sordid and dishonourable, as neglecting 'a proper life', but also harmful to the population of a State: 'the author thinks, a State suffers great loss and injury when the people spend on any empty spectacle money which might be better employed.'[20]

Some appreciated the lightness and spectacle of the aerial walker, seeing their skill and concentration as relevant to the discipline of mind and will. Others saw their danger as all too real. Marcus Aurelius (AD 121–80) is said to have insisted that feather mattresses be used for the protection of wire-walkers, having witnessed the death of a young boy. In Paris in 1385 a rope-walker was balanced between a tower of Notre-Dame and the highest structure on the pont Saint-Michel. Jean Froissart's account concludes, 'He was suche a tumbler, that his lyghtnesse was greatlye praised.'[21] In this balance of skill, will and risk are expectations of who or what can be light. That animals as bulky as an elephant could be taught to walk a rope gives us a strong impression of just how incongruous rope-walking can be. Incongruity is not the only characteristic of the tightrope walker that may have shaped their reception, either. Their mobility and itinerancy would inspire the derogatory remarks directed at their practices; Nicephorus Gregoras (1295–1360) saw a group of rope-walkers take a circuitous tour from Egypt, through Arabia, Persia and Syria and into Iberia.

Sovereignty

The idea of ascent is a common forebear of levitation, especially within the infusion of Neoplatonic thought in Christian doctrine. Spiritual development would be a journey, a path inwards and an ascent via a ladder or a mountain. The vertical, says Denys Turner, historian of medieval philosophy and theology, was the 'spontaneous communal architecture of the divine', remaining today the 'natural metaphor of the individual, as against the communal, relationship with God'. Turner argues that these metaphors of ascent are 'built in to our psychological and epistemological language so intimately that we have, I suspect, quite literally *embodied* them'.[22] Could this be one cause for levitation? Should we consider religious belief an upward thrust enabling the body to hover at least for a little while? Or has religious fervour helped us to mistake remarkable people living in remarkable conditions for levitation?

The mimicry of levity is ambiguous in medieval theological traditions; it could mean sanctity, or the arts of diabolical deception. Christian polemicists such as Embrico of Mainz would exemplify this position in the anti-hagiography *Vita Mahumeti* (*c.* 1100). Written in 1,149 rhymed leonine hexameters in order to resemble the trend of existing hagiographies, Embrico's tract would elide the bodily ascension of the Prophet Muhammad's *Miraj* into heaven with the heresy of the Samaritan and Christian convert Simon Magus. In Embrico's story, Muhammad's ascension is a fraud: God is punishing Muhammad's – in the story, Mammautius's – body for a sin by giving him an epileptic fit. As this is going on, Simon Magus addresses a growing crowd to explain that he has in fact been bestowed with God's love, and angels have taken Mammautius's soul up into heaven. In this regard, Muhammad's ascent becomes a 'cheap imitation' of Christ, or a bogus miracle, just as Magus' levitations were viewed as a distortion, or a mockery of God's power.[23] As we will see, there are levitations that may be understood as good or bad, in motive and consequence, and their provenance matters.

Ideas of levity would proliferate among religious communities and in the spiritual imagination throughout the Middle Ages. In the sixth century, Cosmas Indicopleustes, a traveller-geographer, would depict the cosmos in his *Christian Topography* in the shape of a tabernacle. As Veronica Della Dora has explained, 'The higher part of the structure corresponded to the vaulted heavenly chamber inhabited by God.' The rectangular lower prism encompassed the terrestrial realm. In the Byzantine world, spiritual geographies focused on 'spiritual ascent'. Ascent was tied up with the saints, who were already prone to levitate, and the high places of mountains and other physical summits. As Della Dora explains, mountains have a 'special significance as the closest earthly places to God's abode. Biblical mountains are thus privileged theophanic sites, or *axes mundi* through which the "transcendent might enter the immanent".'[24]

St John Climacus' *The Ladder of Divine Ascent* (AD 600), illustrated in an anonymous twelfth-century painting, combined existing notions of ascent and the divine to deploy a metaphor of ascending a ladder. The device uses the image of thirty rungs of a ladder to depict the vices and virtues one should live by. Leading an ascetic and virtuous life would see someone ascend the rungs to Heaven. Should they fall into vice, they would fall or be dragged kicking and screaming to Hell.

Medieval theological illustrations and scholarship do interesting things with levitators, especially in relation to the figure of Christ arising or ascending to Heaven. These imaginations of the spiritual

ascension of the spirit or body would be set in opposition to understandings of the nature of sovereignty and sovereign power. Classic political theological work has shown in studies of kingship that the sovereign was believed to occupy both an earthly or natural body, and a spiritual form that was endowed by the heavens. The king was both physical and godly, but this was a doctrine that greatly tested liturgical and juridical thinking. Even religious scholarship had its own problems with Christ's potential pre-ascension ascension, as distinct from his literal one. Either his immaterial, spiritual nature and his natural, fleshy nature could have been part of a linear journey comprising a descent from Heaven, death, resurrection and eventual ascension, or a more non-linear climb was possible. This was the view of Faustus Socinus, who in the sixteenth century debated whether Jesus' immaterial nature was able to reside in Heaven even when his natural one was down in his body on earth.[25] Christ, in other words, as well as the king, could have two bodies or several natures.

Socinus' argument also drew on a comparison between Christ's ability to ascend and that of other Christian figures, such as Moses and the disciple Paul. Moses's ascent to Mount Sinai to retrieve the Ten Commandments was understood as an ascent into Heaven; meanwhile, Socinus is unsure whether Paul was raptured into Heaven with his body or not. Such an entwinement also meant that the sanctity of Christ's ascendance was often copied or aspired to, but in ways which gathered more positive associations. Hagiographers seeking to prove the holiness of their saints sought accordance with the life of Jesus. For example, Hilary Powell has shown that St Mildrith achieved renown for leaving a trace of her footprint on a marble stone as she landed at Ebbsfleet on the English Kent coast, resituating the footprints Jesus is said to have left before his ascension.[26] The 'Ebbsfleet stone' is a negative space of presence – the landing an absence that is a permanent print on the rock. The marking inscribed a kind of inverse levitation that

The Ladder of Divine Ascent, St Catherine's Monastery, Sinai Peninsula, Egypt, c. 1150, painted icon.

proved the divine by copying Christ's ascension. We also have the sense that weightlessness may come with the weighty imprint of long-lasting symbolism.

Given the relationship between politics and theology, it is unsurprising that legal scholars deliberating over the powers of the sovereign struggled with the same designations of the king's body. Earlier notions of the sovereign in narrative help him occupy a similar position. A potent story is told through the encounter between Diogenes and Alexander the Great. Alexander blocks out the sun that was warming Diogenes, who is resting on the ground. Diogenes asks Alexander to simply move out of the way, and impresses him with his honesty. Here, the king or prince is elevated to the position of he who always casts the longest shadow, but the tale is one of kingly humility in the common transposition of a sovereign with the sun; he possesses such vertiginous power that he can block out the sun but also bring it back.[27]

Accounts and illustrations of Christ's ascension make these two natures, earthly and spiritual, perhaps most indistinct in the so-called figure of the 'disappearing Christ'. These representations commonly blur the distinctions between sovereign and God, between sky and Heaven, earth and air. From the twelfth century, Anglo-Saxon illustrations have Jesus disappearing into the heavens, his foot dangling down. A cloud and mandorla might cloak his body, but they are not the source of his buoyancy. Ernst Kantorowicz and others have commented on how other symbols and materials denote this bridging between earth and the heavens. Light and atmosphere symbolize an unburdening of human flesh with the lightness of divinity, and the remainder of a body corporate and politic sustained on the ground in earthly offices. In the Caligula Troper, dated to 1060, the Anglo-Saxon chant book portrays the Ascension. In the troper Christ's feet look disposed to climbing an invisible ladder into the heavens. The Apostles look on, their palms raised as if they are pushing Jesus upwards. Other representations

Leaf of Ascension, psalter for Cistercian female supplicant, illuminated manuscript, 13th century, ink and pigments on medium-weight parchment.

W. de Brailes, 'The Ascension', from *Bible Pictures* (1250), ink and pigment on parchment.

of Christ ascending found expression in liturgical rituals and practices, notably the raising of the host (usually a disc of bread), or 'elevation', in the Eucharist.[28]

Jesus' resurrection would provide a similar exemplar of undecided gravity or levity. In Fra Angelico's *Noli me tangere*, Christ takes corporeal presence having risen from the ground. But his figure still demonstrates a suspension, hovering somewhere between dead and alive, between ground and Heaven. As Lisa Rafanelli and Erin Benay write: 'His stance is graceful, almost balletic, and he appears so light-footed and weightless as to be already in the process of Ascension.'[29]

The levitating sovereign can also be found in the Quran and Talmudic narratives and stories, although their ascending powers may be more easily delegated to a host of objects imbued with mystical and magical powers, and even extended to military power. We find these themes within the idea of the magic flying carpet. 'The City of Brass', a story within the *Thousand and One Nights*, tells of King Solomon defeating Dahesh – the keeper of an idol who opposes Solomon – who is cast into a half-living, monstrous statue upon his defeat. Solomon leads his army atop a magic float-ing carpet, although the carpet itself is not imbued with magical powers; rather, it is Solomon who is able to control the elements, mastering the wind that moves them. We learn how his 600-million-strong army mounts the air with Solomon, upon 360 square miles of green embroidered carpet and with thousands of birds above them.

Of course, as the writer and mythographer Marina Warner shows, being on top of a carpet is a common signal of status, and so often the preserve of royalty and celebrity. It is said that the carpet was also the source of higher knowledge – and literally so. Metaphors and figures are often confused in levitation, but the eleventh-century Jewish theologian Hai ben Sherira, or Hai Gaon, recorded that the great Library of Alexandria, founded in the third century BC, kept magic carpets so that the scholars using the library could consult the upper shelves of the enormous ziggurat in which the manuscripts were held. Apparently readers preferred to read their chosen texts while hovering on the air. The carpets were therefore most convenient.

The artisans and alchemists working for their kings and queens were well practised in the art of producing flying carpets, owing to their responsibility for the process of dyeing the wool. It was said that dyeing the carpets with a particular clay with anti-magnetic properties would give them their source of propulsion. Depending on the amounts used in the process, carpets could hover closer to or further away from the ground. As Azhar Abidi has outlined in his 'Secret History' of the topic, the royal carpet makers of ninth-century BC Yemen and Iraq made carpets that could follow the magnetic lines that criss-cross the earth from its poles. The lines 'acted like aerial rails' upon which the carpet was borne.[30]

The German Nazi political philosopher Carl Schmitt's writings on sovereignty – from the early years of the Weimar Republic – have undergone something of a rediscovery in recent times. His work on *Political Theology* is grounded on an important premise: that most theories of the State are, in fact, 'secularized theological concepts'.[31] In this lineage historians like Ernst Kantorowicz, discussed above, find similar themes and close comparisons between the understanding of God and sovereignty as endowed in the body of the monarch, and eventually the State. For Schmitt, sovereignty in a deistic notion of the world resides precisely 'outside' of that world. The sovereign, in other words, is a detached levitator, although Schmitt notes that the American democratic thought expressed in Jefferson's election victory in 1801 swaps a monarch for a population: 'the people hover above the political life of the State, just as God does above the world as the cause and end of all things.'[32]

Following Schmitt, for the political philosopher Jean-Luc Nancy the sovereign is simultaneously heavy and substantial as a summit – not on the summit, but as the summit itself. 'The sovereign rises above the body', Nancy claims, inside and outside the rule of law. The sovereign does not just act from high places – an altar, a throne or a mountain – rather, the sovereign is the summit, *is height*.[33] The sovereign as the most high or 'inequivalent' will help us understand our superheroes, discussed later (see Chapter Five), who also take on many of these allegorical powers.

Both Schmitt and Nancy are undoubtedly capturing, at least in aesthetic form, the political imagination of sovereignty expounded in Thomas Hobbes's *Leviathan* (1651). Hobbes worked on the frontispiece of the book with the engraver Abraham Bosse. In it the sovereign, with the 'mien of the Christ of judgment in Renaissance paintings', literally rises above and behind the earth.[34] Arms outstretched, the sovereign surrounds the population in an almost embrace. For Peter Goodrich, the king is a sun-like figure; overshadowing the earth as a heliotrope – turning to the sun – he consumes all, sucking in light as well as his subjects, for in Bosse's engraving we see the people absorbed into the gargantuan figure. They are 'part of, being numerous, looking upward . . . absorbed into and consumed by the sovereign figure'.[35]

And yet the levitator may not be as simple as this, performing the omniscient, 'synoptic and intellectually detached' perspective Denis Cosgrove identifies in the Apollonian perspective.[36] The levitator, we will see, is certainly detached, and from many things, but it is also a far more ambiguous, and in some instances vulnerable, subject.

Abraham Bosse, frontispiece for Thomas Hobbes's *Leviathan* (1651), engraving.

Levitation is common to other legal icons, frontispieces and illustrations of sovereign power. The depiction by the political writer Jacobus Bornitius (known as Jakob Bornitz) is notably used as the front cover of Goodrich's book on the topic of the art of the law. The image shows sovereignty held in a levitating face, cast as a mask of an 'invisible and absconded power'.[37] Goodrich reminds us that some of the worst examples of sovereignty have seen Greek and Roman emperors publishing their laws as high as possible on a pillar in the Forum, in order that the new rules would be illegible to a largely illiterate population. Indeed, the pillar and the ascetic seeking elevation have coincided: we might note the story of Simeon Stylites, who lived for decades atop a pillar and who is memorialized in the Fortress of Simeon just north of Aleppo

William Burges,
St Simeon Stylites,
illustrating Tennyson's
poem of the same
title, 1861, drawing.

in Syria, as well as many images and artworks, and Tennyson's poem 'St Simeon Stylites' of 1833.

Simeon, immortalized in the ruins, stanzas and other lives he has inspired, had sought a detached life 'patient on this tall pillar', asocial and 'betwixt meadow and cloud'. Sought after for his wisdom and prayer, Simeon rejected the comforts of society. It appears that the more Simeon sought to remove himself to the heavens, mimicking crucifixion by praying sometimes in an 'erect attitude' with his arms outstretched like a cross, and enduring the pain of occupying so small a space, the greater popularity he achieved. However, some note that the smell of his decaying body provided a form of olfactory deterrent to the people he was trying to avoid. The pillar appears to have been remade several times, until by the time of his death in 459 it had reached some 50 ft.

Some find that Tennyson's poem expresses the structure of the column through its linearity, which itself expresses some kind of end-point, reaching upwards. The column is an exclamation mark, as Simeon pushes 'himself to a terminal point, to the closure of the period',[38] just as his pillar was a horizontal point, a 'spot' in a 'human sea into which rivers from all sides debouche'. The Antioch theologian Theodoret highlighted the many movements of peoples from nearby, from Spain, France and even Britain who would make the journey to see the mystic.[39] Edward Gibbon's history of the Roman Empire finds in Stylites a 'celestial life', noting that 'the patient Hermit expired without descending from his column'; he concludes that Stylites' transit to Heaven was rather more direct than most.[40]

Returning to the tendency of emperors to place their laws on pillars, words would be inscribed in such a way that they placed the emperor's rule literally 'above the law, *super* or sovereign', and made a mockery of the laws that he deemed himself above.[41] Nancy and Schmitt's versions of extreme forms of sovereignty are really quite in line with this – what Schmitt calls the sovereign's exceptional powers. For Nancy, 'Its name is a *superlative*: literally what raises itself above from below, and what is no longer comparable or relative. It is no longer in relation, it is *absolutum*.'[42] Affirming our earlier debates about the king's nature, the sovereign escapes any earthly limitations on their powers, such as the law, and does not require our ideas of structure or hierarchy to sustain or constrain them. As Peter Gratton explains, the sovereign is effectively self-supporting; it appears '*ex nihilo*, founding itself on nothing other than its own *rapport* to itself'.[43]

Given all this, the advice for the education of kings and princes was tricky, placed as high as they were, or in Nancy's terms, *at* and *as* height, and above all else. The *Principe perfecto y ministros aiustados, documentos politicos y morales*, written by Andrés Mendo during his time at the Spanish court in the mid-seventeenth century, is a book of emblems that provides a moral education in sovereignty not so much directed towards the education of young princes but a more general understanding of sovereign justice and restraint. Mendo's book features numerous emblems of floating, godly sovereigns, casting seed from their hair. In another a hand strikes down from the skies, aimed at an anvil placed on a barrel, and in a room a floating arm appears out from a cloud. In another the head of a figure, presumably too high up in the clouds, is cut off by a cloud with lightning-like arrows forking down from it.

Jean Paul (Johann Friedrich Richter), the German writer and novelist, would suggest that in the sovereign's education, the elevation of the prince should be balanced with a modicum of humility and modesty. Jean Paul's advice could be found in his book *Levana* (1807), appropriately named after the very goddess of infantile lift Augustine had mentioned. He says of the prince, if 'he is the centre of gravity', giving forms to the various powers of the State, 'He should be a Jupiter who bears his satellites, and his courtly ring, at once round himself and round their common sun.' Like Nancy's comparison to the mountain, princes for Jean Paul also held the high places of a summit: 'Princes are apt to think meanly of other princes, as mountains look little when viewed from mountains.'[44]

Levana was understood as carrying out the first godly intervention following the birth of a child. The essayist Thomas De Quincey would explain that as soon as a child had been born to the world and tasted its atmosphere, Levana would step in, moving 'the paternal hand' to scoop the baby up from the ground: 'the paternal hand, as proxy for the goddess Levana, or some near kinsman, as proxy for the father, raised it upright, bade it look erect as the king of all this world, and presented its forehead to the stars.' This was the function of Levana, who 'always acted by delegation, had her name from the Latin verb (as still it is the Italian verb) *levare*, to raise aloft'.[45] De Quincey, interestingly, compares the baby's comportment to that of a king.

Jean Paul's book is also a fascinating warning of the vices of war for soon-to-be kings eager to demonstrate their sovereign might. Despite the prince's levity, war becomes enticing because no matter how far he can see, the prince finds himself hemmed in; the horizon presents not infinitude but a boundary. Jean Paul advises the prince's educators to ensure that they communicate the import of war as an 'earthquake' that could send the prince's levitation into free fall. War sends everything topsy-turvy, reversing gravity and levity: 'all ancient law courts, all judgment-seats, are overturned, heights and depths are confounded together. It is a last day, full of rising sinners and falling stars.' Should the prince be tempted by the glories of war, it should be made clear that it would merely be a false levity, kept up only by fountains of blood. All that would be left is a 'great soul' that 'hovers there, like the form of an earthly world glorified in the night, and touches the stars and the earth'.[46]

Some leaders, even under communism, would not really heed Jean Paul's advice to young sovereigns, and would see themselves in the position of a secular levitating spirit. Imagery of Mao Zedong's head floating above the adoration of a clamouring public is perhaps some of the most famous of this kind. Equally, Nicolae Ceaușescu's transposition with religious iconography was a common feature of his propaganda posters. Perhaps one of the most bizarre has him standing with his hovering wife Elena, while in the background on one side of the image children – the youth of Romania – appear to be lifting off. On the other side, young adults look like apparitions fading into some doves in flight.

Not surprisingly, then, our ideas of sovereignty, doubled between the king's two bodies, occupy an odd suspended position, both light and heavy but hopefully learned with the modesty of Jean Paul's teaching.[47] Paul Farley has noticed this in his short poem on the present Queen, who

> . . . does the regal wave from helicopters.
> . . .
> On aerial views she is a great authority.

And yet this kind of wit and mockery, the lightness that Farley levels at the heights of kingly and theological power, could be seen as an inappropriate demeanour for dealing with the sovereign, or indeed the workings of religious or governmental law. For the London theologian Edward Stillingfleet, who considered the workings of rule, government and authority in both religion and State in *Irenicum* in 1660, levity should be 'exploded out' of government and law.[48] Stillingfleet warns of a 'superficial lightnesse and vanitie of spirit', which might otherwise sink 'them too much below the command of reason, into the power of unruly passions'.[49] Instead, law and government should be solemn affairs, full of weight. He reminds his readers that the 'Region which is nearest Heaven, is the freest from clouds and vapours, as well as those dancing meteors, which hover about in a light uncertain motion.'

The Blaise of saintly flight

The Swiss poet and novelist Blaise Cendrars, whose memoir *Le lotissement du ciel* (1949) was published in English as *Sky: Memoirs*, was a documentarian of medieval levitation. Cendrars traced birds and stars but especially the floating saints recorded by the

Bollandists in the *Acta sanctorum*, effectively an encyclopaedia
of the saints, taken on by Jean Bolland after it was begun by
Heribert Rosweyde. Joseph of Cupertino (1603–1663) was
Cendrars' patron saint of aviation during his time as a reporter
hiding in Nazi-occupied France. From the twentieth century
looking in, and through the various attempts to trace and catalogue
these individuals, the saintly levitators became Cendrars' poetic
companions. They helped him make sense of his travels in Latin
America, the evacuation of Paris and northern France, the amputation of his hand in 1916, and eventually the death of Rémy, a
pilot, and son to the devoted father Cendrars.

Over half of Cendrars' accounts of levitation coincide with
different kinds of lightness; from the optical, visual, energetic kind
that saw the sovereign transposed with the sun, to the experience
or sensation of weight. In his extraordinary book, he juxtaposes
moments of travel in his biography to the hagiographic accounts
of flying saints. A flash of hovering birds in a Latin American jungle
he compares to the disintegration of matter common in levitation.
Later, it is a meditation on the stars hanging in the sky being eaten
up by blackness. Light and non-light keep drawing him upwards. But
levitation for Cendrars is also an account of outsideness, a removal
of self. He even describes his amputation in these terms: the once
severed hand he perceives 'as an aura, somewhere outside the
body'.[50] His accounts of conflict remind us that the strange presence
of levitators is never far away in war. St Pio of Pietrelcina, canonized
by Pope John Paul II in 2002 and one of the most recently recognized
saints to have achieved levitation, is widely regarded to have levitated during different religious gatherings. But Padre Pio is most
notable for levitating upwards to the height of Allied air force
bombers during the Second World War. After bombers were sent
to blow up a suspected munitions depot in San Giovanni Rotondo,
Pio met the bombers in the air with his hands uplifted, causing
them to turn back, and their bombs to fall away into woodland.

Cendrars continues the Bollandists' trend of recording large and sometimes vast lists of every occurrence of levitation. To write these down is to inscribe levitation as more than a fuzzy experience, but as an actual happening, an event. In St Joseph of Cupertino, Cendrars finds endless levitations alighted by almost anything. A monk passing by with a lighted candle, and even the presence of a lamb, sets Joseph off. Other remains of Joseph reside in the Basilica Santuario di San Giuseppe da Copertino in Osimo in Puglia, Italy. His rising likeness has been painted above the altarpiece; the tubular columns of the basilica's organ form an arrow steering eyes upwards. And even below, in the crypt, Joseph's preserved body is still held up by angel statues in a glass casket.

Light is a common instigator. Sister Maria Francesca is seen levitating with her body resplendent with light. And Father Bernardinus, who died in 1616, was noticed levitating, light filtering through the cracks in the door.[51] For Cendrars, light gives the levitator away, so that a private ravishment is made public.

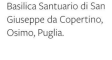

Basilica Santuario di San Giuseppe da Copertino, Osimo, Puglia.

Martin Schongauer,
*The Temptation of
St Anthony*, c. 1470,
copper plate engraving.

The thirteenth-century theologian and priest Thomas Aquinas
would experience dreams of fire and pain, of being girded by two
angels. And, having thrown down his book – a thesis on a change
in the elements of the Blessed Sacrament, as G. K. Chesterton
explains – at the foot of the crucifix at an altar, he would be
met with a vision of Christ, after which he was floated miraculously.[52] Indeed, the name Blaise Cendrars – the pseudonym of

Frédéric-Louis Sauser – combines an evocation of the French *braise*, meaning embers, and *cendre*, or ash. He rises from the ashes.

One of the most interesting saints is probably Teresa, from Ávila, near Madrid. Teresa is notable because she was one of the few levitators who were actually quite self-conscious of their state: her levity was embarrassing to her. She blushed at the thought of it and the nuns around her could not keep her body down. Teresa would also popularize the relationship between levitation and expressions of ecstasy, commonly figured through burning, fiery light, luminous and internal blinding pain. Teresa accounts for the burning affects that Carl Jung would argue the saints endeavour to hold back.[53] Burning holds another relationship to levitation in the lives of the saints, captured in the 'miracle of the book', the miraculous levitation of the books of St Dominic. Heated debates between Cathars and Catholics at the turn of the thirteenth century became even hotter as Dominic (Dominic de Gúzman) and Bishop Diego of Osma, pausing in Languedoc on their way back to Spain from Denmark, waded in on them. Deciding to set fire to Cathar and Catholic scripture in order to determine which was heretical, Dominic's books were said to not only escape burning, 'but in the sight of all leapt far from the fire'.[54]

The relationship between Teresa's levities and her own spiritual writings was incredibly strong, despite her sufferance of vertigo. In Teresa's influential discourse we can find obvious Neoplatonic energies, which she would express through metaphors of rising, weight and an inner verticality of spirit and soul. As with Augustine, Teresa's spiritual ambitions appear 'unimpeded by an earthly, leaden weight';[55] she would find little comfort in the lightness gathered from play or laughter, seeing them instead as distractions. 'Earthly things are but toys,' she would argue, 'and therefore mounts to higher things.'[56] Other female Christian mystics were believed to have levitated too. St Catherine of Siena (1347–1380) is one such woman who experienced, as well as levitation, stigmata,

Pedro Berruguete,
*St Dominic and the
Albigensians*, 1493–9,
oil on panel.

opposite:
Giovanni di Paolo,
St Catherine of Siena,
1460, tempera and
gold on wood.

rays emanating from a crucifix and a flying communion. Consistent with the severing associated with lightness and levity explored throughout this book, St Catherine's head was separated from her body by robbers. Her mummified head now resides in an ornate reliquary in the Basilica San Domenico in Siena.[57]

Teresa's words on ecstasy artfully describe a violent account of possession, of being lifted or raised, which would allow the soul to return to its 'ancient possibility of flying, of rising toward another world'. She explains, 'it comes as a quick and violent shock; you see and feel this cloud, or this powerful eagle rising and bearing you up on its wings . . . and indeed see that you are being carried away you know not where.' While Teresa is eager to identify the cause of her ecstasy and levity as outside herself, she is equally at pains to demarcate her experiences from more earth-inspired flights. It is only God who can make her fly, the soul being 'laden with earth . . . deeply buried in mire, that she has lost the power of flying by her own fault'.[58]

As she is famously depicted in Bernini's *Ecstasy of St Teresa* (1647–52), Teresa lies on a cloud. The cloud is a 'vaporous furniture', writes Gavin Pretor-Pinney in his *Cloudspotters' Guide*, suspending Teresa's erotic/ecstatic moment on presumably condensing as well as spiritual vapour.[59] Like Cendrars, Teresa comprehends her ecstasy as having luminous but also affective qualities. Even if she struggles to communicate her encounters using the lexicon available to her, through an elision of words and meanings, her use of light, spirit, levitation and ecstasy are still highly expressive. She is both outside herself and being burned, turned out and unburdened by a light that depletes her, that is somehow both blinding and visionary.[60]

Teresa's ecstasy is a commonly recounted story of distress and bliss. She experiences a vision of an angel with a spear. The spear tipped with fire enters Teresa, alighting a fire. Drawing the spear out, her longing is expressed as a kind of kindling of fire and light. The experience is so excessive, she finds comfort in hugging the spiritual pain left behind. She recounts this kind of wounding as both an absence and a presence. It is an ecstatic filling of the body/soul with God's presence, pushing or transporting the soul out into a state of bliss. Equally, it is an absence, a longing created by the withdrawal of God's presence from her soul.[61]

Levitators like Teresa would give accounts of being carried away on a flowing river of force. But the saints would also exude flowing materials too; many appearing to release effluvia or smells. Joseph of Cupertino was particularly notable. So was Benoîte Rencurel of Notre-Dame du Laus, Constance Classen notes, who was supposed to perfume the air in which she dwelled. It is said that in 1698, on the Feast of the Assumption, Benoîte was taken into heavenly rapture for a night: 'she floated on waves of light, music, and perfume.'[62]

The lighting of Teresa's intimate spark is a form of release, and why so many compare her experiences to sexual ecstasy. She is experiencing an unburdening by being carried away to become 'a light body, a beautiful body, the Soul with wings, nothing more than a push, a breath, maybe wind itself'.[63] Teresa's flights do not merely hesitate between the ground and air but, for her critics, they drift more definitively towards 'nymphomania . . . and hysteria'.[64] Her sainthood was engulfed by misogynist slander, especially by the German-Austrian psychiatrist Richard von Krafft-Ebing, who authored *Psychopathia Sexualis* in 1886. Krafft-Ebing would pathologize female mystics as hysterics, seeing Teresa's ecstasy not as a rise but a 'sinking', as if she were dragged under by desire into a 'masochistic "hysterical faint"'.[65]

The trouble with levity

We can easily detect the negative sense of levity that was prosecuted during this time. Persecuted might be the more accurate word, for as with Teresa's pathologization as a nymphomaniac hysteric, women would experience the sharpest end of levitative prejudice. The gendered politics of levitation will form a common theme within this book. Folklore and the storytellings of customary and traditional societies show us that levitation was not always conceived as an unequal practice. Indeed we might see the act of the levitator as a form of release or escape from the world as it is – from hardship, inequality, persecution or worse. As Italo Calvino has suggested, the trend for lightness, for levity, may well be a response to the 'precarious existence of tribal life – drought, sickness, evil influences'. The shamanic response to these conditions was a ridding of 'his body of weight and flying to another world, another level of perception, where he could find the strength to change the face of reality'.[66]

There is almost a genealogy to this relationship that we can make in reverse. Let us dwell first on the work of Martin Delrio, the influential Jesuit theologian. His *Disquisitiones magicae*, or *Magical Investigations*, was first published in Leuven in 1599–1600. Delrio's book acted to popularize both the ideas of witches and demon spirits, but also the task of identifying and hunting them. While others have depicted Delrio in pretty narrow terms as a fervent witch-hunter, more recent histories of his life have shown him as a much more careful and textual biographical scholar. One of Delrio's students was none other than Heribert Rosweyde, who began the *Fasti sanctorum* in 1607 – a major inspiration for the *Acta sanctorum*, the hagiography continued by the Bollandists.[67]

Delrio's approach is important in continuing a rather different historical and textual lineage of levitating beings. Instead of saints or sovereigns Delrio focused on demons inhabiting women's bodies

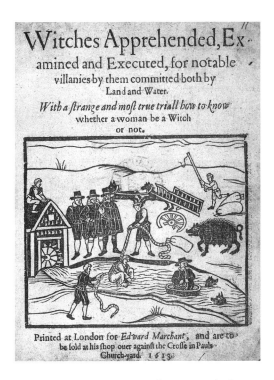

Witches Apprehended,
1613, etching.

or taking their guise. Delrio's interest in witchcraft may have had something to do with his interest in the Roman Stoic philosopher Seneca, who drew on the myth of Medea as a witch. Known for marrying Jason, of the Argonauts, Medea is frequently dramatized riding a flying chariot pulled by serpents. Productions of Seneca's tragedy *Medea* would often make the most of the wires and fly technologies of the theatre.

Italo Calvino finds in the witch another levitative object of male oppression. The witch is a figure of sexual desire, 'where women bore most of the weight of constricted life', and, as Calvino notes, were depicted as flying 'by night on broomsticks or even on lighter vehicles such as ears of wheat or pieces of straw'. Calvino suggests there is a clear link 'between the levitation desired and the privation actually suffered'.[68] In the witch we find a figure of apparent levity but also of grotesque femininity.[69] While the witch would be understood to have the elements under her command, she also appears to be of the air in many different forms of storytelling.

Delrio would repeat the myth of the levitating and airborne witch in an account of a moment within late sixteenth-century northern Europe, of tensions between the Spanish-appointed Governor General of the Netherlands Albert VII, Archduke of Austria, and the combined forces of the Dutch Republic, France and England. It is during Albert's campaign to capture Calais, near the 'Nuletum bridge', which stood as a marker against the people of Boulogne, that Delrio picks up the story. The sentries positioned at the marker begin to notice a dark cloud flying towards them against the wind and a clear sky. The cloud looks and sounds somehow human. The sentries say they 'thought they could hear the voices of many people jumbled together inside it'.[70] One of the sentries decides to send a shot into the cloud. As Delrio's account continues,

> There was a thunder-clap and a woman fell down from the cloud at their feet. She was drunk, naked and very fat, middle-aged, and her thigh had been shot through twice. They arrested her, but she began to pretend she was deranged . . .[71]

Delrio's tale bears a strong resemblance to the fantastic voyages of Robert Paltock's character Peter Wilkins.[72] On board the ship *Hector*, heading for England back from Cape Horn, the captain orders that they fire on a cloud that seems to be following them, hoping the cannonfire will dissipate the cloud. They hear a splash in the water as a figure drops from the cloud with a cry.

In a way, the relationship between the levity of witches and weight is expressed in Delrio's account as a ludicrous contradiction. Somehow the woman flies despite her corpulent body. The witch is an unnatural form that should not fly. Trial by ordeal, as one would expect given the beliefs Delrio exhibits, meant testing the identity of a witch. This was completed not so much by assessing the weight of a potential witch but by their buoyancy: an accused who floated was a witch. For women accused of witchcraft, the trial of ducking or dunking became commonplace in the sixteenth and seventeenth centuries. Of course this sense of weight is very different to the way men were portrayed. G. K. Chesterton's comments on Thomas Aquinas's own weight are suggestive: he describes him as a 'huge heavy bull of a man, fat and slow', or 'stolid'.[73] However, Aquinas's theological and mystical levity does not seem complicated by this in the way women's has been.

Alongside Delrio is often placed Nicholas Rémy, one of the most productive and notorious witch-hunters of northern Europe.

Rémy, a public administrator from Lorraine, is claimed to have executed almost nine hundred witches, but it was a practice that the Church soon began to question. In 1766 a member of the Bavarian Academy of Sciences, Father Ferdinand Sterzinger, presented a direct critique of the witch-hunters, declaring the practice a form of prejudice, and witchcraft the subject of old wives' tales. Delrio, with Rémy, was the simple expression of the 'prejudices of inept souls'.[74]

Of course, the witch and the broomstick would not remain so closely tied to these meanings. In popular culture, the witch and their flight have been renewed and redeemed in different forms. Children and families chuckle at Eglantine's rusty performance as she learns to fly on her broom in Disney's *Bedknobs and Broomsticks* (1971). Eglantine Price, played by Angela Lansbury, is adorable as a rather unconvincing witch, her spells often going wrong and her efforts at levity resulting in an aerial tumble into a group of trees. The witch's broom is also imported into J. K. Rowling's world of *Harry Potter* as a key part of the aerial armoury of the wizarding world, and a skill first learned and practised in school games sessions: in Potter's world the broomstick is used for the sport Quidditch. And, like Eglantine's attempts to become airborne, the broomstick is a mode of levity one must get used to.

But levitation has been depicted as a power that women have borne, or been bestowed with, yet may not want. This subject has even been played on in contemporary works, such as the woman seen as an entirely unwilling recipient of levitational powers in *The Kármán Line* (2014), a short, BAFTA-nominated film by Oscar Sharp starring the British actress Olivia Colman. Colman is ever so slowly lifted off the ground in a form of 'magical social realism', eventually crossing the Kármán line – the boundary between Earth and space where the atmosphere becomes too thin to support the lift necessary for aeroplanes to fly, proposed by Theodore von

Scene from *The Kármán Line* (dir. Oscar Sharp, 2014).

Kármán. The film is a commentary on family detachment and figurative estrangement due to the slow loss of a mother through her premature and levitative death. Colman's character is the entirely unwilling recipient of levitational powers which work to slowly stretch and collapse marital, motherly and familial attachments. From her lounge, after carrying out the usual domestic duties of ironing and of cooking her daughter's supper, Colman finds she is ever so slowly but disturbingly lifted off the ground, eventually passing through the ceiling and her daughter's bedroom. In one scene, we see the last time she and her husband are able to make love, on their anniversary. In another her husband drinks in despair.

Such a melancholy or sad levity is remarkably common. Milan Kundera's *The Unbearable Lightness of Being* (1984) is a magical but painful narrative of a soul's search for lightness, its yearning to rise amid the pain of love, sexual attachments, friendship and intimacy, blurring the Parmenidean dichotomies of heavy and light, positive and negative.[75] Equally, Emine Sevgi Özdamar's *Life is a Caravanserai* (2000) tells a story of a Turkish woman growing up during the 1950s and '60s, moving from childhood to adulthood.[76] The novel is a magical, confusing and disorientating noise of a narrative, through Islamic parables and folklore, refracting a life of family, loss, religion and death, where beds, people and even houses float. Meanwhile, a difficult viewing of desire and embarrassment is to be found in Pier Paolo Pasolini's *Teorema* (1968), which sees Terence Stamp's character entering a bourgeois household and seducing everyone in it. They are indelibly changed by the encounter, their experiences ranging from humiliation and shame to transformation. The film's characters experience a kind of social transcendence, being liberated from their positions – conjugal, marital, familial, economic. By the end of *Teorema* the father has stripped off his possessions and clothes and sold his factory, and creates dust eddies as he stumbles naked on Mount Etna, his cries overlapping the closing credits. The family's maid, whom Stamp's character has saved from suicide at the film's beginning, performs miracles, cures people and achieves levitation above a building in a village. Levitation is therefore about transformation.

Weighing things up

We have a sense, then, that those who levitate are frequently tested, measured, observed and scrutinized. Sometimes those suspected of possessing too much levity are put to the sword, or fire or drowning. Fascinatingly though, until the late nineteenth and twentieth centuries the weighing up of levitators was not only about whether one possessed such powers or not. Levity could be a sign of something more, a signal of a higher or lower kind of purpose or inspiration. If we return to the flying friar whom Cendrars was so interested in, we find that St Joseph was famously subjected to Prospero Lambertini's reforms of the Church's procedures for bestowing holiness by confirming the provenance of miraculous claims in the 1730s. Joseph's life was also brought under the purview of the Inquisition's concerns to weed out all forms of witchcraft or devilry.

Lambertini's protocol of criteria – which are being contested even today as overly stringent by the International Medical Committee of Lourdes, which is tasked with proving unexplained medical cures to be miraculous – rested on the empirical material provided by witnesses, while the assessment of a miracle rested on a juridical decision by the Church's court on a calculation of those testimonies.[77] Fernando Vidal's examination of the medico-legal economy of miracle-proving helps explains things.[78] For we find that by demanding scepticism and empirical evidence, contrary to almost all the reports we can read on Joseph, he was not made saintly on the basis of his levitations, but on the grounds that he had miraculously healed someone, drawing on medical observations and accepted psycho-physiological doctrines of ecstatic rapture of the time.

Joseph's levitations came under scrutiny not to determine whether they had actually happened or were improbable, or whether their existence could be tested, proven or discounted. Of course, many people came forward to attest to his flights. As Lambertini himself remarked, 'unexceptional witnesses deposed to the most frequent elevations and great flights on the part of that ecstatic and rapt servant of God'.[79] What was at stake was their cause. Given Joseph's sensitivity to candles, lambs and other apparently mundane happenings that could set him aloft, the evidence did not convince the Inquisition that his levitations had happened exclusively on religious grounds. Joseph's defence rested on the argument that the influence of music may have led him to contemplate celestial matters. God must have given him the capacity to levitate – so inspired by music – so it could not be held against him. Because it was decided that Joseph's flights had not happened 'exclusively' on religious grounds, the court's concerns did not undermine Joseph's case nor particularly help claims for his sanctity, but they did absolve him of some suspicion. Lambertini – as Benedict XIV – beatified the friar in 1753.

W. Hogarth, inv.ᵗ

A. *absolute Gravity.* B. *Conatus against absolute Gravity.* C. *partial Gravity.* D. *comparative Gravity.* E. *horizontal, or good sence.*
F. *Wit.* G. *comparative Levity, or Coxcomb.* H. *partial Levity, or pert Fool.* I. *absolute Levity, or stark Fool.*

After William Hogarth, illustration for John Clubbe's *Physiognomy* (1763), engraving.

A decade later, in 1763, the writer and cleric John Clubbe wrote a peculiar and intriguing satire entitled *Physiognomy*. The frontispiece was illustrated by none other than William Hogarth, who depicted the weighing scale of Clubbe's imaginative essay – a scale that would attempt to ascertain physiognomic qualities through the different gravities of people's heads. Clubbe's typologies ranged from the extremes of 'Absolute Gravity' to 'Absolute Levity'.[80] The more levity one possessed, the greater the degree of idiocy, Clubbe assumed; this characterization of levitators was not uncommon. Even the overly intellectual is weighed in similar terms, their head 'way up in the clouds'. Hogarth depicted these different positions on the scale through suspended bodies; the most weighty figure stands on his head, dragged down by the density of a very heavy head. The one with the most levity is the 'fool', upright but levitating way up in the air.

The weighing apparatus was a little like those to be found in Britain at the time. Lucia Dacome finds that Clubbe's satire was driven by a fascination with weight-watching as a form of public and personal medical discipline, which became all the rage in late eighteenth-century Europe. Scales were popularized by the Venetian physician Santorio Santorio. His machine was a weighing chair that would assess bodily evacuations or losses by comparing variations in the body's weight. The chair was meant to help regulate the intake of food both by demanding that 'weight watching' became a regular habit for its user, but also by balancing the weight of a user of the chair with the food they wanted to ingest. The more they weighed the more the chair would drop away from their plate of food.

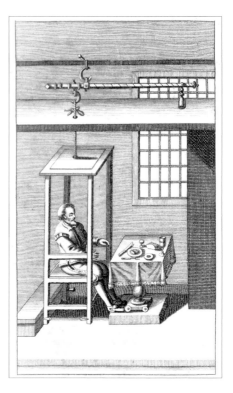

Santorio Santorio's weighing scale, illustrated by John Quincy, frontispiece to *Medica statica* (1718), engraving.

Clubbe's imagined contraption was different to these machines. In his design a steel girdle was to be wrapped around the waist of the person weighed, with a load-stone to take them up into the air. This was a machine that could not be fooled, argued Clubbe. Should the subject wish to avoid their innate qualities being viewed in public then they would have problems, falling 'into their several and respective departments of gravity'. 'Let them squirm about as much as they will', Clubbe suggested, and 'struggle to support their heads from sinking, they can no more keep them up, than a witch can keep her's down.'[81] Even so, Clubbe's scales could be tipped. He noted that one's lightness might be adjusted, for some liquors could make a person light-headed – but not, he suggested lasciviously, 'morning drinkers', who would not be so easily elevated by their beer.[82]

Clubbe had little time for those characters on either end of his scale. He finds those at the bottom to be 'men of weight without importance, these stupid half-burnt lumps of clay'.[83] This heaviest type, however, are not such simple characters, for even the 'grave men' of absolute gravity and weight, once put in motion, 'bounce and fly; for anger is a kind of yeast in lumpish constitutions'.[84] At the other end of the scale, just before absolute levity, is a 'wretched form of man', the '*pert fool*', a 'gnat'. Clubbe finds the lightest people to be the most annoying: like a buzzing fly, 'he is at your elbow and your mouth; in your path when you walk, and perches at the back of your chair if you sit down.'[85]

These imaginative scales were also gendered. The practice of weighing in the eighteenth century was a peculiarly male and public phenomenon. The Coffee Mill of St James's Street, London, became a particularly fashionable place for weight-watching. But as the historian Lucia Dacombe argues, women were largely absent from the books that recorded people's weight. Both sets of scales – Clubbe's parodying ones and the real scales used in urban centres – tended to make equivalences between character, demeanour or spirit through weight. Some believed that the 'characteristically precarious equilibrium' of women 'could not be regulated by means of weighing'.[86] As Clubbe suggests in his writing, 'When I say *all* people I mean only those of the masculine gender'; the female sex, he would add, 'cannot be weighed with decency'. Clubbe's point of view corresponded with a wider one. Women's 'tempers, passions and manners' did not need to be weighed, or therefore visibly measured, because they were already and always on show. The surface of the woman was more giving or revealing than the male, more volatile. The female form easily expressed women's 'eager propensity to speak their minds' and thus their demeanours could 'discover themselves'.[87]

Gravities and levities

Lightness in early scientific thought is taken as a positive quality which, in some ways, seems so much more matter of fact, so much more obvious than theories of gravity. As Steven Connor suggests, 'Even modern writers find something provocatively lopsided in the idea that gravity might have no active opposite.' Levity was pitted against gravity in a doctrine of reciprocity of opposing vertical forces. The last vestiges of these ideas, and their soon-to-be-outmoded proponents in the face of modern chemistry, could be found in the debates over phlogiston.

The Enlightenment sought to leave the medieval behind in a simpler set of distinctions between mysticism, faith and the mechanics of the universe. Throughout this book we will see that these are almost always false demarcations and side more in favour of a commingling. Even Isaac Newton was not completely one-sided in his adoption of a gravitative world-view, away from a more levitative understanding of the universe. When Newton's *Principia* (1687) was being composed he also wrote elsewhere of a cosmology that the historian Frank E. Manuel describes to be 'of a far greater diversity of beings than those recognized by positivist physical sciences and nineteenth-century Unitarians'.[88]

Anticipating the new millennium, in a piece of extraordinary prose, Newton imagines a heavenly city occupied by bodies of the 'Children of the resurrection', where heavenly and earthly spaces are brought into one:

> as fishes in water ascend and descend, move whether they will and rest where they will, so may Angels and Christ and the Children of the resurrection do in the air and heavens. 'Tis not the place but the state

Albert Tissandier,
*Ascension du 26
Septembre*, 1876,
graphite.

which makes heaven and happiness. For God is alike in all places. He is substantially omnipresent, and as much present in the lowest Hell as in the highest heaven . . . We usually conceive it to be above.[89]

The above penetrates our world, in Newton's view, envisioning other celestial beings subsisting as far above the earth as they pleased, moving where they will, to 'rule the earth and converse with the remotest regions'.[90]

Perhaps one obvious place where religion and science would come together can be found in the aesthetic appreciation of the new balloon prospect. Despite its association with mania and spectacle, the balloon ascent also combined scientific measurement and rationality with exclamations of delight, rapture and an imagination overwhelmed by the experience. The views were

heavenly. Thomas Baldwin was an early aeronaut who hired
Vincenzo Lunardi's balloon to ascend from Chester in 1785. He
would describe his ascent into the heaven of the lower levels of
the atmosphere, where 'innumerable rays of light darted on the
eye as it glanced along the ground: which, tho' of a gay green colour,
appeared like an inverted firmament glittering with stars of the first
magnitude.' From this perspective the balloon prospect could even
be compared to the view from the seat of the sovereign. Stephan
Oettermann remarks upon the Montgolfier brothers' decision not
to call in on the king during a flight in 1783: 'What is a king (even
one with an empire on which the sun never sets) compared to an
aeronaut who can, if he chooses, see two sunsets in one day?'[91] For
Thomas Monck Mason, balloon ascension was akin to rapture – or
perhaps we mean rupture, a severing of mind from body, thought
from sensation. 'He almost feels as if', Monck explains, 'the usual
community of sentiment between his mind and body [have] been
dissolved.'[92]

If we return to the ideas of kingship and indeed the gravities
which appeared to keep the law, perhaps we can review the role
of the levitator in relation to such forms of power, sovereign or
otherwise. If we regard satirists like Clubbe to have the role of
'responding justly' to contemporaneous events, we might review
just how we understand the *Physiognomy*.[93] In what ways might
the levitator help provide a form of satirical critique, just as the
sovereign may use lightness to make mockery of the law? Goodrich's
suggestion is that both levity and gravity may exist in the same
space; each medieval figure of sovereign power seems to prop the
other up.[94]

George Wither's illustrations from his *A Collection of Emblems*
are remarkably similar to those in Mendo's *Principe perfecto*:
figurative objects and symbols float above the world. But held
within these are traces of satire. The emblem shown here depicts
traditional Christian legal norms, of sovereignty and the godliness

of law; however, in the building at the left of the image, a man is
found dangling from the bedroom or closet of a woman. Perhaps he
is on his way to an extra-marital dalliance. This is how Goodrich
interprets Wither's intent, finding the emblem remarkable not
for its depiction of love, but for an 'illicit assignation' that under-
mines the appearance of law and apparent trust and 'good faith'.[95]
Sharing the same space we find the assertion of solemn and
weighty legal matters and the possibility of their own undoing:
'the lightness of critique, the willingness to satirize, the risk
of ridicule, lampoon and laughter'.[96] This is not uncommon to
levitation. Even the high seriousness of the balloon ascent – a
heavenly or scientific marvel – was the butt of satire. The balloon
was frequently depicted deflated like a bottom or rounded like a
breast, and subject to what Bayla Singer describes as a form of
'low' humour. Cartoons, sketches and rumours depicted not the

ecstasy of spiritual transcendence but sexual intimacy. Singer
tells of a British sketch of a balloon containing two aristocratic
passengers who are leaning back against the balloon car: one of
them comments, 'It rises majestically,' with the other responding,
'I can feel it.'[97]

And so, in the strange magic of the medieval and early modern
levity that would run through the legal principles, notions of
sovereignty, and spiritual leaders of the period, we also perhaps
have a form of thinking that we can take forward through the book.
In the context of contemporary writing, Italo Calvino identifies
several trends: a 'weight, density and concreteness of things,
bodies, and sensations' and 'a weightless element that hovers
above things like a cloud or better perhaps the finest dust, or
better still the field of magnetic impulses.' Feelings of lightness,
the emotions, drives, passions of uplift, ecstasy, suspension,
longing, bodily possession, do not easily fit with seriousness
or solemnity. Levitation is a tension, the product of equal and
opposite forces, to the extent that levitation is not often about
joy or indeed heaviness but more ambiguous sets of feelings and
those torn between the poles of sentiment.

Capturing these contradictions in a book on levitation requires
what Masciandaro has called a particular kind of medieval possession that encourages an *unknowing* of our established ways of
thought or writing, and an embrace of 'poetry as knowledge and
philosophy as joy':

> the scholarly being I am thrown into is a grave levitation,
> the lovely becoming light of weight in all senses: metaphoric,
> literal, and above all in the truest most palpable sense of the
> phenomenal poetic zones of indistinction between the two
> . . . not flight from but the very lightening of *gravitas* itself,
> the finding or falling into *levitas*.[98]

2 Faking on Air

IN 1902 THE Edison Manufacturing Company recorded what was thought to be the first American motion picture footage of or about India, in the form of Thomas Edison's film *Hindoo Fakir*. The footage is remarkable. During the movie we see a 'Hindu' magician or mystic floating his female assistant in a series of cleverly cut-together sequences, which are punctuated by the magician's exaggerated and excitable gestures. His assistant rises, floats and eventually flutters in the air. She does so first after being placed on several spikes, which the 'fakir' has thrust into the ground. After dabbling in some magic to presumably hypnotize the woman, and bestow her with lighter-than-air powers, the fakir knocks the poles on which she is resting away. And to demonstrate his assistant's true levity, he runs his hands over and under her floating body, before passing a hoop along her length to emphasize the point. A viewer doesn't have to look too closely to see that the woman swings gently backwards and forwards, owing to the wires that suspend her. It is still a fantastic trick.

Things become even more fantastic. The fakir brings out a basket which he places in front of a set of stairs and a shadowed doorway, which is blacked out to hide the fact that some of the mechanics of the trick are not only cinematic but physical. He gestures with his hands and the woman suddenly appears in the basket. The lid is closed, and after he performs several bows to the basket it begins to levitate into the middle of the frame. The fakir thrusts his sword into the basket. He does this several times, presumably to signal his assistant's demise. After a few more bows the basket returns to the ground and we see that the woman is quite fine.

Levitation is as much a part of the film as is transformation or transfiguration. As soon as the basket settles on the ground the fakir picks the woman up and she disappears into dust, which the fakir retrieves and sprinkles into a bowl. Out of the bowl emerges a flower, a lily, from which his assistant arises with wings, which she deploys to flutter about at the top of the frame and then drifts from side to side across the backdrop. The magician urges her down with his hands; he bows and they leave the screen.

Some authors hold that the magician is very likely to be A. N. Dutt, who toured the United States with his magic show and was also known as Ram Bhuj. Dutt would take inspiration from Indian yogic traditions and bring them to an American and European audience.[1] It is through the travel of levitation into different cultural contexts that the lacings of Indian and Eastern belief are able to travel too. But this was an older trend: the authors Peter Lamont and Crispin Bates point to the 1820s and the circulation of several traveller accounts of Indian mystics, conjurers and jugglers who possessed extraordinary skills and other-worldly powers. The traveller and scholar Ibn Battuta, Marco Polo, and the Mughal emperor Jehangir, as well as many others, helped sow the seeds for the zeal with which the Indian levitator was consumed in the mid-nineteenth century.

Levitation had been popularized in the West before Edison's movie, and even the circuiting magicians and jugglers travelling from India whom we will examine. Antoine Galland's early eighteenth-century translation of the *Thousand and One Nights* would help provide an earlier context of Middle Eastern mysticism and levitating forms, such as flying carpets. The magic carpet would of course be received into the context of rising balloon experiments and public spectacles as well. Surprisingly, the magic carpet is not as present a figure in the *Nights* as one might expect. As Marina Warner has shown, the carpet has instead emerged as a symbol, its qualities of flight becoming 'a shorthand for dream ecstasy and fulfilled desire, and for creating thrills with erotic and transfiguring resonances'.[2]

In this chapter we follow the optical diversions, refractions and corrections accomplished in how levitation emerged in a confluence of several artistic, philosophical and magical influences which had made a circuitous path between East and West. What is more, we will explore how, as levitation was drawn into the genre of the stage magician, it relied upon increasingly complicated technical apparatus and special effects to achieve the illusion of weightlessness, and the allusion to non-Western mysticism.

The fakir

A. N. Dutt was also known by other names: Linga Singh, Ishmael, as well as variants on 'Hindoo' or 'Indian Fakir'.[3] By 1902 he was the latest in a series of Indian magicians to delight Western audiences in an evolution of the type. From the early nineteenth century, following a great number of travel writers who had recorded the Indian theatre of Orientalist street conjuring, Indian magicians had voyaged to Britain and Europe. The reception of the conjurers changed during the course of the century by intersecting Indian and British sensibilities of caste and class.

The *jaduwallah* or *jadoo wallah* tended to be Muslim, of low caste, and tended towards juggling performances that had a tinge of the fraudulent and corrupt. They were immortalized in Wilkie Collins's novel *The Moonstone* (1868), in which a troupe of jugglers haunt the book's protagonist and shadow the diamond (the lost moonstone) with an eerie and Eastern exoticism. Brahmins, or high-caste Hindus, performed feats that were typically more heavily spiritualized, and apparently involving supernatural forces rather than the lower form of devilry. Even in *The Moonstone* the *jaduwallah*s are tricksy characters, but not in the way you might expect. In a critique of British imperialist narratives of race, the *jaduwallah*s are revealed as Hindu Brahmins in disguise, seeking to protect and restore the stolen diamond of their deity.[4] The lowly jugglers are recast through the novel as heroic protectors. And so, as the identity of the *jaduwallah* would prove to be swappable in fiction, reality would follow. Henry Mayhew's interview with a London juggler in *London Labour and the London Poor* (1861) – among other interviews with strongmen, conjurers and street performers – found that the juggler was of course British. And following the exploits of the Indian juggler Ramo Samee, the same juggler had shaved his head high to the temple to 'allow him to assume the Indian costume'.[5]

Sheshal, the 'Brahmin of the Air', or the Air Brahmin, as other magazines and periodicals of the time also called him, is said to have been drawn in 1832 at the British Government House in Madras, a colonnaded building set in English-style parkland. The Brahmin, described as a 'slender, middle sized man' and as having attained a 'considerable age', toured other rich houses in Madras demonstrating his feats. He would assume his position behind a cloth screen, which was removed to reveal his floatation. The widely circulated story described the apparatus the Brahmin used for his seemingly impossible levity:

Sheshal, the 'Brahmin of the Air', artist unknown, from Harry Houdini, *The Unmasking of Robert-Houdin* (1908).

the wrist of his right arm . . . rests upon a deer skin rolled up and fixed horizontally before him to a perpendicular brass bar.

This brass bar is fitted into the top of a small four legged stool, near one end of it. While in this attitude he appears engaged in prayer, holding in his hand a number of beads, and having his eyes half closed.

Other commentators on the act, including Thomas Frost, would confuse Sheshal with an earlier Brahmin who performed almost exactly the same act. Frost attests that the other Brahmin would release a 'a gurgling noise, like that occasioned by wind escaping from a bladder or tube, and when the screen was withdrawn he was again standing on the floor or ground.'

The traveller, author and barrister Louis Jacolliot appears to have discovered an earlier performer of the trick in the Hindu holy city of Benares (now Varanasi), which he would recount in *Occult Science in India*, published in English in 1884. The performer's name was Covindasamy. His levitation appears to have been so stable, so still, in fact, that Jacolliot compared him to a bronze statue of the Buddha that was regularly purchased by Western tourists 'without a suspicion that most of them come originally from English foundries'. Jacolliot goes on:

> For more than twenty minutes I tried to see how Covindasamy could thus fly in the face and eyes of all the known laws of gravity; it was entirely beyond my comprehension; the stick gave him no visible support, and there was no apparent contact between that and his body, except through his right hand.[6]

Seeking the source of the trick was part of the spectacle. Given the opportunity to examine Sheshal's apparatus, audiences supposed that the meagre support the Brahmin used was probably a metal rod, hidden beneath the deerskin on which his arm rested. A writer believed that this would have been connected to a metal frame hidden beneath Sheshal's clothing, concealing a wire ring on which he must have been sitting. The world's most famous magician, Harry Houdini, agreed. Before we turn to Houdini, who researched and debunked the illusion but also practised levitations of his own, let us discuss the rising rope, another apparatus with which the Hindu levitating on an impossibly slender support would be coupled.

The rope trick

Influential stories reached the West, revolving around spectacular tricks wherein a rope was caused to rise and become suspended in the sky. This disregard for gravity was completed when someone – usually a small boy – was made to climb the rope. He would sometimes disappear and often return to the earth in dismembered pieces, before being revealed as whole again, much to the relief of the audience. One of the most prominent accounts of this kind is a story from the court of the seventeenth-century Mughal emperor Jahangir, during a visit by jugglers from Bengal. Stories such as this would come to feature in the work of the Theosophical movement, centred in Western Europe, which we will come to later. As Jahangir, the fourth Mughal Emperor, attests, the jugglers produced a chain of great length at his court, before they 'threw one end of it toward the sky, *where it remained as if fastened to something in the air*.'[7] In this instance, a dog ran up the chain before disappearing; other animals followed: a panther, lion, tiger and a hog.

Ropes, of course, figure prominently in levitation, but this time they are impossibly strung: one can see their beginning, but the rising rope ascends up to a point where the means of suspension vanishes. Once more, light and lightness are key here in two important ways. The dismemberment of the boy climbing the rope uses light in one sense as spectators were often made to look into the sun when following the child skyward. Light, not *lightness*, encloses the mystery of the trick in an aura or protective shell, 'to impede profanation by the gaze of the curious'.[8]

The viewer cannot see what is happening. Sceptics suggested that the crowd must have been hypnotized; outside observers simply see spectators gazing upwards at nothing. Light functions to cut: it is what Marchetti might call 'a sword, blade of flesh and steel', searing vision and decapitating – or at least appearing to.

Such rope tricks captured the public imagination. The *Times of India* would propose a competition, with a prize of ten thousand rupees for the successful repetition of the act. The London committee of The Magic Circle offered five hundred guineas, too. As with the *jaduwallah*, many Western performers tried to capitalize on the act. In Britain, 'The Great Karachi' would become the most famous to do so, and would be subjected to the investigations of the psychic investigator Harry Price. In December 1934 *The Listener* would publicize The Magic Circle's original competition and went on to publish Price's write-up of Karachi's demonstration at the house of the philosopher C.E.M. Joad.

It is worth saying that despite the numbers of witnesses, investigations and exposés on stick leaners, levitators and rope tricksters extraordinaire, the truth closest to reality would often be lost. Peter Lamont explains how the earlier stories of Sheshal, whom we saw earlier, despite being subject to a range of accounts that explained his levity, continued to baffle Victorian audiences. Two decades after the original stories, the *Daily News* featured another piece on the Hindu levitator: 'the Indian Juggler walks into your garden, and suddenly appears six feet from the ground, sitting cross-legged, with nobody and nothing nearer to him than the grass. How does he do it? We cannot explain.'[9] The cultural circuits through which these conjurers of levity would pass, from Orient to Occident, may provide some answer to this problem of cultural forgetting, in which levity's originality was continually reasserted.

Another fakir of the East was the Fakir of Oolu, who was actually one Alfred Sylvester. Sylvester began his profession as the assistant to another Victorian conjurer, Professor Pepper (John

Henry Pepper). The Fakir of Oolu managed a similar levitation feat, which was really a 'modified version' of Sheshal's 'man that sat in the air'. In this case, it was a 'lady that sat in the air', against the Oriental set design of London's Egyptian Hall. Thus, Lamont argues, the deed was 'invented by an Indian, modified by a Frenchman, and was now being performed by an Englishman dressed as an Indian'.[10]

Temples to levity

Sylvester is an interesting example of the itinerancy that defined many performers of levitation. His obituary in an Australian newspaper provides a window onto his movements, especially as he died at the age of 54 in Melbourne in 1886, following a tour to the British colony. His career was a natural alchemy of scientific and photographic expertise, stage shows, exhibitory illusion and the peripatetic urge common to many conjurers of the time. Having studied medicine and chemistry, he went on to become the principal lecturer at the extraordinary Leicester Square institution the Royal Panopticon of Science and Art. The Royal Panopticon opened in 1854 in the wake of the Great Exhibition at the Crystal Palace. Unfortunately, the new institution closed after only two years, becoming the Alhambra Theatre; this eventually gave way to demolition in 1936.

Whether Sylvester's spectacular stage inventions were seen in the vast domed space is unknown. Sylvester was an important stereoscopic photographer during the time, until his warehouse at New Dorset Place on Clapham Road in London burned down. But we know that institutions like the Royal Panopticon were well suited for the expression of lightness and levity, and it is worth spending time on the material contexts within which levitations were formed and performed. A sketch of the building's mosque-like rotunda illustrates the vast fountain that rose in height to some 99 ft (30 m), made 'brilliant' by the light that cleverly illuminated it.

The 'detached particles' of the fountain, wrote one publication, came to descend back to the ground 'like a shower of many tinted gems'.[11] The fountain rose above a backdrop of what one journal would describe as a 'Saracenic style' that 'glitters with blue, and crimson, and green, and white, and gold'. The glass of the dome created a 'starry effect' by drawing the eye upwards to the golden colours and rainbow, alongside suspended chandeliers. Like the acts of mystical and mesmeric levity, the building was of course a copy: the *Illustrated London News* reported it was a daguerreotype imitation of a mosque in Cairo.[12] The outside was described as a 'mongrel edifice', its towers topped by minarets.

Several curiosities adorned the Panopticon that add up to an idea of Victorian engineering undergirding the possibilities of splendid levity. A primitive glass elevator was one: a so-called 'photographic ascending room' that took visitors to a photographic display at the top of the building. Alongside a diving bell and magnificent organ, the hydraulic elevator – one of the first in London – provided visitors an elevated perspective on the cavernous room. Out of the windows they would enjoy wide views of London. Inside the rotunda other curiosities were gathered around the central gallery.

In many respects the Royal Pantopicon expressed a visual culture of display that had become commonplace in Britain, France and Western Europe and that we could call panoramic. Before it was built, London spectators were used to viewing displays in the round through panoramic displays of paintings that would enwrap and immerse the viewer in scenes of the London skyline, such as those by Robert Barker (1787 and 1792). In these moments the viewer was moved into the air. For the urban dweller this raised and oblique position on the city meant a greatly expanded visual perspective. Such panoramas rendered the public speechless. Others took their collective breath away. Vincenzo Lunardi's balloon was exhibited in the Pantheon – a building on Oxford

A Representation of Mr Lunardi's Balloon, as Exhibited in the Pantheon, 1784, 1784, etching by Valentine Green and aquatint by Francis Jukes.

Street designed by James Wyatt – in 1784, allowing visitors to arrive and gape at the hovering balloon beneath the building's rotunda, positioned just underneath the oculus. As Caren Kaplan suggests, 'visitors to the first panoramic installations could imagine that they were rising in a balloon and were free to see as far and wide and as often as they desired.'[13]

Buildings designed for viewing were diverse, ranging from Bentham's prison panopticon to the serious museum, to those of more daring spectacle and curiosity. As Stephan Oettermann identifies, however, emphasis would begin to be given to the more solemn places of display, the scales appearing to be 'tipped clearly in favour of earnest attempts to educate and *enlighten*'.[14]

The Royal Panopticon was something in between a setting of the serious and the spectacular, and in one of the galleried levels opposite the fountain could be found several sculptures. The most notable for us was the *Veiled Woman* (1854) by Raffaele Monti, the Milanese artist who had become well known for his sculptures displayed at the Great Exhibition, becoming an associate of the

Panopticon in 1851. Monti had fought in the Italian War of Independence before relocating to Britain in 1848. Today he is more well known for his *Veiled Vestal Virgin*, purchased by the Duke of Devonshire in 1846 and now on display in Chatsworth House, and *The Sleep of Sorrow and the Dream of Joy* (1861), now housed in the Victoria and Albert Museum. Similar to *Veiled Woman*, *The Sleep of Sorrow* depicts a woman sleeping among several flowers, while another semi-naked woman, draped in cloth, rises above her, both arms outstretched. It was one of the first works shown in the reconstructed Crystal Palace, as a sequel to Monti's role as an official sculptor for the original Great Exhibition display, the Crystal Palace having been designed by Chatsworth's head gardener, Joseph Paxton. As we will see, Monti's work with Paxton continued into other commissions. Bizarrely enough, Monti's personal movements would coincide with those of another important levitator. In 1855 the sculptor kept a studio at 45 Great Marlborough Street in London, which, almost ten years later, would be occupied by a Mr Samuel Guppy, the soon-to-be-husband of the infamous Victorian medium and levitator Agnes Guppy.

Monti's extraordinary combinations of drapery and flight were used to construct a political allegory. Whether the public realized it or not, Monti was using levity to represent 'the ethereal dream of a united Italy rising from the exhausted dreamer below', as Gabriel Williams argues.[15] Richard Tonson Evanson, a medical practitioner and peer, expressed his delight at the exhibition and Monti's sculptures in a book of poetry, *Nature and Art* (1868).[16] His words reverberated with lightness:

> Yet while in sleep grief thus contracts her brow,
> A gleam of sunshine lights her soul even now;
> A glimpse of Heaven, a thought that blest time
> When her Redeemèd soul shall soar sublime;
> All earthly cares and woes behind her cast,

Raffaele Monti, *The Sleep
of Sorrow and the Dream
of Joy*, 1861, carved
marble.

While she attests her heavenly rest at last;
Though now earth's veil still clouds her opening eyes
As she ascends, nor yet has reached the skies;
That most angelic form ascending there –
A marble figure – yet it floats on air . . .'[17]

Evanson was probably ignorant of Monti's Risorgimento politics,
translating the sculpture as a narrative of female redemption and

the Neoplatonic ascendance of the soul we have found so common to levitation. Contemporary scholarship finds Monti's work for the Royal Panopticon in the form of his *Veiled Woman* (1854) to be a bridging piece between *The Sleep of Sorrow* and the *Veiled Vestal Virgin*. Combining his hallmark veiled face with a levitating body, Monti employs all of his skill to impart a sense of weightlessness onto the heavy marble, 'intensifying the impressions of weightlessness and virtuosity' and suppressing the statue's natural centre of gravity.[18]

While the finesse and political subtleties of the sculpture were not quite commensurate with the confident display of emerging technologies and curiosities of engineering and science in the Royal Panopticon, Monti's *Veiled Woman* could and would find other admirers. An author of a review in the *Practical Mechanics Journal* found a likeness between Monti's sculpture of levity and Thomas Moore's Eastern-inspired narrative poem *Lalla Rookh* of 1817.

All this gives us a taste of the London in which Sylvester's shows were given. It makes sense that he would find a home in another Oriental-style Piccadilly venue, the Egyptian Hall. Built in 1812 by Peter Frederick Robinson, the hall was positioned in the same part of town as the Royal Panopticon. Its exterior was decorated with plaster Egyptian sculptures and hieroglyphics, supposedly inspired by the temple of Hathor at Dendera; its interior eventually housed Napoleon's military carriage. Inside and out, the hall was the nadir of British 'Orientalist fantasies'.[19] Even before it was used to host events, entertainment and stage shows, it displayed curiosities from Victorian travellers such as the Liverpool curioso William Bullock, who had commissioned the building in the first place, to house his collection.

The exhibits were oriented towards titillation through bodily and natural curiosity, and included a supposed mermaid (consisting of several animals sewn together), the original 'Siamese Twins', 'the Living Skeleton' and the American dwarf General Tom Thumb. The hall would eventually come under the ownership of the magician John Maskelyne, who used the venue to expose and debunk precisely the tricks Sylvester used the hall to perform. Bullock's first collections took full advantage of the transatlantic trade for which Liverpool was a key port, before he relocated them to London. The hall was a microcosm of Liverpool and London, staging a confluence of mobile worldly goods.

The Times popularized Sylvester's show at the Egyptian Hall as a sensational levitation feat. In it, he first appeared to float a rod above his hand,

Playbill poster showing a levitation trick at the Egyptian Hall in London, 1894.

before revealing his true intention to his assistant. He would place her on a high stool before resting her elbows on 5-ft-tall poles. Rather like the Hindoo Fakir's mesmerism of his assistant, the Fakir of Oolu would then remove the stool, and the audience would find the assistant supported by the two poles. To gasps from the audience, the fakir then removed one more of the poles. After this reveal, the woman would be made to perform several different positions and movements, reminiscent of Ariel, Mercury and Cupid, before lying, as if on a couch, at a right angle to her one flimsy support. Making the 'mysterious power of suspension more mysterious', Oolu would run the pole above, over and behind his assistant's body, as if to prove the absence of a proper and explanatory support for her levity. This concluded, the so-called 'denizen of the air' would then be 'restored to consciousness with all the customary symptoms of awakening from mesmeric sleep. The Fakir vouchsafes no explanation or comment, but retires in silence.'

Sylvester's Fakir of Oolu show proved immensely popular and it would travel far. He would go on to visit Melbourne, Sydney, New South Wales, New Zealand, Tasmania and South Australia, as well as India, before returning to Melbourne in 1882, where he resided until his death. It is clear that Sylvester's tour of the Antipodes created quite a stir. In fact his name would remain in common parlance, to mean a huckster or a trickster. Debates recorded in the New South Wales legislative assembly frequently refer to the Fakir of Oolu during heated discussions, especially when it concerned the budget!

We can trace major criticisms of these kinds of acts, and they tend to orbit around the notion of fraud. Late nineteenth- and early twentieth-century investigators of stage levitation and the rope trick would accuse their exponents of trickery. Some would suggest that the trick was performed through hypnosis, not of the levitee but of the witnesses to the event. Here there are strong resonances with the exposure of levitating mediums, which will be explored in the following chapter. For others it was not the trickery of the trick – so to speak – that irked them, but rather the claims of the originality of the act.

Hypnosis and Houdini

Harry Houdini stands out as both a purveyor of the conjurings that would make Sylvester and so many others very famous, and as a critic of these arts of deception. Houdini's 'unmasking' of the French illusionist Jean-Eugène Robert-Houdin (1805–1871) marked one of his most famous attacks. Robert-Houdin's suspension trick bears a strong resemblance to the cases we have described so far, especially those of Eastern-inspired fakirs. In his trick, however, it was Robert-Houdin's son, and not a female assistant, who was raised or suspended almost on nothing. First, his son would stand on a stool. Two poles were placed by his arms, to anchor him. Robert-Houdin would spray his son with a special ether, which he would inhale, becoming quite unconscious. He would appear to have succumbed to what posters proclaimed was a state of 'suspended equilibrium by Atmospheric Air', or it could have been through the 'Action of Concentrated Ether'. Adding drama, musical sound effects accompanied the act. Robert-Houdin would then remove the stool and each support holding his son up, leaving the boy to appear weightless. To top off the trick, Robert-Houdin would rotate his son's body, so that he appeared to be comfortably resting on the air. Sound familiar?

Robert-Houdin worked hard to defend his invention of this trick, drawing on the wider cultural and scientific context of the development of anaesthetics in medical surgery. His use of this analogy to magic suggests a wider cross-fertilization of science and the arts. 'Seeing that the surgeons had invaded my domain,' Robert-Houdin proposed, 'I asked myself if this did not allow me to make reprisals. I did so by inventing my ethereal suspension.'[20] His memoirs even suggest that some bystanders mistook his trick for reality: he comments that they regarded the 'etherization too seriously', protesting 'in their hearts against the applause, and wrote me letters in which they severely upbraided the unnatural father who sacrificed the health of his poor child to the pleasure of the public'.[21] Of course his comments only helped to amplify the magician's powers to confound his public and bloat his reputation. But Houdini's critique was not directed in this way. What particularly angered Houdini was that Robert-Houdin claimed the trick as his own, where rather 'he gives the impression that but for the sensation created by the use of ether as an anaesthetic he would never have thought out the new trick.'

Martin Scorsese's film *Hugo* (2011) suggests that Robert-Houdin's trick was also copied by others, such as the stage and

Ben Kingsley as Georges Méliès performs the levitating trick with his wife Eugenie in *Hugo* (dir. Martin Scorsese, 2013).

cinema magician Georges Méliès and his wife, who bought the Paris theatre where Robert-Houdin had performed so many of his tricks. They would name the building after him; the Méliès-owned Théâtre Robert-Houdin was located on the boulevard des Italiens, not far from the Grand Café. The couple were influenced by Robert-Houdin's earlier performances at the Egyptian Hall, where Sylvester had also played. They also inherited his ideas and mechanical toys when they purchased the building and its elaborate stage machinery.[22] In *Hugo*, Ben Kingsley is shown in a flashback portraying the Méliès' staged levitation, in the Square de l'Opéra-Louis-Jouvet.

If Méliès could be accused of adapting or advancing Robert-Houdin's trick too, in many respects Houdini's critique is really quite unfair. His accusations pinpoint the crudity of Robert-Houdin's accomplishment, detecting that he almost certainly used a steel corset attached to a steel rod set into the ground. Houdini suggests that this probably accounted for the rigid performance of Robert-Houdin's son, and the sympathy of the audience, who confused the rigor-mortis-like comportment they perceived with the effect supposedly induced by the ether that Robert-Houdin – the cruel father – had administered to his innocent son.

From what we know of the many other historical cases of this suspension-and-levitation trick we have discussed, it also becomes apparent that Houdini's investigations of Robert-Houdin's deceptions miss something. Many other stage and street conjurers were up to exactly the same thing, just perhaps not as dramatically or successfully as him. What's more, the history of magic – and indeed tricks like this one – is surely a story of the improvisation and adaptation of techniques, trickery and concealed machinery, to the extent that any claim of originality is so obviously fraudulent. In fact, Houdini himself was just as guilty of this. Before his 'unmasking' of his namesake, Houdini would attempt his own performances of the art of suspension, adapting, as many others had done, a levitation/suspension trick known as the Trilby, based on the hypnosis- and mesmerism-themed novel *Trilby* by George Du Maurier, published serially in 1894 and as a book in 1895.

Both the trick and the novel played off against one another. Alexander Herrmann's stage shows, performed with his wife Adelaide, were the first to make the transposition, and were believed to have partly adapted Robert-Houdin's suspension routine as well. Like Sylvester and Robert-Houdin, Herrmann would also enjoy a long run at the Egyptian Hall in London, from 1870 to 1873. These would be known as his 'Thousand and One Nights'. On Herrmann's death in 1896, the *Chicago Tribune* would report an exposé of the trick. The piece describes how Herrmann – posing as Svengali – would lay his assistant, his Trilby, on a plank before using various hypnotic spells to cause Trilby to float, rise and sink at will.[23] The *Tribune*'s demystification of the process had perhaps already begun. For while its readers may have appreciated the visual spectacle of Trilby floating around in the air above a darkened stage, 'one could hear the machinery creak. Then one spent the rest of the day wondering what the machinery was like.'

Despite his misgivings about Robert-Houdin's originality, Houdini had also sought to adapt the Trilby trick for himself. Houdini researchers imply that his role as an assistant in the Marco Magic Company's tour of the Canadian Maritimes in the year of

The Great Herrmann's version of Maid of the Moon, 1908, lithograph.

Harry Kellar performs the levitation trick through mesmerism, 1894, playbill.

Herrmann's death saw the beginning of his reworking of the act. Houdini and his wife Beatrice (or Bess) eventually left the magician in Marco's (Edward James Dooley of Connecticut) employment, and went out on their own after the folding of the company. They took the Trilby levitation trick with them. Other circuits of exchange are evident in levitation tricks. William Robinson, one of Kellar's engineers, had helped create Astarte: Maid of the Moon, another levitation act. When Robinson went to work for Herrmann, he brought the Maid of the Moon act with him too.

Reports of Houdini's levitations are vague and mixed with the mystery with which the stage conjurers sought to cloak the act. In the 1953 biopic of Houdini, starring Tony Curtis, Harry is shown to levitate Bess, who is played by Janet Leigh. And here starts some of the intrigue, given that few Houdini scholars had knowledge of Houdini practising this trick. A further image can be found of Houdini apparently levitating the actress Wanda Hawley in 1919. Houdini was then working on the film *The Grim Game*, and both actors would have been present on the Famous Players-Lasky studio lot in Hollywood at the same time. The image appears to be a publicity stunt to promote both movies.

Screenwriter Alfred Giebler's 1919 story for the journal *The Moving Picture World* emphasizes the Houdini enigma.[24] Giebler's write-up accounts for a day of missed leads, glimpses and whispers of Houdini's presence, as he struggles to find Houdini on the Players-Lasky lot. This is how he records his conversation with the company's publicity manager, Adam Hull Shirk:

> 'Adam,' I said, 'I've come out to see Houdini.'
> Adam looked at me with a speculative eye.
> 'Do you know what you're up against?' he asked.
> . . .
> ' . . . Houdini's a regular fellow. But you know that not being where he's supposed to be is the way he makes his living, and he's always practising it. It comes natural to him; it's the best thing he does. And besides, he is a magician; he's upsetting this whole place.'

Shirk shows Giebler the photo of Houdini levitating Hawley:

> 'That's the kind of stuff he does, comes along and raises people up on the air. We're afraid he'll do that to some of us some time and then go away and forget us. Wouldn't it be terrible, now, if Miss Hawley had been left in this position? Of course, the air is nice and soft –'[25]

After a day of chasing, all Giebler is left with is the Houdini-Hawley photo as a trace of Houdini's magical presence.

Of course the familiar gender politics of the levitator are not absent from Houdini, or any of the other stage shows the levitation/suspension trick was shown in either. The relation is remapped from the novel *Trilby* upon the Trilby suspension trick. As several critics have made clear, much like her stage counterpart the Trilby of Du Maurier's book is an aestheticized and sexualized object throughout. She is Svengali's Trilby, an object of capture, becoming an accomplished operatic singer only when hypnotized by Svengali, so coining the name's association with misogynist possession. For some scholars of *Trilby*, there are other resonances with the representation of female levitators. For, like the workings of light that literally and figuratively slice up and expose femininity as surfaces and abstractions explored already in this book, so Trilby is 'cut up into idolized body parts', her feet fetishized and painted, her mesmerised body beatified as a living dead.[26]

The magician's assistant

What should be clear by now is that until relatively recently magicians themselves did not levitate; their powers were better demonstrated by floating others. The more physical, visceral form of magic that would involve contemporary magicians levitating their own bodies and displaying other feats of endurance is a more recent phenomenon, as practised by David Copperfield or the British street magician Dynamo. Early twentieth-century cinema and stage production fell into older stereotypes, where a female assistant would be levitated and simultaneously objectified.

Beyond his earlier stage work, Georges Méliès' cinematic wizardry would feature several particularly sexualized levitations of flying women. As Elizabeth Ezra makes clear, even if Méliès' films would not go to the 'supreme' forms of perversion of others, three types would occupy his cinema: 'winged creatures such as fairies, butterfly-women, celestial bodies in the form of stars or moon goddesses, and the lifeless bodies that float in the air.' Most of them, argues Ezra, 'provided an excuse to show young women clad in tights and diaphanous garments'.[27]

His *La Sirène*, or *The Mermaid* (1904), features a levitating mermaid in repose set against the backdrop of an underwater scene. A conjurer passes his hands underneath her body, to illustrate that no supports are in place and underscoring her floatation. The film blends theatre, cinema and the non-existent fourth wall. The scene is highly reminiscent of Edison, as well as Sylvester, Hermann, Robert-Houdin and Houdini. Common to Méliès' films is the disappearance and reappearance of levitating women, which demonstrates that their ethereality is under the command of the male magician. Edison and Méliès may well have learned from one another, given that both of their works regularly featured levitating women, caterpillars and transformations. They were certainly competitors.

In *Alcofribas, the Master Magician* (1903), a woman appears out of a flying chalice, before she is hypnotized or mesmerized and made to lie on a bed of coals. Billows are given to the coals. The flames lift the unconscious woman into the air, before she disappears, only to reappear again floating under a waterfall with two compatriots, with whom she dances in the air. Notably, the name Méliès gives to his magician, Alcofribas, is derived from Alcofribas Nasier, the pseudonym and anagram of François Rabelais. The sixteenth-century writer published *Pantagruel* in 1532 under this guise.[28] Méliès' connection to Rabelais' world is really not unexpected. Rabelais' character Pantagruel, the son of the giant Gargantua, is the protagonist in a satirical take on the *Odyssey*. The book is a nautical tale full of strange grotesque characters, some of whom devour and ingest air. Rabelais, as Mikhail Bakhtin reminds us, renders a baroque or grotesque body open to the cosmic elements, which move unseen.[29] In *Pantagruel* words are the most unlikely of things to become solid, able to congeal as objects in the air, quite frozen. Coming across floating words 'that are not yet thawed', onto the deck of his ship Pantagruel throws 'whole handfuls of frozen words, which seemed to us like your rough sugar-plums'. When the crew pick them up and warm them within their hands, they let the words loose again: 'we really heard them, but could not understand them, for it was a barbarous gibberish.'

Méliès' play with vaporous and solid transformation became even more sophisticated as his technique developed. His *Les bulles de savon animées* (Soap Bubbles, 1906) demonstrates an advancement in his cinematic magic. First, a woman seemingly condenses out of the steam a magician lets rise into the air. Standing the woman on a table or altar, the magician then blows bubbles from a pipe, except the bubbles are the levitating heads of women, hovering in the air. Méliès may have drawn this imagery from elsewhere. A little more than twenty years earlier, Gustave Moreau's watercolour *The Apparition* (1876) had appeared: a portrait of the emerging presence of the head of John the Baptist hovering in the air in front of Salome, the stepdaughter of Herod II and Herodias. Moreau's painting is perhaps made reference to in Méliès' cinematography. Salome is an interesting figure of female seduction and the immorality of lightness. It is her provocative dance that leads Herod to grant her any wish, and her light-heartedness or impetuousness that leads her to demand John the Baptist's head.[30] The executioner lurks in the background of the painting.

Moreau's other imagery of Salome dancing helps imbue her form with a levitating quality to make her quite ethereal. But the public sensation generated by Moreau's paintings would pale in comparison to Aubrey Beardsley's illustrations for Oscar Wilde's play *Salome*, written in Paris in 1891. Beardsley's *The Climax* shows Salome having just kissed John the Baptist's severed head, which drips blood into a puddle on the ground; his hair has turned into snakes, reminiscent of Medusa's. Meanwhile, in this image Salome

Aubrey Beardsley,
The Climax, 1894,
line block print.

is very obviously levitating: her body is several feet above the
ground. Her hair also appears weightless and statically charged.
In the end, Wilde became concerned that Beardsley's images were
so distracting that his play would be seen as an illustration of the
pictures, rather than the other way round.[31]

It is important then that we understand the kind of context
within which Méliès' filmography would be received. In *Les Bulles*

Gustave Moreau,
The Apparition,
1876, watercolour.

de savon aimées he encourages his floating heads up to the table
to reside with several standing woman. The magician quickly
disapparates the female heads, before they appear again, sitting
on the table, this time adorned with wings. In an act of male
violence, the magician takes their wings, forcing the women to
disappear again.[32] The finale of the film sees the magician crouching
down into a cross-legged pose on top of a casket. Displaying that he

can even use his powers on himself, he transforms into a bubble, which slowly rises towards the top of the screen. The magician then emerges from the bubble, triumphant. Méliès' genius was to even levitate his flying women above his theatre by projecting them on the wall over the entranceway in order to attract audiences to his spectacle.

Other experiments in moving images at about the time of Moreau would also make things appear as if they were in the air, or reveal that the air is where some of us reside. Eadweard Muybridge's chronophotography of Leland Stanford's horse Sallie Gardner, on the Palo Alto track in California, was able to prove a bet and show that a galloping horse will have all four legs off the ground at once. Sallie Gardner is frozen onto photographic negatives in *A Horse in Motion* in 1878. Sallie Gardner was of course not a winged horse, as in wider tropes of levitating horses, but imagining her airborne signals the liberation of the jockey from terrestrial pull. As Laura Hillenbrand, author of *Seabiscuit: An American Legend*, evokes so beautifully,

'Thurston, the famous magician, East Indian Rope-trick', 1927, lithograph.

> The racehorse, by virtue of his awesome physical gifts, freed the jockey from himself. When a horse and a jockey flew over the track together . . . For the jockey, the saddle was a place of unparalleled exhilaration, of transcendence. 'The horse,' recalled one rider, 'he takes you.' . . . On the ground, the jockey was fettered and muted, moving in slow motion, the world a sensory vacuum after the tenfold high of racing speed. In the saddle, emancipated from their bodies, Pollard, Woolf, and all other reinsmen sailed eight feet over the world, emphatically free, emphatically alive. They were Hemingway's bullfighters, living 'all the way up'.[33]

The trend of levitating a female assistant would continue in the stage shows of Harry Kellar and Howard Thurston. Thurston would adopt many of Kellar's tricks, including levitation. Kellar bestowed the title of successor on Thurston, upon his retirement in 1908. But it is not only women who are exposed to the power plays of a domineering male magician figure. Paul Auster's extraordinary novel *Mr Vertigo* (1994) combines the tropes of modern American myths of rootless travel and commercial entrepreneurialism in a band of stage conjurers – the aim is to accumulate wealth, and quickly – with those of Neoplatonic ascension. It is a rags-to-riches story several times over. And yet the book is also an exercise in magical realism that upsets several of the relations we have been discussing so far, because in *Mr Vertigo*, Walt the Wonder Boy, the hero of the book, really does levitate. In 2011, Kristian Smeds's production *Mr Vertigo* adapted Auster's book for the Finnish National Theatre. Smeds moved the audience onto a rotating stage in the middle of the theatre, so that they were looking out at the space where they would ordinarily have been seated, upending the usual relationship between audience and actors.[34]

Dangled

The gender politics of levitation are not limited to the stage or the cinema. Early balloon demonstrations are particularly interesting, especially in the period when the shine or novelty of ballooning was beginning to wear off. Sophie Blanchard, the first professional woman balloonist and wife to the balloonist Jean-Pierre Blanchard, would eclipse his fame by following a similar pattern to later female aviators as the novelty of the woman in the air drove audiences to their shows. Jean-Pierre himself was believed to have gone bankrupt, Sophie carrying on the business to pay off his debts. The image here shows Sophie during her ascent in Milan in 1811 for Napoleon's 42nd birthday celebrations. William Maclure believed that the whole population of the city had turned out to see her, even if he thought that her ascent only left a 'superficial impression, which leaves a vacuum causing the craving after another wonder'.[35] Here Sophie is shown held up by the thinnest of strings from the balloon above her. If you cut them away would she still float, still dangled by the invisible threads of her marital embroilment?

There have been many Blanchards. Early female balloonists navigating relationships with their fiscally ill-astute and manipulative partners is not uncommon. None is rendered quite so clearly as in Jane Urquhart's novel *Changing Heaven* (1990), where the character Arianna Ether – a female balloonist and parachutist – is loosely based on the English balloonist Lily Cove. Of course, Blanchard and Cove were not levitating, but their many flights would be taken with so many different tones and tenors of lightness that they might as well have been. In Urquhart's book, Lily Cove becomes the character Polly, better known by her celebrity name Arianna Ether. Arianna was a female balloonist, touring the country with her domineering manager – also lover – Jeremy. Like Sophie Blanchard, Arianna performs parachute jumps from the balloon.[36] The real Lily was also managed by an experienced balloonist and parachutist, Captain Frederick Bidmead.

In the early parts of the novel, balloon flight provides metaphors from which Arianna's myth is built, but also through which she appears subjugated to the force of her partner. Jeremy was once just as famous as Arianna and had been known as the 'Sinbad of the Air', but is now jealous of her success. As Arianna, Polly appears almost weightless; as she arrives in Haworth, Yorkshire, the wind

Luigi Rados, *Sophie Blanchard in Milan*, 1811, lithograph with stipple engraving.

threatens to carry her away. In the book, Arianna is described as having been tall and thin, with fine white, silky and curly hair. There are rumours that 'she had levitated in the cradle, so lighter than air had she been, from the beginning, that her mother had to use twenty blankets secured by large stones merely to confine her to her bassinet.' People also said that as a child, iron shoes were made especially for her, to be worn when she played in case she became too animated. When she slept, her parents did not dare leave the window open even a crack, lest she should float away through the smallest opening, given her thinness. She chose not to read much at all, because the words, as she perceived them, could weigh her down.[37] These rumours are masculine representations that inscribe Polly/Arianna with a vulnerability and a frailty. Both Arianna and Cove fall to their untimely deaths, Cove during the Haworth Gala in Yorkshire in 1906.

Changing Heaven shows us that levitators can create ruptures in time. Urquhart's Arianna could be George MacDonald's character in his 1864 story 'The Light Princess'. Bewitched by an evil aunt at her christening, the princess's gravity is taken from her. The only thing that could cause her to regain it was her crying. But unlike the melancholy of Urquhart's characters, the princess never cries. She is as gay and light as the wind, her laughter singing its way through the book. The precautions Arianna's parents were said to undertake are soon found to be necessary for the princess, when the queen accidentally leaves a window open:

> the little girl was wrapped in nothing less ethereal than slumber itself. The queen came into the room, and not observing that the baby was on the bed, opened another window. A frolicsome fairy wind, which had been watching for a chance of mischief, rushed in at the one window, and taking its way over the bed where the child was lying, caught her up, and rolling and floating her along like a piece of flue, or a dandelion seed, carried her with it through

the opposite window, and away. The queen went down-stairs, quite ignorant of the loss she had herself occasioned.

The young princess was found to have floated 'by the elvish little wind puff', only to nestle safely under a rose bush, where her giggles shake little petals from the roses.

Arianna seems to have some of the same properties as the princess, but they are ambivalent qualities.[38] Her tethering to Jeremy is tortuous, his affection for her as changeable as the weather. Their love is a rough sea, an elemental tumult of air and the water she fears. Equally, Jeremy renders her flight within a Neoplatonic and Christian tradition, in which her ascent is shown as the soul's desire to rise to the heavens, to join with God. Her return by parachute, Jeremy exclaims, resolves her redemption to 'absolute purity, the *lightness* of the cleansed female soul'. Before Arianna's ill-fated flight in Haworth, Jeremy prepares the crowd for the feat:

> 'And so, my friends, what you are about to see is not simply a young, pretty woman sailing away in a balloon. Oh, no . . . no indeed. What you are about to see is the very spirit of British womanhood ascending to her rightful place with the angels in the clouds. Remote, untouchable, apart. Who are these women who help us, after all, if not angels? Should they not be given the power to fly like other angels? And if this is impossible for all, should not there be one who can represent the rest?'

Arianna's levity is thus a highly gendered one, her lightness signalling how out of place she is on the ground.[39] Somehow she holds together a highly ambivalent lightness. Arianna falls to her death in a nearby lake. Lily Cove's death was thought to have occurred because her parachute lines may have been interfered with by a jealous lover.

Publicity poster for *The Light Princess*, National Theatre, London, 2013.

National Theatre

The Light Princess

a new musical

music and lyrics by **Tori Amos**
book and lyrics by **Samuel Adamson**

Supported using public funding by
ARTS COUNCIL ENGLAND

MacDonald's story contains similar tropes. The princess is ultimately saved by a prince who, on account of falling in love with her, sacrifices himself and in so doing causes the princess to cry and thus regain her gravity. In many senses she is an object, pushed and pulled around by her parents who find her lightness in many ways useful, for they can pick her up and position her when they need to – should her light-heartedness become too much. On one occasion the princess offers to be bound to the earth by a string so they can float her like a kite. But the story of 'The Light Princess' has been redeemed by its reimagination in what the musician Tori Amos would describe as a feminist fairy tale: a musical production of the book by the National Theatre opened in 2013 starring Rosalie Craig, with music and lyrics by Amos.

Drone du Soleil

In the Cirque du Soleil-produced film *Sparked* (1994), a lamp maker tinkers with his contraptions before the power goes out in his workshop. One by one the lampshades around him seem to gain a life of their own and float, or hover, behind him, like luminescent ghosts. Before too long he realizes he can conduct or orchestrate the shades, which follow the attitude of his head and the positions of his arms before he whirls them around the room in a torque of colour and motion. But this is no trick. The video reminds us that no CGI was used in the making of the film: the lampshades are levitated by artfully operated and apparently autonomous quadcopters. There is a knock at the door and the lampshades return to their bases or the inventor's worktop, ending the suspension of the dream.

3 Science, Spiritualism and Scepticism

I F THE PREVIOUS CHAPTER showed how levitation has been held up and supported by a considerable apparatus of wires, steel corsets, cables and a litany of rumours and stories circulating across continents, this chapter deals with a different set of materials, and quite unusual and opposing ways of imagining them. For while we saw how certain levitation events were subject to the gaze and imagination of a public and a print media, the act lacked the scrutiny to which levitation will be put in this chapter through science and paranormal investigation. The study of levitation has involved its own apparatuses and contraptions to capture, see and weigh. To some extent this pits the machinery of investigation against the machinery of trickery and fraud. And yet we have seen that levitation is performed within intense systems of belief, faith and spirituality, as well as completely oppositional logics and rationalities of scientific explanation. It is too simplistic to suggest that these competing epistemologies and world-views have always been incompatible. In fact, we will see that they have almost always found some form of sympathy for each other.

A theory of levitation

In 2007 the artist Goshka Macuga unveiled a curious sculpture in carved wood and fibreglass of the nineteenth-century co-founder of the Theosophical Society, the Ukrainian Helena Blavatsky. The sculpture would be shown at the Saatchi Gallery in London, in Frankfurt, New York and Adelaide, before being sold at auction at Christie's to the Andrew Kreps Gallery in New York for £37,500. Blavatsky is depicted between two chairs, performing an infamous Victorian parlour trick of levity.

Blavatsky and her followers might have disliked her appearance alongside other mediums of the séance in this book. The Theosophical Society was founded in 1875 with the goal of bringing together thinkers and philosophers to consider spirituality, comparative religion, science and philosophy, and hitherto unexplained powers and forces. Except Blavatsky was keen that they distanced themselves from what she described as the 'cradle and hotbed of Spiritism and mediums', seeing them as dangerous 'for humanity'.[1] And yet the group would spend a great deal of energy investigating and theorizing the causes of levitation.

Goshka Macuga, *Madame Blavatsky,* 2007, carved wood, fibreglass, clothes.

Blavatsky set out the key to levitation in her book *Isis Unveiled* (1877). Written as a stream of consciousness, it would mark a treatise on the world's major faiths, claiming they belonged to an older and higher wisdom. Blavatsky was, as was the movement, especially sensitive to non-Western theologies. She had first moved to India in 1882, setting up a branch of the movement in Adyar in south Chennai (Madras). This did not mean Theosophy was simply opposed to science, however. In fact, Blavatsky was keen to identify different forces that could make levitation possible, a levity which she accorded not to a random and unidentified force, but to natural and spiritual laws comparable to gravity. 'Thus levitation', she argued, 'must always occur in obedience to law – a law as inexorable as that which makes a body unaffected by it remain upon the ground.'[2]

Blavatsky would make constant allusions to more accepted versions of physics in order to explain these laws, seeing levitation as a natural phenomenon of lift like a whirlwind, or a tornado. These elemental spirits would be relied upon by the more passive medium seeking to levitate something or someone; while for the skilled 'adept', levitation could be achieved by a 'magneto-electrical effect'. In this instance, one who was able to control the polarity of their body would float.

For more unintended or unconscious levitations like those we discussed in relation to the ecstatic saints, Blavatsky seeks advice from anthropology and finds the potential for natural gestures to follow lines of thought and concentration. To this extent, levitation is the body following a 'mental aspiration and rises into the air as easily as a cork held beneath the water rises to the surface when its buoyancy is allowed to assert itself'. Levitation becomes not much more than the focused will of what Theosophists named aethrobasts.

While Blavatsky was keen to advance the possibility of several motive forces of levitation, she also ruled out others. In a letter to *The Theosophist*, Blavatsky takes care to explain that the inflation of the body by air will not cause it to float in the air like the physical phenomenon of a body floating on water. She explains that a body pumped full of air would simply lie on the ground, 'without showing the slightest tendency to rise', and thus 'so would the ascetic's body, though pumped full of air from crown to toes'. A more plausible floatation would be the potential of altered polarities caused by the inhalations and exhalations of yoga.[3]

All this appears to circle off levitational powers from the quotidian forms of public spectacle we saw in the last chapter, which Blavatsky finds to be repugnant or of a 'lower purpose' – what she goes on to describe as 'merely an instrument of hanky panky'. Of the escapades of public demonstrations such as Harry Kellar's stage feats, she considered that they offered merely the baseless thrill-seeking of low heights: 'it exposes the operator to the risk of breaking his neck, and it is applied in such an exhausting and inartistic way as to leave those who exercise it, utterly prostrate, at the end of an exhibition.'[4] Such warnings are common. Inayat Khan, leader of Universal Sufism, regarded levitation cautiously. Making similar assertions to wider cultural ideas of lightness and weight, Inayat Khan warns of a superfluous levitation, or levity for its own sake: 'It does not give a person great exaltation to become so spiritual that he floats in the air by levitation, if he is no better than a balloon.'[5]

The glare beat upon me

> There is a lady, Mrs Guppy,
> Mark, shallow scientific puppy,
> The heaviest she in London, marry,
> Her, Spirits three miles long did carry.
> — 'Old Ghosts and New', *Punch*

Light and dark, heavy and light: these are the contrasts exposed in the work of many female mediums of the age of the séance and spiritualism. For the Italian medium and levitator of tables, chairs and other objects Eusapia Palladino, exposure is a deliberate and appropriate word, because her story speaks to the more-than-scientific light to which her performances were subject, and the scrutiny of a misogynist press and academy attempting to defame her through sexual insinuation. The same could be said of London-based medium Agnes Guppy, who ignited middle-class intrigue in the wake of her apparent transportation and levitation from a friend's home in Highgate to Lamb's Conduit Street in Holborn on 23 June 1871.

The depiction of Guppy's femininity is of real interest here primarily because she was not a waiflike figure or viewed as ethereal and thus liable to float off on the air. Nor was Palladino. Many characterizations of Guppy's flight played upon the size and weight of her body, repeating some of the earlier themes of fatness and supernatural flight associated with the witch of early modern Europe. The combination of weight and lightness was a prime object for satire, making Guppy's levitation seem somehow more absurd. 'Fat, fair and forty', was one expression used to describe her, drawing on a popular satirical phrase for attractive married women beyond their prime, yet sympathetic to engaging in extra-marital liaisons.[6] *The Spectator*, debunking an article in the *Quarterly Journal of Science* on levitation, implied that Guppy's weight may have led to a 'revulsion of feeling against the hardiness of earthly conditions'.[7] Guppy's size or her 'corpulence' apparently hinted at her low class and low morals. Mr Guppy, writing in the *Daily Telegraph* to defend her, would comment:

> my wife is not fat; it is all good solid flesh, with very little bone. And I ought to know. And if she *were* fat, I have not offered her for sale, and therefore newspaper owners and correspondents should keep their cattle-show language for suitable occasions.[8]

Both Guppy and Palladino may not have been quite as large as their critics were fond of depicting, for they both wore rather layered and bulky clothing, useful for their acts.

Palladino was born in 1854 in Minervino Murge in southern Italy, and at a young age she became famous for levitating furniture. She would also exhibit a strange light and produce strange substances in the relative darkness of a séance sitting. Palladino's prowess earned her renown but also exposed her to the cynical investigations of many scientists and sceptics of the time, including the Society for Psychical Research. The wider accounts are telling for the sexual advances which they suggest lay at the heart of Palladino's success. In this context, darkness provided the grounds for rising sexual tensions, undermining Palladino's position. For those attempting to photograph the phenomenon, light was a threshold or limit for how levitation could be actually witnessed. Mrs Guppy, bizarrely characterized as a madam, was linked to keeping a brothel in Liverpool on Bayhorse Lane.

Palladino achieved notoriety because of her ability to defy several of the investigators who were intent on unmasking her capabilities as tricks. Others were convinced by her. As with St Joseph, of interest to us is the weighing up of evidence around Palladino's and Guppy's levitations. Within Palladino's various sittings, physical contact was required: the séance-goers grasped Palladino's hands. But there were questions as to whether at any point they had lost contact, so as to allow her to raise the table using her own hands. Palladino underwent investigation in Cambridge and Naples by representatives of the Society for Psychical Research, in Paris by the Institut Général Psychologique – this included both Pierre and Marie Curie – and in New York by Hereward Carrington and others. She was well known for having converted the influential racial criminologist Cesare Lombroso; of both Guppy and Palladino, Alfred Russel Wallace was also a fan.

Mediums put a lot into their performances, whether they were channelling spirits or talented actors – it is perhaps not so interesting to ask. Instead, we can note that Palladino was a highly proficient medium, or perhaps the right word is *sensitive*, at channeling forces through her body's expressive movements and gestures. Carrington speaks of Palladino's tiredness, her burning hands seeming to 'contract or shrivel'. For many mediums like Guppy their presence seemed to appear bigger, their bodies were somehow more expanded and projected into the room.[9] Palladino added to her 'hoarse panting cries, shrugging up her shoulders and sneering', with gasping, while her foot scraped the floor backwards and forth.

In the darkness, several witnesses would see dark shapes emerging from Palladino. Some have drawn on interesting sets of philosophies and cosmologies to try to make sense of these events, blurring scientific investigation with spiritualist leaps. For many, Palladino's table levitations, along with the projection of her shape, arms and fluids, suggested an externalized force, in a way comparable with the new understandings of electricity and magnetism and also resonant with spiritualist movements in Theosophy. For the psychic investigator Hereward Carrington,

we have here nervous energy or 'fluid' existing beyond the periphery of the body – that is, in space, detached from the nerves. And if a motor current can exist and travel in this manner, why not a sensory current? It would only have to travel in the opposite direction. For these reasons, therefore, I am disposed to regard the phenomena of exteriorised sensibility as highly probable, if not actually proved.[10]

And while the summary of Carrington's report concluded that Palladino was a fraud, several of her witnesses suggested further investigation was necessary. It was possible that the witnesses might have hallucinated, to the extent that their 'complete conviction' would not be possible. Wallace would also weigh in, suggesting that earlier experiments held at Cambridge in 1895 'only prove that Eusapia might have deceived, not that she actually and consciously did so'. Indeed, Harry Price, the most incontestable of psychic and paranormal investigators, described Palladino as 'alternately fraudulent and genuine'. Price went on, 'with all her deceptions, Eusapia was often genuine and her tricks were of some psychological interest.'[11]

Palladino was investigated through a mixture of witnesses observing the sittings of a séance, and others who took part under controlled conditions. And several séances were photographed using new advances in photographic technology. Many tried to catch out the formidable Mrs Guppy, too, by suddenly producing a light in the midst of a sitting. But the camera can be understood as a prosthesis for revealing other kinds of matter that the eye could not perceive. In the context of Palladino's apparent powers, the presence of unknown or unexplainable forces and substances, such as plasma, was the mysterious drapery around which her ability to levitate was confused. According to a variety of theorists of spiritu-alist powers of the time, such as Camille Flammarion, these were best understood as a quasi-substances lurking below or beyond our powers of perception. Flammarion was himself an ardent balloon-ist; having chosen to ascend on Ascension Day in 1867, it is clear that he saw ballooning to be another form of transcendence. 'In the midst of these blue heavens', Flammarion recalls from his experience, 'I rise from my seat . . . and leaning my arms upon the edge of the car, I glance downwards into the immense abyss.'[12]

For Flammarion, Palladino's powers – and those of others like her – tended to exist only in the absence of light. Darkness was necessary in order for these powers to fully condense themselves, to 'take shape, affect even a certain resemblance to the human body, to act as do our organs, to violently strike a table, or touch us'.[13]

For levitators, light and its absence produce strange effects, composing and recomposing forces only the camera can expose with artificial light. Magnesium or potassium chlorate were substances commonly used. Photography would try to light the scene, albeit imperfectly, while writing would seek to decompose it further into a mode of scientific description that various observers and authors would follow. A parallel mode of detection and evidence-gathering is used to record encounters with Palladino, which describe as much unreliability with the equipment as with the medium herself. At the beginning of one séance, Palladino announced that her sitters would experience something they did not expect, a surprise, which would be archived on photographic plate 'as an unimpeachable record'. Flammarion then takes over the narration of events:

> We wait pretty long before anything happens. At length, the medium trembles, sighs, recommends that we breathe deeply and thus aid her, and we feel, rather than see, the moving of the violin through the air, with a slight vibrating noise of the strings. Eusapia cries, 'It is time, take the photograph, quick, don't wait, fire!' But the apparatus does not work: the magnesium won't kindle. The medium grows impatient, still holds out, but cries that she cannot hold out much longer. We all vehemently clamor for the photograph. Nothing moves. In the darkness, which is needed in order that the plate in the camera shall not have to be veiled, M. de Fontenay does not succeed in lighting the magnesium, and the violin is heard to fall to the floor.[14]

Guillaume de Fontenay was one of several investigators of Palladino's activities, photographing her during a séance outside Paris in 1897. Fontenay is interesting in the context of photography because he was seeking to innovate a means of reproduction without a camera or lens. Although he pursued various methods of spirit photography, he was relatively critical of the announcements around the discovery of 'V-rays' in 1913 by Louis Darget, who developed photographs of what he considered were the forms of simply thought, believing that our thinking would radiate projections into the air that could be caught by the lens of a camera.[15]

We have to understand levitation through photography because in some respects they evolved together. Photographs of levitators like Palladino and the Welsh medium Colin Evans could be subjected to scientific scrutiny and, just as much, amateurish interest and public celebrity. Images would circulate in popular magazines and publications. Photography would go hand in hand with precise typologies and categorizations of different kinds of levitation, strapped down into the bullet points, tables and charts of analysis that Olivier Leroy would employ in his *La lévitation* (1928).[16] Furthermore, we might see in the striving to capture levitation and other spiritual effects through photography the precise means to give form to levity, to objectify it or inscribe it with and by light. As Marina Warner explains in an interview, spirit photography aimed to show that phenomena such as levitation were material phenomena: 'The light touched the paper, and there was this thing that somehow became object.'[17] For Evans, an infrared camera would pick out his levitation against the darkness at a séance in London in 1938. By contrast, Palladino would insist on darkness, 'calling for less light – *Meno luce!*'[18]

Palladino gave a biographical account of herself in 1910 to *Cosmopolitan*, but her voice is drowned out by a chorus of other investigators and commentators. These wider accounts are telling. Palladino's lower-class, peasant background and lack of education – she was apparently barely literate – were often mentioned alongside insinuations that she used her sexuality to advance her success. To some extent this may have been used to authenticate the innocence of the levitator, as a sexualized and unintelligent vessel for the bestowal of other-worldly gifts.

However, Palladino's interview in *Cosmopolitan* is fascinating. While doing little to reinforce the rumours about her, she literally and figuratively describes the modern construction of the masculine, scientific, desiring gaze, a view that is as penetrative as it is illuminating:

> I have been asked, too, why I prefer darkness to light. My answer is much the same. In the beginning when they wanted to get good results they turned down the lamps. It was so arranged by those who made the preparations, and now I have grown to want the darkness. I think it is the best condition. It brings me greater ease and peace. Light seems to have a disturbing effect upon my mind and body, and the influences are less concentrated. Sudden light, when I am sinking into sleep, is injurious to me. I feel pain in my eyes and head. My heart flutters. I find it hard to breathe. I tremble. But when gentlemen insist upon having the light I am willing, if it is not changed, to have the glare beat upon me.

Further on in the interview, Palladino tries to articulate the feelings the witnesses aroused in her:

> Always the people stared at me, and said things to each other that I did not understand. But always they were kind. Now I come to America, and I weep.
>
> The boys who laugh, are they your journalists? I desire to meet only men. I am not at my ease among those who lack weight in the front of their foreheads, where the soul is. I must have attention, concentration. I have received that from the learned men of Europe. Among them, above all others, I like to sit. I prefer men to women, but it is not a question of sex or country, but of intellect and earnestness. I do not object to doubt. I am accustomed to it. It fades away. I know when they come into the room with me who are the doubters. I like to convince them, and for

this reason it is these that I ask to hold my hands and feet, to look everywhere, to do anything they please to satisfy themselves.[19]

She would suggest, 'I am an instrument, to be played upon, like a piano.'

A psychical laboratory

It was not just the medium who was caught under the glare of scientific scrutiny, but scientists themselves. Many could be led to distraction, seduced or simply fooled through misdirection. In 1894, the physicist heavily involved in the development of radio, Oliver Lodge, would propose a 'psychical laboratory'. It was devised expressly for the purposes of investigating psychic phenomena and any alterations that occurred in the physiology of those under such scrutiny. Hereward Carrington, member of the American Society for Psychical Research, was struck by the idea and would propose that such a space could make special attunements and measurements of the medium's own weight, as well as the other bodily circulations and rhythms that might be caused to alter during moments of levitation. More practically for the sceptics, Palladino and those like her could be caught in the moment of fraud.

Lodge himself would be involved in several sittings with Palladino, but the so-called Milan Commission may have inspired his suggestion. The commission met in October 1892 in Milan, at the apartment of one M. Finzi, to conduct several experiments on Palladino, and included other Milanese notables such as the director of the Observatory, Giovanni Schiaparelli – known for his observations of the planet Mars and the mistranslation of his description of natural waterways using the Italian word *canali* (channels) into the English 'canals'. His work would partly inspire Bogdanov's socialist novel *Red Star* (1908), discussed later in this

Alexander Aksakof as controller of a sitting with Palladino in Milan, 1892.

book, and especially Percy Greg's science fiction novel *Across the Zodiac* (1880). Alexander Aksakof, councillor of the Russian tsar (and pictured here with Palladino) was there, as was Charles Richet, a professor of physiology in Paris, who won a Nobel Prize in 1913 for his work on anaphylaxis.

The committee reported several moments of unexplained levity, the first regarding several actual levitations of the table and the chair Palladino was sitting on. The second was related to her weight during the settings. The Milan team used scales to investigate. Palladino was seated on a chair, which was placed on a weighing platform with her feet tied together; a balancing weight was set a short distance away. The apartment's owner, Finzi, read the weight while Schiaparelli watched the balance and especially Palladino, so it could be determined whether she was pivoting off the ground or another surface. By today's standards, Palladino's weight, including the chair, was pretty light at only 58 kg, or 9 stone. But soon the team found that the opposing weight required lightening: Palladino seemed to have diminished her weight by over 8 kg.

The committee's findings were far from conclusive. They could find no explanation for the levitations they observed and photographed, or for the diminishment of Palladino's weight. They did concede, however, that the apparatus manufactured for the sitting was far from perfect. First, they found that movement on the scale away from a subject's centre of gravity could cause some variations in measured weight, albeit within quite narrow limits. Moreover, they could not say whether or not during the

moments of Palladino's lightening she had managed to gain hold
of someone's hand or a surface. As with many of the other sittings
Palladino would attend, however, the investigations had been far
away from proving conclusively that she was a fraud.

Like the seventeenth-century philosophical proponents of the
oppositional pairs of levity and gravity, others would continue to
investigate levitation through the measurement of weight. As we
have seen, the investigations of parapsychic phenomena intrigued
many other inquiring minds from outside the arena of psychical
research, including those developing photographic techniques,
and even engineers and cultural theorists. Notions of the soul's
weight were also not a million miles away from spiritual and
levitational inquiry attuned to the lightness of the body upon
death, as if the soul could fly away, leaving the body ever so slightly
lighter than before.

The Hungarian-born writer, novelist and commentator Arthur
Koestler's philosophical meditations on Eastern mysticism aligned
with scientific debate on the more speculative ends of the spectrum.
Koestler took seriously the potential for levitation alongside other
spiritual forces. His geographic and theoretical travels to India
and Japan later in his life resulted in several interventions in the
magazine *Encounter*, edited by Stephen Spender. He would also
collaborate with the Birkbeck physicist J. B. Hasted in the 1970s on
levitation and weight. These activities would develop tendencies
we can see in his more substantial published works.

Brian Inglis's obituary of Koestler ascribes his interest in
psychical research to several absurd incidents and coincidences
dating back to his childhood that led his interest in the paranormal;
these included his anticipatory escape from a domestic fire and, on
another occasion, his flight from an exploding can of baked beans.[20]
His biographer Michael Scammell suggests that at a party Koestler
tried to convince George Orwell, who would be particularly critical
of Koestler, to attempt to levitate.

Koestler's writings on the Holocaust, especially in *Arrival and Departure* (1943), perhaps capture the escapist and funambulist qualities of his understanding of levitation. In *The Yogi and the Commissar* (1945), Koestler pitted totalitarian rule against the freedom of yogic spiritualism. Moreover, there are the qualities of the *luftmensch* about Koestler, which we will discuss in the final chapter, given his biographical demeanour as the prototypically mobile and rootless European intellectual.

Koestler's wider writings reflect his interest in almost spiritual states of consciousness, which Inglis traces back to Koestler's account of a ride in an ambulance at an early age when he first felt what he describes as an 'Oceanic Sense'.[21] This is one of the most explicit attempts in Koestler's oeuvre to give name to a levitational feeling. In his celebrated novel *Darkness at Noon*, published in 1940, the oceanic sensation is found amid the stark bureaucratic world of an allegorical Soviet Union in the character Rubashov, sentenced to a world of show trials, prison, torture and death:

> It was a state in which thought lost its direction and started to circle, like the compass needle at the magnetic pole; until finally it cut loose from its axis and travelled freely in space, like a bunch of light in the night; and until it seemed that all thoughts and all sensations, even pain and joy itself, were only the spectrum lines of the same ray of light, disintegrating in the prism of consciousness.

Ironically, in *Darkness at Noon* this form of ecstasy is decried as counter-revolutionary, a 'petit-bourgeois mysticism', a 'refuge in an ivory tower'. Resistance must not be too light, because, as Rubashov explains, 'in a struggle one must have both legs firmly on the earth.'[22] Through such a derogatory sense of levity, it may be that Koestler was trying to convince Orwell to accept its possibility, while Orwell would respond by questioning Koestler's intellectual speculations on levity and socialism. In Koestler's suicide note he would write that the 'oceanic feeling' was sustaining him, 'beyond due confines of space, time and matter and beyond the limits of our comprehension'.[23] Orwell named the totalitarian state in *1984* Oceania, after Koester's 'oceanic feeling', a sensation Orwell was keen to deride.

Koestler's work on levitation, as we will see, was more than intellectual: it was a practical and empirically experimental concern. It was heavily inspired by his travel experiences, during which he would immerse himself in Eastern spiritual traditions and write about them at length.[24] It is important not to give the impression that Koestler did not display any sense of scepticism. From India he would describe encountering a man who had claimed to have seen someone levitate over water, floating on a well, 'either in a crouched position or standing on his head'. Koestler was interested in the fact that the young man, who was a physicist engaged in postgraduate research, also practised yoga and had several clear memories of witnessing another yogi levitate as a child. The man seemed able to hold the views of science, religion and mysticism together without too much conflict. Koestler went on to consider that for a 'pious Hindu', whose swimming experience was probably limited to a dip in a temple tank or river, seeing anyone swim – let alone float on or above the water – would be to witness a 'miraculous achievement'.[25]

Koestler would also show deep frustration with the fact that many accounts of actual yogic levitation lacked serious evidence, witnesses or accurate records. He bemoaned Ernest Wood's Penguin book on *Yoga*, which asserted that levitation was a 'universally accepted fact in India'. That the record of so many levitations drew not on accompanying records and testimony but the words 'I remember one occasion', Koestler complains, are 'typical of most writers on the subject'.[26] Could levitation be the product of hazy childhood memories, Koestler wondered, given that nearly all the descriptions he came across were from early recollections? Paralleling our earlier discussions of absolute levity, could levity not be subjected to some form of measurement? Could experiments be performed simply to weigh the body in levitation? he wondered. Should levitation actually occur, then 'the loss of a few pounds would be decisive proof of the power of mind over gravity,' he supposed.[27]

Back in London, Koestler cemented exactly this proposition in what he called 'Project Daedalus' (interestingly, the same name the U.S. Air Force gave to its high-altitude experimental parachute programme; see Chapter Six). Koestler found an initial apparatus for his project by purchasing a set of weighing scales of the type commonly found in railway stations. He would eventually procure a machine that was a weighing-scales-cum-bed designed by the electronics engineer Geoffrey Blundell. The idea was to determine not exactly full levitation, but a partial one. For a body to become ever so slightly lighter on a weighing scales seemed a more realistic proposition. The scales were installed in Koestler's basement flat in Montpelier Square, where Ruth West, who would work for the Koestler Foundation, also lived. As West described in an interview for *Vanity Fair* a while after Koestler's death, she was there 'to teach people how to levitate', but wished they were conducting their experiments in Tibet, where 'you *would* find levitators anyway'.[28] The machine West and Koestler used automatically printed small changes of weight on a chart. Inglis suggests that volunteers were invited to 'join in the research into – *not* levitation . . . but, "mood-induced fluctuations in body weight".'[29]

It is worth pausing in this narrative of Koestler to remember that imaginations of levitating Tibetan lamas would continue to be exoticized well into the middle of the twentieth century. Hergé's comic book *Tintin in Tibet* (1958–9) sees Tintin begin the story by dreaming of his friend Chang surviving an aircraft crash in the Himalayas, who, we find out later, has actually been saved by a

yeti who shelters him in a cave. Tintin, his trusty dog Snowy, and
the rambunctious Captain Haddock head off into the Himalayas
to find Chang, where they are rescued by Tibetan monks high up
in their mountain sanctuary. The comic book demonstrates a
stereotypical European colonial engagement with the indigenous
societies its Belgian travellers encounter. Once in Tibet, the Sherpas
guiding Tintin seem superstitious and afraid. One of the monks
they encounter is prone to lift off from the ground in a levitational
and ecstatic vision, confirming Tintin's premonition of Chang's
survival. Indeed, the yeti that had saved Tintin's friend from the
elements, Tintin considers in the last frames of the book, may have
yet held a human soul.

Koestler's machine is believed to have ended up in the hands of
J. B. Hasted of Birkbeck College, who was conducting research into
a range of phenomena, including extra-sensory perception (ESP),
during the 1970s. Of course, this was the age of the metal benders
and the televisual popularization of telekinetic powers, ESP and
paranormal activity, during which Hasted ran a series of trials. Some
of these were discredited, even by members of the Society for
Psychical Research community in correspondence with the famous
American magician and celebrity sceptic James Randi. The most
notable was a set of experiments conducted with Uri Geller who
visited Birkbeck in late June 1974. The eminent Birkbeck theoretical
physicist David J. Bohm was also involved in the same set of
experiments.[30]

Hasted appears to have improved on the Koestler scales in the
form of a machine that is now owned by the Science Museum of
London, stored in their archives at Wroughton, outside Swindon.
Notes from the Science Museum's acquisition of the Hasted
weighing scales suggest that they may also have been based on the
design of a weighing machine from Sunningdale Ladies Golf Club.
It is difficult to find much evidence for this other than the fact that
Rosalind Heywood, one of Hasted and Koestler's collaborators from

the Society of Psychical Research, lived in Sunningdale, and has admitted to her immersion in what she described as the 'cozy golf and bridge playing world' of the Sunningdale social set.[31]

Several of Hasted's reports indicate that his machine was also built by Geoffrey Blundell, and furthermore, they acknowledge the support of the Arthur Koestler Foundation, and specifically Ruth West and Deborah Du Nann. Whatever its origins, the weighing machine, or bed, indicates the existence of other scientific concerns to explore levitational phenomena, and a curious adaptation of other technical and scientific instruments to do so. The Science Museum's records indicate that the machine made use of an earlier instrument devised to measure heart rate and blood pressure changes in a subject lying reposed on a bed: this was the ballistocardiograph, developed in the late 1930s by the American Isaac Starr as a spring-coupled and un-dampened bed. The apparatus was sensitive enough to pick up the forces of the action the heart exerted on the body. The machine would be commercialized by Japanese electronics manufacturer Nihon Kohden in the early 1950s.[32]

The intention was for the bed to weigh its user. A Hasted report describes the bed as follows: 'Each corner is suspended

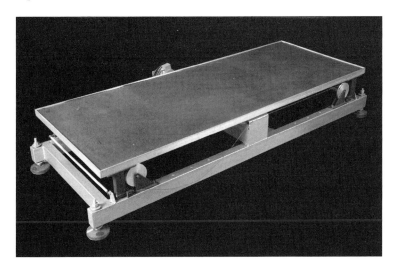

The Hasted Bed, 1978–80, Science Museum, London.

by a tensioned wire, the wires pass round pulley wheels and are attached to a single load cell. Electronic controls enable a high sensitivity suppressed zero output to be recorded, after adjustment to the body weight of the subject who is seated or lying on the bed.'[33] Hasted's research on levitation and other psychic phenomena sought a path of explanation and speculation through the burgeoning writings of quantum physics.[34] One of Hasted's published papers on levitation and wider parapsychic phenomena speculated whether the many-universes interpretation or 'relative state formulation', advanced initially by physicist Hugh Everett in 1957, could provide some explanation for paranormal phenomena such as levitation. Hasted's referee suggested that this interface or connection was never actually made in the paper; it was only conjecture. In fact, Hasted relied on the many-universes theory to propose what could be responsible for the levitations reported in the sittings of mediums such as those we explored earlier. Hasted believed that some levitations would require a force or energy many times beyond that of which a normal adult was capable; levitation was even more likely because a human being would not otherwise be capable of lifting some of the objects. His solution to this problem, that the total energy exerted was beyond that available to a single universe containing a single human being exerting themselves, was that many universes – and thus many mediums – might be interacting with one another. When a table is levitated, he proposed, the minds of the participants could have enabled a switch to another universe of higher potential energy.

Hasted's investigations would include the case of the Enfield Poltergeist, believed to have haunted a home in Enfield, north London, from 1977–9. Hasted's interest was piqued because the apparent haunting of the house also included the levitation of several of its occupants, especially the eleven-year-old girl Janet Hodgson. A school crossing officer observing from over the street had seen the girl appear to move up and down in front of the window. The officer did not believe Janet was jumping because she appeared horizontal. The paranormal researcher Maurice Grosse claimed to have seen Janet levitate from an armchair into the middle of a room in which he was sitting. Likewise, a tradesperson named Mr Rainbow also gave testimony to the effect that he had witnessed Janet and other objects, seen from his position between 100 and 200 yards away in the street, float in the room and whirl about. Their motion frightened him. It is worth saying that there are many stories of young girls levitating. Perhaps one of the most apt combines the lightness of witches in the apparent levitation of six Portuguese sisters committed to the Danvers State Lunatic Asylum in Massachusetts in 1928. A creepy photograph showing the sisters levitating pressed up against a wall now circulates the Internet, apparently taken by the sisters' brother.

In Enfield, the house and the girls achieved almost celebrity status, subject to the inquiries of the press, television and other psychical researchers. Yet many of the occurrences have been proved to be, or are extremely likely to have been, hoaxes by the girls. It is evident that the girls perpetrated the flinging of objects: several things had hit the *Daily Mirror* photographer Graham Morris in the head, convincing him that further investigation was required. The girls also impersonated the deep voices which others heard – said to be of a dead neighbour – as well as other unexplained noises. The photography on the front of Guy Lyon Playfair's book – Playfair was one of the Society for Psychical Research investigators who examined the Enfield case – shows Janet apparently in a bedroom, apparently levitating.[35] A photograph of Janet's floatation, which was subject to a huge amount of speculation and analysis, was very obviously captured while she was jumping. The photographic image may well be the only thing that ever held her in space as she leaped from the bed.

Hasted's team were able to subject Janet to several tests at Birkbeck, and with more rigour than was possible in the Enfield

D. D. Home depicted in
Louis Figuier, *Les Mystères
de la science* (1880).

house. Hasted sat Janet on his weighing bed and asked her to
change her weight. His report suggests several anomalous readings
of apparent weight gain of almost 1 kg (2 lb) – not an insignificant
amount for a small child – for several seconds. Hasted could not
explain this. While the kinds of material we have so far seen appear
quite shaky, to say the least, the lack of plausible explanation for
the pieces of evidence that *were* found raises an interesting issue
for our understanding of levitational research. Could and should
such phenomena be subjected to ordinary methods of empirical
scrutiny? And if they are and achieve positive results, how do we
value the evidence?

Carl Jung's observations of several mediums during sittings in
darkness would support his affirmative belief in the possibility of
levitation, based on the primacy of his own sight and the testimony
of others. 'To reject the recorded evidence on this subject', he
argued, regarding the many observations of D. D. Home's famous
flights, 'is to reject all human testimony whatever; for no good in
sacred or profane history is supported by a stronger array of proofs.'
Home's levitations were certainly subjected to an enormous number
of witnesses and testimony. Alfred Russel Wallace, William Crookes,
Arthur Conan Doyle and even Napoleon III, whom Home enter-
tained at Versailles, were all followers.[36] Home had also shared a
passionate friendship with Viscount Adare (Windham Wyndham-
Quin, Lord Dunraven), and it was he who saw Home's most famous
levitation. It was 13 December 1868, at Ashley House in Westminster,
when Home's witnesses saw him leave an upstairs window only to
fly in through another and laugh as if nothing had happened.

The investigators Guy Lyon Playfair and Maurice Grosse have
noted that the tools of inquiry would often break down during
the Enfield case. BBC cameras and recorders seemed to utterly
fail in ways that were at odds with the usual manner in which such
technology would fail, or with faults that would normally have been
picked up by routine maintenance.[37] In drawing a comparison with

the investigations of Palladino, discussed earlier, and the report of the Society for Psychical Research's first president, the Cambridge utilitarian philosopher Henry Sidgwick,[38] Playfair and Grosse would discuss the tendency for whatever evidence had been obtained – however slim – to disappear, in what they termed 'evidence evaporation'. Doubts seem to nag away at the evidence no matter how convincing it might have first seemed. Such doubts, they suggest, haunted the researcher, to the point that they would demand to revisit the case. 'Negative evidence', they argued, 'not only sticks like mud, but increases in viscosity with the passing of time, even when based upon allegation, insinuation, second-hand hearsay or outright lies.'[39] Their complaint gives credence to the notion that parapsychical research may actually demand other forms of proof, because it has a tendency to be treated unfairly in comparison to other branches of science, and to be subject to as much irrational scepticism as serious and fair evaluation.

Playfair and Grosse could have been drawing on Sidgwick's letter to the editors of the *British Medical Journal*, who had published an editorial titled 'Exit Eusapia!' in 1895, following the Cambridge experiments.[40] The piece poured scorn upon the efforts of Sidgwick and others who were apparently duped by the medium. Sidgwick wrote a staunch reply defending the methods of psychical researchers. The letter in response from the journal is revealing, for while it accepts that it might have misrepresented the views of the investigators, it questions that their attentions should be diverted to such a topic in the first place. Sidgwick's efforts were only wasted time, lacking commitment to the problems of urgent concern, having 'their origin in delusion when they are not the result of jugglery and imposture, and which in any case are unworthy of the notice of serious men'.[41]

4 Reverie, Dreams and the Surreal

IN 1977, AFTER A PUBLIC DEBACLE, a debate in the House of Lords and a vast Sotheby's auction of the house's mammoth collection (the 'Sale of the Century'), the Society for Transcendental Meditation bought the former Rothschild mansion Mentmore Towers, set on a hill on the border of the Buckinghamshire and Bedfordshire countryside. Like other Rothschild homes in 'Rothschild-shire', Mentmore was a copy. Built by Joseph Paxton, famous for the Crystal Palace and the gardens at Chatsworth, it was a Victorian piece of gothic splendour, hosting tsars and prime ministers – Benjamin Disraeli's diaries have him enjoying the Mentmore hunt – adorned with a grand fireplace by Peter Paul Rubens, an orrery clock from Versailles palace and a vast collection besides, but the model for Mentmore was Wollaton Hall in Nottinghamshire. Mentmore's purchase must sound incongruous to this history. The society was led by the Maharishi Mahesh Yogi, a spiritual leader born in central India, who would inspire such notable followers as the Beatles, Clint Eastwood and the filmmaker David Lynch. Transcendental Meditation (TM) would draw on the long history of practices of yogic meditation in order to emphasize and, to some extent, institutionalize and commodify training and procedures for the building of personal creativity, well-being and spiritual health. TM also had a political arm (discussed later). Most importantly for us, it was also a society with a predilection for experiments in yogic flight.

At first blush TM may not be as out of kilter with Mentmore's surroundings as it sounds. The great hall, decorated with Moorish and Islamic carvings, was ringed by a gallery and its ceiling covered by Paxton's characteristic glass roof. The room was all about upwardness. It was all elevation, as a watercolour of Hannah de Rothschild, who in 1874 inherited the estate from her father, Baron Mayer Amschel de Rothschild, makes clear. Hannah, who would become the richest woman in Britain upon her inheritance, is dwarfed by vertical space as much as her wealth.

In a brochure for the Mentmore-based society, several mattresses can be seen lying on the floor of the great hall, and the smoking or billiard room. These were from those practising yogic flying. The transcendence pictured in Mentmore's great hall was the first stage of the society's process to enlightenment. The room became known as the 'flying room', and jokingly referred to as 'London's third airport' by the press. Their comment was close to the mark, given the British government's commission had identified a site just a few miles to the north of Mentmore, at Cublington, for the future of airport expansion in the southeast of England in 1971.[1]

The society's many activities at Mentmore Towers included renting it out for film and television productions. Terry Gilliam's *Brazil* (1985) would film a restaurant scene in Mentmore's Grand Hall, on a platform built several feet above the ground, to lift the actors a little closer to Paxton's vaulted glass roof. Reportedly, the society liked the design so much that they asked if the set constructed for the film could be retained, but the production team had to dismantle it in the Grade I-listed building.

The scene and Gilliam's film exult in the strange and the fantastic. Jonathan Pryce's Sam Lowry is *Brazil*'s protagonist, living in a dystopian future, continuously daydreaming himself out of his caged existence as a worker within a topsy-turvy bureaucratic and

Flight meets bureaucracy in *Brazil* (dir. Terry Gilliam, 1985).

totalitarian society. These are common themes within Gilliam's filmography, and are also similar to those that appear in Koestler's novels, discussed earlier. Lowry frequently sees a vision of himself as a metal-winged, godlike figure, soaring through the clouds with dexterity above the presumably British countryside. His trance usually involves him saving a beautiful woman and battling some kind of monster within the depths of the world below him.

It is worth mentioning that this species of soaring levity is not quite the sort that Gilliam would experience in his own dreams. Gilliam admits that in those, he usually hovers just a few feet off the ground, even if he is able to traverse the world from this limited height: 'I'm not a high flier,' he says in an interview.[2] Finding the muscle memory of the dreams so real, and confusing imagination for reality, as many characters do in his films, Gilliam once sat down with a friend and tried to show him his abilities. Unfortunately, his levitation did not come off.

The levitator usually needs something to push off against, and for Lowry it is his confinement. Lowry is restrained within the torturous work that subdues him. He endures the indifference of his overbearing and ageless (following her copious plastic surgery) mother and her friends in the restaurant scene – maternal relationships are important here. The landscape of the movie plays a part in this too. From the corridors of his apartment building to his work in the records department of the Ministry of Information, the film sets denote both enclosure and massiveness. On the one hand, there are the claustrophobic and burrowed-through ducts and endless cables, perforating even the most domestic of spaces. Law enforcement officials happily explode openings in ceilings and floors – all designed by Norman Garwood – in order to prosecute their law. Outside these tunnels, the sets and matte paintings depict vast canyons of a vertical metropolis, echoing the American sketcher and architect Hugh Ferriss's gargantuan renderings of the future city, which owe much to Fritz Lang's film *Metropolis* (1927).

Matte paintings, models and the use of forced perspective help achieve the sense of a monstrously large modern and urban dystopia. Lowry's character is caught very much within the cogs of this machine, and only his dream flights can free him. Even a zip-wire escape with Robert De Niro's character Tuttle, who abseils down a disused cooling tower in the film's finale to save Lowry from a lobotomy at the hands of his friend Jack Lint (Michael Palin) – all a dream – offers the possibility of flight from this noirish vertical hell.

Lowry's dreams of levity and escape are not uncommon, and correspond with psychoanalytically informed theories of flight which understand levitation as an expression of some form of longing for intimacy following detachment. In this chapter we examine the relationship between levitation and the strange, through dreams, Surrealism and psychoanalysis.

Transcendence

Bizarrely, another important levitative figure repeats itself at Mentmore, and appropriately so, given the working relationship between Joseph Paxton and the sculptor Raffaele Monti at the Great Exhibition. In the decorative coving which Monti was employed to carve at Mentmore, his veiled vestiges would look down on the vaulted great hall, perhaps puzzled by the scene of the society's followers hopping on the floor below, or the ecstatic orgy scenes portrayed in Stanley Kubrick's *Eyes Wide Shut* (1999), shot in the residence. Without the delicacy of his standing sculptures,[3] Monti's carvings can also be seen in the surreal music video for the song 'Avalon' by Roxy Music, directed by Howard Guard in 1982. They are caught in a flash between a whirling female muse and the falcon Bryan Ferry releases into the Buckinghamshire dawn.

Within TM, the emphasis is on a series of stages through which one rises higher in one's aspirations. The portrayal of yogic flying by the society's proponents, its detractors and the wider public media, would frequently be mixed up with wider associations of yogic mysticism and actual levitation. Yogic flying has been taught by the society since its days at Mentmore Towers, where it was offered as part of its course TM-Sidhi, to which numerous notable figures and intellectuals were invited, presumably as a way to help the programme achieve popularity and legitimacy.[4]

As so often is the case with levitation practices, TM adherents have mixed mysticism with efforts to gain some form of scientific acceptability of their beliefs. Today they claim that scientific research supports the existence of positive physiological changes, measurable by an electrocardiogram. They suggest that during yogic flying 'there is a marked increase in brain wave coherence that coincides with the body lifting up.' Scientific research on yogic flying was also central to the society's home in Mentmore, where it positioned itself in the late 1970s as the Maharishi European Research University (MERU). A series of seminars on 'Science, Consciousness and the Creation of an Ideal Society' would run exploring the benefits of 'higher states of consciousness', on themes such as defence, government, biochemistry, psychology and physics, and was advertised in journals such as *New Scientist*. Laboratories had been set up in the servants' block of the house to explore these practices. And while the seminar series had sought to make TM intriguing to a new generation of academics, through their political activities they also wooed some of the great and the good, including Nobel Laureates such as theoretical physicist Brian Josephson and the chemist Ilya Prigogine, but also the renowned psychologist Hans Eysenck, to witness their activities.

The parapsychology team (now the Koestler Parapsychology Unit) that Koestler's estate would support in Edinburgh made several enquiries to Mentmore, seeking to bring TM-Sidhi under their scrutiny. Susan Harding and Michael Thalbourne were interested in the apparent paranormal abilities of those practising siddhas operating at 'higher states of consciousness', especially levitation, or 'flying'. Despite TM advocates' obvious intention to prompt scientific discussion or explanation of their practices, they do not seem to have been receptive to the Edinburgh team. While we can only take the published writings of Harding and Thalbourne at their word, they suggest that TM had rejected their application because 'the organisation has an unfavourable attitude towards parapsychology.'[5]

Claims of the benefits of Transcendental Meditation and flying, both to the individual and society, have always been part of the TM message. As far as their political ambitions went, they aimed right for the proverbial top of the mountain. In Britain, these activities were once again centred at Mentmore, where in 1992 they launched the Natural Law Party from the former Rothschild mansion. In the United States, their claims and aims were even more radical than in Britain. John Hagelin has been the scientific leader for Transcendental Meditation through the Natural Law Party, running for U.S. President in 1992, 1996 and 2000. Part of his campaign would rest on the basis of the crime-prevention or -easing results of the meditative and levitation practices he and TM proposed. The 'Maharishi Effect' made wild predictions for TM's success. It would enable Hagelin to suggest that there was a relation between the numbers who practised TM and yogic flying, and the local or even global crime rate:

a group of 200 practicing [sic] the TM-Sidhi program together in a city of four million (100 × 200 × 200) would be sufficient to produce a measurable influence on the whole city; a group of 1,600 in the U.S. would influence 256 million (100 × 1600 × 1600) people, the whole population of the U.S.; and a group of 7,000 would influence 4.9 billion (100 × 7000 × 7000) people, the population of the world at that time.[6]

Today TM spokespersons advocate their programme as a method of counter-terrorism and peace-building, 'helping to avert negative intentions before they rise to action'. Proponents of TM even argue that their positive energies overflow into national security,[7] while the national debt might ebb away through the benefits of TM's coherence, suggests Natural Law Party candidate and former magician Doug Henning. Henning ran as a candidate in the 1992 general election in the UK in Blackpool South, and then in Rosedale, outside Toronto, in the Canadian elections in 1993. Henning was less inclined to relate TM to science than magic. He explained that through the mysteries of TM he could disappear, because 'your body just stops reflecting light'. And, moreover, 'When you reach your full potential, and you think, "I want to levitate," you can levitate.'[8] With the Maharishi Yogi, the Society drew up plans for a theme park: Veda Land. The park was to be located near Niagara Falls, with Henning acting as director of Maharishi Veda Land International, a subsidiary of the for-profit Maharishi Heaven on Earth Development Corp. Their plans would include a levitating building, a meditation university, a tower of peace and a flying-carpet ride. Henning died in 2000 and the party was deregistered in Canada in 2003.

If TM's version of not-quite-levitation would allow society to transcend the vices and inequities of conflict and war, at its heart TM advocates a kind of transcendental evolution of the very nature of the human. Yogic flying is the first and most earthbound stage of this transition. Golden Dome, possibly a spoof website and named after the new headquarters of TM in Fairfield, Iowa, makes an artful addition to the long association between levitation and human transcendence: 'The basic trend has been for man's body to hold his head ever higher', the website states, and 'then the head (or mind) lifts the body higher'.[9]

In this projection, the siddha of today is merely at stage 1, achieving short hops to higher levels of consciousness in some ways reminiscent of Stanley Kubrick's transcendent evolution from ape to star man in *2001: A Space Odyssey*. Stage II moves five hundred years from now, where hovering is to be achieved during meditation, and the beginning of the mastery of the laws of nature at 'the quantum gravity level'. Three thousand years from that point, humans will have learned to float through the air as if a superman, and will have learned to master nature at the 'unified field level'. Finally, in AD 9595, humans will arrive at siddha level IV, achieving total mastery over the laws of nature, allowing corporeal transportation at will, and the transformation of matter. The figure does not just levitate on this scale, but like the medieval symbology of the disappearing Christ, the human can almost dematerialize altogether to some kind of semi-spirit form. All that is left is a foot – just about – in both worlds.

Bedtime

Levitation can often come in slumber, in the fall of the body to sleep and the realms of the dream or the unconscious. Sigmund Freud helps tie up the relationship of the psychology of levitation with sleep and also with sexuality. He famously regarded Leonardo da Vinci's yearning for flight as 'deflected expressions of sexual impulses'. Freud finds that Leonardo's memory of a vulture flapping its tail against his lips condenses with Leonardo's understanding of the first pleasures he derived from being nursed by his mother. In this light, levitation and levitational dreams may express supressed Oedipal sexual desires following early motherly or parental detachment.[10]

For Freud, flight and levity were expressions of sexual excitement embodied in the male penis, rising up 'in defiance of the laws of gravity'.[11] The different vehicles of the aerial age were seen as symbolic representations of how the human imagination had revolved around the 'phenomenon of erection'. In *The Interpretation of Dreams*, Freud writes that the dreamer might 'treat the sexual organ as the essence of the dreamer's own person and make himself *fly*'.[12] In the rise of levitating bodies – and aroused body parts – sex is paradoxically vertical, because, like levitation, it often happens lying down.[13]

As we saw earlier, the magic carpet was a popular transportation aid in the *Thousand and One Nights*. Contemplating the carpet may allow us to see the curious relationship between psychoanalysis and the treatment of levitation as a mental but ultimately curable event. For Marina Warner, there is a strange commonality between the sofa and bed or daybed, for confession, hallucination and vision:

> the oriental sofa becomes a nesting place for dreams and pleasure, a daybed, a low-lying couch for reclining and abandoning oneself, alone or with others – to love-making, autoeroticism, smoking, gossiping, daydreaming, to storytelling, reading and studying, and to quietness and reflection.[14]

For Warner, interesting levitated perspectives are to be found in the artwork of the Danish artist Melchior Lorck. Commissioned by Ferdinand I to produce intelligence about the Ottoman Empire, Lorck gives us an earlier view of floating figures through the detachment of an elevated perspective on Turkish cities, in the works he created between 1555 and 1559. Lorck's images are not the emotionless and rational abstractions you might expect to be the case in the history of the aerial view, but contain sometimes odd and magical juxtapositions. Warner focuses on two. In one, a curious image of a levitating tortoise hovers above a Venetian scene. In another, Lorck presents a remarkable watercolour of the city of Istanbul from above, this time showing another intimacy: a pair of lovers can be discovered on a balcony engaged in an intimate act. In a way reminiscent of the legal emblem we

Melchior Lorck, *Tortoise, and Separate View of a Walled, Coastal Town in the Veneto*, 1555, charcoal.

considered earlier, we find the collision or collusion of a subtle satire with the seriousness of Lorck's reconnaissance images.

The British Museum's collection of Lorck's works show his special affinity for flight. Several decades fall between Lorck's engraving of a crucified man in 1550, after Michelangelo's depiction of Haman on the altar of the Sistine Chapel of 1511, and his *Surgi Fortun* (The Instability of Fortune, 1574). Both subjects, however, are twisting and appear to be almost taking off. The engraving of Fortune depicts her floating on top of water with a coastal city beyond. Fortune seems to be weaving the elements with one hand, and mastering a sea creature in another.

We will come back to the relationship between crucifixion (and other kinds of death) and levitation later, because first we can find further preoccupations with levity and the blurring worlds of sleep, dreams and reality. Franz Kafka writes in his diary of 16 December

1911 that while falling asleep, he had a vision of a 'group of people isolated in the air, like a mountain with the earth extended somewhere beyond them'.[15] So entranced was Kafka by this dream that he forced himself to focus on one of the figures, who was wearing a distinctive ceremonial dress. For June O. Leavitt, Kafka is not employing the psychoanalyst's lexicon of terms; instead his ideas are more resonant with the writings of the Theosophists, with whom Kafka was beginning to engage.

In March of that year Kafka had attended one or more lectures of Rudolf Steiner in Prague. Steiner was then head of the German arm of the Theosophical Society, which Madame Blavatsky had founded. Kafka would go on to attend an appointment with Steiner at the Victoria Hotel. During the session he confessed to Steiner that he was experiencing transcendent or clairvoyant states, losing grip with the fabric of reality, and becoming more interested in his spiritual or 'mystical' life at the 'the boundary of the human in general', as Kafka describes in his journal.[16] While Kafka's diary entries suggest he found the conversation with Steiner disappointing, his writings would continue to display the elements of Theosophical influences.

One of Kafka's early short stories, 'Descriptions of a Struggle', set in his home town of Prague, is particularly interesting for the levitation of the story's narrator. Having been dumped unceremoniously on the cold ground of the street and standing, swaying, by the statue of Karl IV, the narrator is lifted by an idea. He tries experimenting with little swimming movements and finds that he enjoys them. His head rests in the cold air; 'it was my right knee that flew best; I praised it by patting it.'[17] For Leavitt, it is apparent that Kafka is narratively experimenting with Theosophical ideas of the etheric body, which might explain the distance he begins to exhibit from his actual physical body, as seen in the affection he gives to his knee. His flight demonstrates an immersive experience of Prague through his flying, etheric self, as his memory becomes a little vaguer, his thoughts a little slower.

The narrator works hard to keep himself airborne, just above the railings as they make their way across a bridge towards Petrin Hill. He increases his speed and swims in circles 'around every saint I encountered', and then holds himself 'just above the footpath by imperceptible flappings'. He is reassured that he can 'throw himself into the air'. Interestingly, the location of Kafka's levitational narration is also the site of Tereza's ascension in Milan Kundera's *The Unbearable Lightness of Being*, as she walks up Petrin Hill, overlooking the city. The saints lining the heavily statued

Jaroslav Róna, *Franz Kafka*, 2003, bronze.

Charles Bridge are encountered from much further away in Tereza's passage. Rather than her circling them, they reproach her, 'shaking their fists and lifting their stone eyes to the clouds'.

Communist Prague and Hollywoodized New York could perhaps not be further away from one another in other filmic imaginations of levitation. In Ivan Reitman's 1985 comedic hit *Ghostbusters*, levitation once again carries the usual associations of ecstatic dispossession and sexual fantasy, and back to a bed. Bill Murray is Peter Venkman, the reluctant figurehead of a group of disgraced parapsychologists, kicked out of the department of psychology at Columbia University for their 'sloppy' and 'questionable' methods. Men, as we have seen in this book, tend to investigate levitators. So, typically, it is Sigourney Weaver's character Dana Barrett whose 22nd-floor apartment is haunted, and who solicits the Ghostbusters' help. Almost all of the ghosts levitate in *Ghostbusters*, from the first haunting in the New York Public Library that leads to the opening titles. Throughout the film, there are strong expressions of male sexual fantasy. As the level of spectral activity increases and the Ghostbusters receive more work, during a montage Dan Aykroyd's exhausted and asleep character Ray dreams of being awoken from sleep by a young woman floating above him. The ghost quickly disappears before he finds the flies to his trousers are unbuttoned and he is taken to a dreamed ecstatic bliss.

Barrett's eventual levitation is permitted by a transformation which occurs not on a bed but a couch in her apartment, as she puts the phone down to her mother. Monstrous male hands burst out of the sofa, pinning her down and silencing her scream, before thrusting her towards the kitchen, where a hell hound waits to, we assume, devour or consume her. Some moments later Venkman arrives to pick Barrett up for their date. Barrett now reveals she is – wince at the innuendo – possessed by the 'Gatekeeper' Zuul, and very eager to join with the 'Keymaster'. The keymaster is actually Vinz Clortho, now inhabiting Rick Moranis's character Louis Tully in order to realize the coming of Gozer, a Sumerian god. Offering her body up to Venkman, who now claims to be the Keymaster, Barrett/Zuul rises and floats above the bed. Her body is driven upwards by the growls of Zuul's voice, which is inhabiting her with a beastly dog-like voice. Her

Dana Barrett levitates as Zuul in *Ghostbusters* (dir. Ivan Reitman, 1984).

hands clasping her body, Barrett/Zuul is turned slowly upside-down to face Venkman below.

Later, in a phone call to Spengler, Venkman quips that Barrett 'sleeps above the covers' and reveals that he ended her levitation, 'shooting' her with several ccs of Thorazine to put her to sleep. Barrett/Zuul does submit to sleep's fall, but only until she is awakened by the climax of the environmental protection agency officer, who has shut off the protection grid to the Ghostbusters' custom-made storage facility. The interruption to the ghosts' prison releases their pent-up energy, which explodes through the roof, creating fireworks on the Manhattan skyline. If you haven't had enough of the innuendo yet, on this awakening, Weaver's Barrett/Zuul walks in slow motion to her apartment window, before that too blows out in a massive explosion, only for the Keymaster/Louis Tully to turn up for further consummation at the end of these multiple orgasms.

Given all this, perhaps it would seem incongruous that levitation, suspension and free fall should be drawn on as a way to market the more wholesome sphere of domestic home improvement. As we have seen, levitation has a strong relationship to dreams and the space of sleep. The 2014 advert 'There's No Bed Like Home', produced for IKEA by Mother London and directed by Juan Cabral, features a woman tumbling out of several beds that are to be found levitating in the sky above London. The woman free-falls between the beds, as if a parachutist, and eventually falls her way to her own bed at home, where she wakes up, refreshed. Famous lines from Shakespeare's *The Tempest* narrate the sequence, evoking the relation between dreams and oneiric flight.

Maybe this is not so at odds with the discussion so far. If levitation is a suspension, disorientating and rootless, where all coordinates might be lost, the fall of sleep is a move away from suspension. The fall from levitation has direction. It is a zeroing in. The fall of the woman, however terrifying, is the more grounding act – back to bed, back to reality. IKEA is obviously not the originator of the deployment of these tropes within the alchemy of advertising: countless bed and mattress manufacturers and sellers frequently market their products on the principles of weightlessness.

Nightmares

Along with the relationship to dreams and sex, levitation is also tied to nightmarish experiences and encounters. Indeed, psychobiographers of Freud and others have been keen to show that Freud himself was particularly fearful of flying. Had he not been, he might have left Austria in 1933 when Hitler came to power. His fear may have come from an 'abnormally' strong attachment to his mother, the fear of severing that attachment by flight and travel, and the suppression of other emotional and sexual impulses.[18] Levitational flight and ascension in dreams can come with feelings of horror-ful vertigo.

Exploring levitation in a different direction from Freud, Carl Jung saw the psyche itself – the complex of unconscious and conscious thought – as obeying quite different laws to those of gravity. If gravity was a force that dragged the body down, the psyche could act against it. For Jung, the psyche could be understood *as* 'weightlessness'. Jung's interest would be developed through his explorations in other unexplained phenomena, such as flying saucers and other objects that appeared in the skies – topics he would eventually devote a book to. His work would also delve into experiences of human levitation through his encounters with the famous medium Daniel Dunglas Home, and particularly the experiences of the wounded during the First World War. For Jung the psyche and gravity were 'incommensurable' or irreconcilable because of their different natures; the psyche he understood as '"anti-gravity" in the truest sense of the word'.[19]

Jung's interests were also personal. During 1944 Jung found himself experiencing several levitational visions while in a delirious

state, ensconced in hospital following a heart attack and with a
broken foot. Jung would describe a moment of ecstasy, experienced
from a position floating several hundred miles above the earth. In
this 'weightless, levitated condition' Jung felt 'safe in the womb of
the universe'.[20] Moments of traumatic experience, from blasts to
shrapnel wounds, would give Jung perhaps the greatest examples
of the primacy of the psyche over the body. Many of the wounded
described sensations of levitation and out-of-body experiences,
which would replace their nightmarish trauma with the bliss of
levitative ecstasy. For Jung these indicated a 'shift in the localiza-
tion of consciousness, a sort of separation from the body'.[21] His
field notes on patients recorded during and after the war show Jung
to have been fascinated by accounts of levitation as a 'sensation or
hallucination':

> the wounded man seeming to rise in the air in the same position
> he was in at the moment he was wounded. If he was wounded
> standing up, he rises into a flying position, if lying down, he
> rises in a lying position, if sitting, he rises in a sitting position.
> Occasionally his surroundings seem to rise with him – for
> instance the whole bunker in which he finds himself at the
> moment. The height of levitation may be anything from eighteen
> inches to several yards. All feeling of weight is lost. In a few cases
> the wounded think they are making swimming movements with
> their arms . . . During levitation the mood is predominantly
> euphoric.

Paul Fussell has noted that the mental and physical injuries of
the war also set many people in flight, including the wounded for
whom travel became exhilarating and even cathartic. The British
soldier Maurice Wilson, who had earned a Military Cross, 'and later
had his arm and chest ripped open by machinegun fire', would
experience a similar wanderlust, but aimed specifically at the ascent

of Everest.[22] Leaving the war on the verge of 'nervous breakdown', Wilson appears to have found peace in a period of fasting for 35 days. By luck he would come across stories of the 1924 expedition to climb Everest, the journey that would claim George Mallory's life. Wilson felt, as many others would, the pull or allure of the mountain. Those who have gone before and followed Wilson have experienced the same desires – what the mountaineer Frank Smythe described as the longing to 'expand consciousness, to escape from fleshy shackles, to rise above all earthly considerations'.[23] The ascent of Everest could be a form of levitation, and Wilson would devise a plan to take him to Everest by plane. He believed he could levitate the rest of the way.

In Salman Rushdie's *The Satanic Verses* (1988) the character Allie yearns – like mountaineers do for Everest – for the character Gibreel. Their sexual union is transcendental and ecstatic, a transporting 'outside'. In Rushdie's book she becomes the first woman to climb Everest, where she encounters none other than Maurice Wilson's spirit; she comes across his ghost sitting in the lotus position, chanting a mantra. Rushdie gets some of the details of Wilson's ascent wrong, but he is keen to endow Wilson's fictional spectre with the levitative powers that in life he may have never have gained. Wilson hangs about Allie, strolling on the ground or hovering in the air. On one occasion he seems to belly-flop into the snow before gliding 'upwards as if he were riding an invisible anti-gravity toboggan'.[24] Rushdie's book conflates sexual ecstasy with the ascent of Everest and that of death. Allie's climb does not ape the weightlessness of Wilson's ghost, but finds transcendence in the labour of the climb, as she feels light despite, or because of, the arduous ascent. Allie feels 'something lifting off the top of my head'.[25]

Wilson believed that his ascent could be partly achieved by aircraft to northern India, or rather that is where his circuitous route took him as he fought against different national bureaucracies, including the British, who refused to ease his permission to travel across Persian airspace and eventually crash-land or parachute into Lhasa. Wilson bought a Gipsy Moth plane to take him there, naming it appropriately Ever Wrest; he was forced to land in the last airfield in India closest to the borders of Nepal.[26] He hoped that the last leg of his trip would be aided by mystic levitation. Instead, it was terminal. After travelling from Darjeeling into Tibet in disguise, and finding his way to Rongbuk monastery, Wilson died on Mount Everest's slopes in 1934. Receding ice has allowed his body to be viewed on various occasions during the decades.

Building on the themes of the psyche and the space of slumber, many levitators have intruded on our dreams, submitting the dreamer, often female, to a sometimes horrifying hover. These imaginations are ancient. In the Roman coinage of Antoninus Pius, minted in AD 140–44 to celebrate the 900th anniversary of the foundation of Rome, can be found representations of the god Mars, hovering naked, spear in hand, above a half-naked Silvia, a vestal virgin about to be raped by Mars.[27]

An interesting figure can be found in the idea of the banker, the suited financial worker who is suspended by the cushion of his fiscal adeptness, and in some portrayals, supernatural and other-worldly forces. We could turn to the unlikely stage of the Joss Whedon-created television series *Buffy the Vampire Slayer* (1997–2003). The Emmy Award-nominated episode 'Hush' featured only eighteen minutes of dialogue in the 45-minute run time, because the voices of the inhabitants of Sunnydale – a town somewhere in California – have been stolen away by the visitation of several eerie figures known as 'The Gentlemen'. The men are perhaps so distinctive because they also appear suited. Sporting cufflinks and black ties, they are the perfect expression of financial workers or public administrators turned, or innately, monstrous. As the story unfolds we learn that these nocturnal visitors hold their origins within children's fairy tales. Buffy and her friends discover that a princess's scream once killed them, and thus only the human voice can hurt these figures.

To negate this threat, The Gentlemen steal the voices of Sunnydale's populace using a magic wooden box. It is a child's or teenager's nightmare, exemplified in the nursery rhyme song Buffy hears in a dream that anticipates The Gentlemen's arrival:

> Can't even shout, can't even cry. The Gentlemen are coming by. Looking in windows, knocking on doors. They need to take seven and they might take yours. Can't call to mom, can't say a word. You're going to die screaming but you won't be heard.[28]

The tropes of voice and (sexualized) female disempowerment feature in the discussions of cultural critics working on *Buffy* and the wider canvas of u.s. television series. The Gentlemen invade domestic spaces, infiltrate the night, and ultimately mutilate the body. By the end of the episode Buffy destroys the wooden box and ends the lives of The Gentlemen with her own scream, which causes their heads to explode.

For our purposes, The Gentlemen retain our focus because they are another figure of levitation. They appear as skeletal-looking men in baggy suits. Their skin is sunken to follow the contours of what is left of their muscle and bone. The figures take human hearts for their sustenance when the town is asleep, carving them directly out of their owners' bodies. Of course, The Gentlemen do not walk or run, but levitate, floating a foot or so off the ground. Their movement is a menacing glide. They also manifest a veneer of politeness; their gestures and cruel smiles mask their wicked designs on the human body, as they loom over their sleeping or voiceless victims.

If there is something perceptibly surreal about this imagery, perhaps it should come as no surprise that figures such as these have also been rendered in twentieth-century artworks. The

Surrealist movement was perhaps the most active in capturing the energies of levitation, and particularly the conflicting relationship between levitation and gender as overtly present within *Buffy*.

Remedios Varo was a Spanish anarchist Surrealist known for her startling expressions of fairy tales and magical fables. Varo (1908–1963), with other women artists (such as Leonora Carrington), would escape first Spain and then Nazi-occupied Paris to take refuge in post-revolutionary Mexico during the Second World War. Varo's flight was completed with the aid of the Emergency Rescue Committee, who would also help other writers and activist refugees leave Europe. Her escape followed an inspiring but suffocating relationship with the poet Benjamin Péret, a close friend of the Surrealist leader André Breton. These attachments tended to suppress Varo's and others' creative energies.

While conceived within a framework weighted with masculine stereotypes, Surrealism nonetheless helped women to imagine alternative gender and sensory orders. If the surreal was acceptable and laudable, why not the surreal possibility of a feminist alternative to patriarchy? As Whitney Chadwick writes of Remedios Varo's feminine imagery: 'the women in Varo's paintings . . . are alchemists, magicians, scientists and engineers who travel through forests, along rivers, and above the clouds in jerry-built conveyances that run on stardust, music, and sunlight.'[29] In Varo, feminism and levity are seen as innate and sensual qualities or tactical adaptations. She felt compelled to imagine peculiar figures positioned in unlikely ways on tiny sets of wheels. It is appropriate, given her interests, that Varo was also influenced by Freud and Jung, as evident in her *Woman Leaving the Psychoanalyst* (1960), where the moniker FJA is inscribed above the doorway the woman leaves, initialling Freud, Jung and (Alfred) Adler. Titles by Freud, Jung and the famous Theosophist and theorist of levitation Helena Blavatsky were also among Varo's collection of books.

Levitation reflected Varo's interest in science as well as spirituality. Her *The Phenomenon of Weightlessness* depicted an Einstein-like scientist with a floating earth-shaped globe orbited by a moon. Vari's work would even be used as the front cover of a textbook on general relativity entitled *The Riddle of Gravitation*.[30] Even if her work appears far removed from psychoanalysis, we might see in Varo a kind of sublimation, 'that is to say, the process by which "solid bodies" become "volatised", what is thick, crude, dense "evaporates".' To this extent, 'everything tends to lose weight' in her works, both physically and spiritually, to the point that her beautiful imagery is chock full of ethereal floatings, 'levitations, flights, ascents and heights'.[31] Things, cobblestones, instruments, floorboards, domestic spaces and other objects are arisen and seem to stay so.

In *Bankers in Action* (1962) there are clear similarities to the depictions of The Gentlemen, although the bankers appear to be

Remedios Varo,
Bankers in Action,
1962, oil on masonite.

Remedios Varo, *Capillary Locomotion*, 1959, oil on masonite.

more in flight than the sinister glide of The Gentlemen. The bankers carry canes and sport bowler hats. Their faces, however, are far more impassive than sinister. A woman in a shawl watches them cautiously, hidden from view behind a wall. This is perhaps one of the most ominous of Varo's works,[32] and displays a sombre atmosphere of male possessive or exploitative behaviour that Varo would explore elsewhere. *Capillary Locomotion* is one of the most enigmatic of these themes. Three men levitate in a corridor. Or at least they appear to be levitating, until we recognize that they are in fact floating on their long beards, which brush the floor below them, curling up as if a monkey tail. The men, the hair on whose heads appears vaporous and cloud-like, ride their beards as if bicycles, their moustaches held as if handlebars. Above them, from a window, another man peers out and ensnares a woman, who is lifted by the beard. Her hands reveal the asymmetry of power with the men; they remain desperately outstretched, palm downwards, fingers reaching to retain her autonomy. The men hold their own in a grip.

It might be a stretch to make any suggestion of comparison with the administrative evil Varo would have witnessed in Nazi-occupied Paris or even Francoist Spain.[33] Nonetheless, Varo's Surrealism expresses distinctive anti-capitalist themes. Ricardo Ovalle's notes within a catalogue of Varo's work recall a story of when she was visited by a banker, who requested that she consider a commission to paint a mural on the history of banking. Ovalle recounts that Varo considered the idea for a moment before suggesting, 'Well, yes, I believe that can be arranged. I imagine a man at the entrance to his cave with a pile of bones he is protecting with a huge club.'[34] 'Naturally,' writes Ovalle, 'the potential client never returned.'

Mexico

There is a thread which we should follow that concerns just where levitations and meditations about them come from. What cultural or political milieu gives shape to the levitator? Common to levitation are the points of passage, the mobility and transit – perhaps escape, or escape's desire – which give rise to the fantasy of levity. Post-revolutionary Mexico before and during the Second World

War provided one such milieu for Surrealists wondering about and experimenting with levitation. Under President Lázaro Cárdenas, Mexico functioned as a haven for women artists in a self-declared atmosphere that was to be conducive to artistic expression;[35] this was especially the case for the wartime refugees to whom it granted asylum and citizenship. Varo and the British artist Leonora Carrington became friends, and arguably produced their best work during their time in Mexico.

Carrington's story is as chaotic as Varo's, sharing the same energies, whether by choice or force, during her early life. Born into a privileged household, Carrington was sent to and subsequently expelled from several institutions, including the convent of Holy Sepulchre near Chelmsford, Essex. There, she developed some of her interests in folklore as well as Catholic mysticism, and a fascination with the miraculous. It was these interests which shaped her ambitions to achieve some form of sainthood. Her poor behaviour and a reported attempt to levitate would lead to expulsion from the school, with Carrington later admitting that 'I probably overdid it. I liked the idea of being able to levitate, mainly.'[36]

Carrington's early turmoil would continue, even as she found artistic freedom in Surrealism. We can identify some levitational force in her rejection of her Surrealist partner Max Ernst, who reduced her role to one of muse, rather than actor, within his art. Having followed Ernst to Paris, and enduring his arrest and transportation to an internment camp in 1939, Carrington had a mental breakdown and was incarcerated in a Madrid mental institution. After being released into the care of a nurse who took her to Lisbon she would be granted escape and refuge in the Mexican embassy, and eventually travel to Mexico. Within this vortex of turbulent events, commentators find a certain magic to Carrington's interests, one of which was alchemy. Her artwork and masterpiece novel *The Hearing Trumpet*, first published in 1974

and within which her friend Varo would find form in the character of Carmella Velásquez, suggests her retreat from masculine appropriation and mental as well as physical imprisonment.

Carrington's and Varo's immersion in Mexican art and culture also lends an animation or spiritual vitality to their works, which imbue everyday and domestic objects and spaces with spiritual force, energy and playfulness. Living furniture is especially common in Carrington's work, as are earlier Renaissance artistic techniques of opening up interior spaces by cutting away walls and roofs to show life going on within. Carrington was especially interested in the paintings of Stefano di Giovanni (known as Il Sassetta), who would feature a representation of St Ranierius levitating in the skies of Florence to free or liberate prisoners, in his polyptych of the *San Sepolcro Altarpiece* (1437–44).

Il Sassetta, *The Blessed Ranieri Rasini Freeing Poor People from Prison in Florence*, 1437–44, tempera and gold on poplar wood.

Others have also shared Carrington's experience of Mexican spiritualism and medical incarceration. Antonin Artaud (1896–1948) is an interesting and provocative figure who had a volatile relationship with the Surrealists. Artaud was also troubled by severe mental illness, suffering 51 treatments of electroconvulsive therapy at the hands of Gaston Ferdière, director of the Rodez psychiatric hospital northeast of Toulouse in France in 1945. Artaud had been moved about between different psychiatric institutions, being taken to Rodez by a sympathetic friend, the Surrealist poet Robert Desnos, from the Ville-Evrard in a suburb of Paris.[37] Under Ferdière, a poet who wanted to treat Artaud with a combination of art therapy and electroshock treatment, he seems to have thrived, before later turning on the doctor for his inhumane practices. In Rodez, Artaud would write much of his work about his journeys to Mexico, especially his encounter with the Tarahumara (Rarámuri) people.

Artaud's accounts of his travels to Mexico are somewhat confusing. Some even question whether he ever went there at all, given that some of his accounts were written in Rodez, and several years after the fact. Artaud was interested in alternatives to European world-views, which tended to prioritize the scientific and militaristic, and whose traces could be found in Europe's colonial history in Latin America in the time of Cortés. Artaud wanted to explore magic, to discover the 'indigenous soul' of Mexico.[38]

In Mexico, Artaud would celebrate the 'magic spirit of primitive civilizations', exploring elemental figures and forces, from snakes and volcanoes to birds, in which Artaud saw the Mexicans devoting their symbolism to 'freedom and space'.[39] Within his descriptions of the Tarahumara, he finds parallels to Hieronymus Bosch's *Nativity*. There are continuous tensions with organized religion in Artaud's work. He explains in a letter to Henri Parisot – the publisher and translator of other Surrealist and imaginative works, including by Lewis Carroll – in 1945, written in Rodez, that his interest in

and travel to Mexico could be situated within his loathing for
Christianity: 'I went to the heights of Mexico to rid myself of
Jesus Christ.' He would similarly claim an earlier desire to visit
Tibet, to wash the holy spirit out of him. Artaud's spiritual
commitment was, however, complicated. Throughout his life his
passions frequently oscillated between an embrace and rejection
of Christianity.

In 1925 Artaud wrote a strange letter to the Dalai Lama. This
was one of several letters he addressed to spiritual leaders, among
them the Pope and the 'schools of the Buddha'. He would write
again to the Dalai Lama in 1946. The first letter was published in
the Surrealist magazine *La Révolution Surréaliste* in April 1925.
Artaud's address, intended to be read aloud, is an exaltation of the
Tibetan Buddhist leader. His language is replete with Neoplatonic
emphasis, which we have seen in the celebration of height, mountains and summits. His letter features levitation, too – the strange
power believed possible by Tibetan Buddhists and encountered
by Tintin in Tibet in Hergé's story.

The address to the Dalai Lama doubles as an attack on
Christianity: 'make for us a spirit entirely turned towards those
perfect summits where the Spirit of Man no longer suffers!'[40] Artaud
would also claim: 'We are surrounded by coarse popes, literati,
critics, dogs. Our spirit is among the dogs, who think always with
the ground, who think hopelessly in the present.' Artaud strives for
liberation from these depths. He requests,

Lama, teach us the material levitation of the body and how we
may no longer be held by the ground! It is with the inner eye
that I look at you, O Pope, at the summit of interiority. It is
inwardly that I resemble you: self, impulse, idea, lip, levitation,
dream, cry, renunciation of ideas, suspended between all forms
and hoping for no more than the wind.[41]

One of Artaud's most interesting encounters in Mexico was with the artist María Izquierdo, with whom he would collaborate and create a series of watercolours, which were taken back to France to be shown at the Galerie Van den Berg in Montparnasse, Paris, in 1937.[42] Two of Izquierdo's paintings could occupy a discussion on levity through the prism of gender. *Allegory of Work* (1936) and *Allegory of Liberty* (1937) directly reflect on Mexico's violent revolution. In both works are featured floating, in-between or liminal figures signalling some kind of post-revolutionary and pre-Hispanic Mexico. Women are the subjects of violence and oppression in this imagery. In *Allegory of Liberty*, the imagery features the Aztec-inspired sacrificial decapitated heads of women that are stolen by an angel and taken towards the heavens. In *Allegory of Work*, we almost see repeated the disappearing Christ, and yet this is an undoubtedly male giant figure, with both legs sunk firmly in the volcanic landscape. A floating orb hides his genitals; the body – like Hobbes's sovereign – is somewhere in the clouds. A naked woman holds her hands to her face.

The desire for height was one that Artaud began to critique. In the Christian tradition, Artaud complains, could be found the emphasis upon the soul's 'ascension into the sky as a spirit'. He understands Christ's ascension as a vaporization, a dissolving into heavenly nothingness. The ascension, from this perspective, is nothing more than 'an infinite vertical line', and so he scolds Christ and God for their pretensions to innateness, their seat high up in the 'abysses of infinities'. He would mock these ideas in a poem:

> *Myself* Antonin Artaud
> I am a pure spirit
> and I make my body
>   rise
> looking at it as I do
> like all the asses of the holy spirit of God

who believe that man is a double

composed of a

wellrounded spirit

and then of a body,

an organism

that is

regulated

by the spirit

of master eternity on high.[43]

Artaud renounced Christianity on 1 April 1945 at the age of 48, and by the time of his 1946 letter the Dalai Lama had become all but a 'bastard' to him. The second letter to the Dalai Lama is written in a very different tone of address. Isabelle Gros suggests that Artaud's turnaround may have a lot to do with his treatment in Rodez. His addiction was apparently remedied with doses of violent electroconvulsive therapy and the Christian morality he had begun to despise.

Nuclear mysticism

In the foyer of the Dalí Theatre-museum in Figueres, Catalonia, one can look up and see the most extraordinary ceiling panel. It is as if the work of the Futurists has been reversed. If you were to invert Tulio Crali's *Nose Dive on the City* and its aesthetic command of the view from above, or the vertigo-inducing imagery of the metropolis in Gilliam's *Brazil*, this is what you'd get. Looking upwards in the Dalí museum, one sees Dalí with his wife Gala. At first, the soles of their feet present themselves, as if almost about to tap you on the head. After that the eye is drawn up, up, up to the disappearing perspective as their bodies vanish into the plenitude of the heavens. Like the Christ-like figure drawn next to them, they are in ascension, and it is magnificent.

The image should be compared with Dalí's own singular portrayal of *The Ascension of Christ* (1958) because it uses a similar perspective, although in the latter the perspective has shifted so that the body of Christ can look horizontal. Far from being a unique idiosyncrasy of Dalí's work, and in the context of Surrealism, levitation would be absolutely crucial to his growing interest in religious mysticism and the science of the atom. Dalí's apotheosis in Figueres would also bring his imaginative visions or reveries almost full circle, as he had spent so much of his youth daydreaming from the rooftop of his parents' house in the city. Physical ascent was common as a source of inspiration in Dalí's youth: he describes being beckoned, drawn upwards to the Molí de la Torre, a farmhouse topped with a polygonal tower, as an attraction of 'dizzy height'. Raising his eyes to it in an 'ardent gaze of promise and fidelity', he whispered, 'I'm coming!'[44] These whispers becoming a daily ritual, Dalí's ascents blended anticipation with fear, before experiencing 'delight' in being lost in the views over the surrounding mountain-tops and peaks.

Some Surrealist works offer perceptual shock through bizarre and strange compositions of genre, style and myth. Salvador Dalí's many encounters with levity, religion and science would do exactly this, most fully expressed in his nuclear-mystical work that sought to master gravity through 'quantum realism'. Dematerializing matter, as in atomic experiments, Dalí would also spiritualize his works, animating the inanimate with ideas of energy and radiation. His 'mysticism', he would declare, 'is not only religious but also nuclear and hallucinogenic'.[45] 'Mine St Teresa of Ávila!' he declares.[46] Dalí's works are mash-ups of Renaissance figures and physics, expressed perhaps most clearly in his *Crucifixion* (*Corpus Hypercubus*), an image of a levitating Christ crucified upon a three-dimensional Cubist cross. Gala plays Mary Magdalene, gazing upwards.

Although we will come back to Dalí later in the book, the levitations he would make of the female muse are of a very different

character to those of Varo and Carrington. Dalí was more than happy
to visually suspend partially unclad women on a photographic plate,
or graphically dismembered on canvas. Instead of rejecting a masculine appropriation of the levitator, Dalí does precisely what Varo and
Carrington were seeking to resist. The female levitator is an object
of his sexual lust. Like the male magician, Dalí as the painter can
contort and command the levitated female at will.

Were it not for the collapse in confidence of the film's investors,
we might actually have seen Dalí levitating on the movie screen. He
was cast in possibly the most well-known film that was never made:
Alejandro Jodorowsky's *Dune*, based on the Frank Herbert novel of
1965. Jodorowsky, who purchased the option for the film in 1975,
had somehow persuaded Dalí to play the emperor in the movie.
Dalí was signed alongside Mick Jagger, Orson Welles and Gloria
Swanson. Early artwork, some by H. R. Giger, famous for his
designs for *Alien* (1979), had been started. Had the film come to
fruition, Dalí might have been seen hovering on a Holtzman
Suspensor, the technology that allows heavy furniture, vehicles
and other structures to gracefully float in the *Dune* universe. The
suspensor works upon the Holtzman effect.[47] In Herbert's own
guide to the terminology of *Dune*, he explains that the Holtzman
field generator is 'able to nullify gravity within certain limits
prescribed by relative mass and energy consumption'.[48]

Bubble

Perhaps the most obvious expression of the relation between
levitation and dreams and sexuality can be found in the photographer Melvin Sokolsky's gorgeous fashion work for *Harper's Bazaar*
in the mid-1960s. Sokolsky had caught the eye of the art director
for *Harper's*, Henry Wolf. Beginning at the age of just 21, between
1963 and 1965 Sokolsky developed his *Bubble* and *Flying* series of
photographs, which were first used for the magazine's Spring 1963

edition. Shot in March of that year, the imagery featured fashion models dressed in the latest trends levitating within Plexiglas bubbles or orbs over New Jersey looking back towards Manhattan, and later Paris.

This of course sounds similar to Georges Méliès' cinematography and his *Les bulles de savon vivantes*. Sokolsky's bubbles present a set of similarly ethereal floatings of the model Simone d'Aillencourt, struck in different poses, having been craned into extraordinarily enigmatic positions above buildings, rivers, streets, crowds, dinner tables and outside windows. Sokolsky would then take the cable out of the imagery by minimal retouching.[49] As with the other levitated women discussed in this book, the case of bejewelled high-fashion models plucked from the earth reflects a not uncomplicated relationship between levitation and objectification. The images do not show shock or surprise at the model's flight, as if it were natural to come across a hovering woman adorning the lower skyline of the city, and there is much more to the imagery than visual desire. In 'Over New York' (1963) Simone is more goddess, more a representation of empowerment as a fiery spirit, than anything else. But it is generally men who subject the model to such a semi-indifferent gaze. Some of the models appear to be pushing against their Plexiglas enclosure, perhaps attempting to resist their transparent confinement within a plastic prison.

Peculiarly, or naturally, for us, Salvador Dalí and Gala had visited Sokolsky's studio and it is clear that both men had drawn inspiration from each other. Dalí would demand of Sokolsky that he must make 'Dalí fly'. But Sokolsky was inspired by another source of artistic stimulation, a masterwork by the Dutch late fifteenth-century artist Hieronymus Bosch – who had so intrigued Artaud – *The Garden of Earthly Delights*. Sokolsky claimed to have dreamed of the remarkable figures from the middle part of Bosch's triptych. The airborne figures ascend towards the sun against a blue ether, and a naked couple sits in a transparent bubble.[50] Sokolsky is

clearly merging both figures; he would have a recurring dream of floating in an egg above unknown worlds.

In his later 1965 series, shot in Paris, Sokolsky began floating the models in a different way, using a steel tripod manned by two men, who would counterbalance a floating model suspended by a canvas corset strengthened with riveted aluminium hoops. In one of his images a woman floats above a Paris building; below her, as in our other levitational images, we see love portrayed by a couple embracing. Not all of the images present the women's levity as icy or indifferent to their condition. In 'Happarition', a woman, orbless, levitates above a party of friends in a restaurant, in apparent or apparitional happiness, as if a bystanding ghost affected by the activities but not able to take part. The friends do not notice her. Sokolsky would return to these themes at different moments in his career, in his later *Dream* series, set against Surrealist-inspired interior sets that he built and designed.

In one of Sokolsky's photographs, the flame from a fire-breathing male, 'the fire dragon', engulfs a model's protective bubble. The model strikes an interesting pose. Her hands push upwards against the bubble while her legs are crossed. He is half naked while she is dressed. Her left foot is flat against the floor of the bubble while her right leg, crossed over her left, is poised on tiptoe. She could be almost *en pointe*.

5 Super

A FOOT APPEARS BENEATH a cloud. It is attached to a muscled calf. But the foot does not dangle; it points downwards like a pencil tip about to begin scratching on a cumulonimbus. The image, rendered in a Russian print of the ballerina Marie Taglioni, speaks of the levity her performances displayed in an already existing milieu of lightness. According to Jennifer Homans's monumental history *Apollo's Angels: A History of Ballet* (2010), the imagined and rendered worlds of myth in the beginnings of nineteenth-century Romantic ballet would conjure 'countless weightless and insubstantial creatures, winged spirits, sprites, sylphs, and fairies who dwell in the air, trees, and other natural realms'.[1] In the dream worlds it created, Romantic ballet was light and airy. At the same time, equally, it was earthly, grounded and sensual in the entwinement of bodies, limbs and technological machinery. Three particular inventions of body and technology stand out: the *en pointe* and ballet shoe; the use of smoke and stage effects such as wires; and the tutu.[2]

Pre-Romantic ballet productions had created similar and almost real *en pointe* effects by using stage machinery to create fake clouds, so that the dancers would appear as if submerged within the vaporous architecture of the skies. In *Flore et Zéphire*, Charles-Louis Didelot's 1796 ballet, which featured stage technologies

Achille Devéria, *Marie Taglioni / (Sylphide)*, 1830s, lithograph coloured by hand.

designed by the engineer Liparotti, wires were attached to the dancers to enable their weightlessness. Alexander Pushkin devoted a poem to the Russian ballerina Avdotia Istomina, who performed Flore in Didelot's 1804 production: 'Obedient to the magic strings, / Brilliant, ethereal, there springs . . . Istomina, the nimbly-bounding.'[3]

As a 'geometry of rapture, pliability, and impossible levitation', *Flore et Zéphire* was a triumph of levity, but it distributed the 'vicarious thrill of weightlessness and ethereality' differently among the dancers. The female's lightness, her defiance of gravity, could make the male dancer seem bulkier and weightier, while the ballerina's 'limbs stretched and folded in a seemingly impossible origami'.[4] The danger therein is that the female body appeared to be absent from labour, unlike the male's more obvious muscular performance. For Anna Furse this is a form of corporeal camouflage, for the dancer is 'actually sweating buckets, near vomiting with breathlessness and bleeding in her shoes'.[5]

Peter Milton, *Points of Departure I: Mary's Turn*, 1994, etching and engraving.

This was trickery indeed. Marie Taglioni's performance of *La Sylphide* in 1832, an adaptation of Charles Nordier's novel *Trilby, ou le lutin d'Argail* – not to be confused with George Du Maurier's novel of the same name discussed earlier in the book – would make her famous.[6] Her performance produced the sensation of lightness but through the introduction of remarkable bodily force, directed not upwards but down into the ground, 'making the body appear to float or ascend'.

Taglioni's version of a sylph sees the dancer flit, skim and hover as she practised, trained by her father Filippo to dance on her toes, almost *en pointe*, combining feminine lightness with directed muscularity. A Russian commentator, entranced by Taglioni's movement, compared her motion to aerial flight, 'the fluttering of wings, the soaring in the air, alighting on flowers and gliding over the mirror-like surface of a river'. Taglioni would also popularise the tutu, a garment enhanced by Paul Lormier in *La Péri* in 1843. The tutu's floating qualities come from the layering of its fabric, which was gauze manufactured in Paris and London; muslin, first imported from India; and tarlatan from Tulle in the Corrèze region of France.[7]

The Impressionist Edgar Degas would make Parisian Romantic ballet sing in his paintings; for Peter Conrad, Degas' ballerinas also 'levitate like frothy clouds in a shining sky'.[8] Indeed, the artist Peter Milton makes Degas the observer in a Paris snooker room as the American artist Mary Cassatt plays snooker in *Points of Departure I: Mary's Turn* (1994), inspired by the 1909 photo by the well-known American photographer Gertrude Käsebier. With Degas looking on, it is Mary's turn to play and the balls begin to hover; just as ballerinas seem to float between a picture frame on the wall behind. Milton's genius is to see Cassatt as an expression of one of Degas' character traits, in this instance his misogynist self. As the artist explains, *Mary's Turn* materializes this relationship, while it can also work to 'raise their antithesis'. Levity is able to turn the gravities of relations the other way up, to the extent that 'a billiard game is coaxed into an exercise in levitation by the sure touch of Mary Cassatt'.[9]

Carlotta Grisi would become the Peri in 1843 – the same figure as that in Thomas Moore's poem *Lalla Rookh*, briefly mentioned in the previous chapter, in which the character Lalla, the Peri, leaps into the arms of her lover from a cloud. Grisi appeared to spectators to have transformed from a body with weight into a 'dove's feather, drifting in the air'. As Homans argues, though, this is a paradox, it is a 'weighted weightlessness and muscular spirituality that made Taglioni seem both earthly and elsewhere at the

Edwards Foreign Repository, *Mademoiselle Carlotta Grisi in Coralli and Gautier's Grand Ballet of the Peri*, 1843, lithograph coloured by hand.

same time'.[10] The ballerina's celebrity was a contradiction. Taglioni's display of grace, technique and earthbound muscularity was sometimes dependent on a just as earthy and elaborate stage machinery of ropes, weights and wires. The playfulness we will see within the various body cultures of levitation in this chapter, as well as the discord of the levitator, are captured here. These are levitators that are somehow light and heavy; ethereal yet dense and muscular. They are female but also male; omniscient, but far more vulnerable and passive than first supposed.

Male ballet dancers could also achieve something of the same lightness, although more through leaps and jumps than flitting *en pointe*. The Russian dancer Vaslav Nijinsky was asked whether it was difficult to appear to levitate, as he did in productions such as *La Sylphide* with Anna Pavlova.[11] Nijinsky replied, 'No! No! not difficult. You have to just go up there and pause a little.'[12] On the eve of Nijinsky's attempted move to the United States in 1940 for the continuation of his psychiatric care, Nandor Fodor, the Hungarian parapsychologist, would remark on Nijinsky's extraordinary powers of lightness, when interviewing his wife Romola. Her intriguing account recalls an instance when she told Nijinsky that it was a 'pity he could not see himself'. Nijinsky's answer to his wife recalls the ecstatic levity recorded in earlier chapters. He explained, 'But I do. I always see myself. I am detached. I am outside.' During his performance he was almost another personality, a different man. For Romola, 'He looked and acted like a stranger.'[13] After undergoing electroshock treatment, Nijinsky would eventually settle in Virginia Water, Surrey, and some locate him in Sunningdale, Berkshire, our potential home of the inspiration for J. B. Hasted's weighing machine. The ballet dancer's prowess of levity has not really ebbed. The biography of Suzanne Farrell, the American ballet dancer, was appropriately titled *Holding on to the Air*. In it she recalls her tutor, the choreographer George Balanchine, instructing her to 'just hold on to the air when you're up there [*en pointe*] . . . You're riding on the air.'[14]

Innocence

We have seen levitation frequently made sense of as some kind of evolution, some transitional change or shift towards a different kind of human condition. In the context of age, the child and childhood are interesting as levitative figures. Unsurprisingly, the education of children has been understood as a levitating act, or at least a rising, an elevation. Even birth has been viewed as an event of levitation. *The Trauma of Birth* (1924) by Otto Rank, a disciple of Freud, is an influential book suggesting that the origins of much trauma reside in separation from our mother at birth. Rank would argue that dreams of flying may be a response to the transition from the levitative suspension of the foetus's life in the womb through birth, 'the latter flying sensation, changing the violent birth trauma into an easy floating out'.[15]

Few words of advice are as instructive to us as those that can be found in the works of Jean Paul, who set out his ideas on education in *Levana*, which we considered earlier in relation to the education of princely young men. Booksellers may have picked up on the possible pun, by suggesting that the book 'will itself literally be picked up by parents who will presumably read it and then follow its teaching to bring *up* their own children'.[16]

Jean Paul's teaching sought to elevate the child: to lift their spirit, their passions, their thought and instincts. Education could be thought of as an 'educational ascent' from the child's fallen condition.[17] Joel Black has argued that Jean Paul's treatise should be seen as typical of Enlightenment teachings of educative and intellectual elevation.[18] Education would be required to lift the child out of the decaying quagmire – what Jean Paul called the 'spirit of the age' – of the laws of gravity. He also assumed he was dealing with particularly *light* individuals, comparing them to heavenly bodies.[19] For girls, Jean Paul asserted, childhood is a moment to indulge in lightness before the fixity of their years of duty, service or marriage: 'If a boy may be a zephyr, why may not the girl be a zephyrette?' he asked.[20] Lightness would be harnessed by motion, play and laughter.

Within the characters of late nineteenth-century and twentieth-century children's literature we see a moral and ethical framing of lightness to counter adulthood. A childhood innocence and gaiety is privileged – remember MacDonald's 'The Light Princess'. Aware of the dangers of excess, greed and apparent old age, J. M. Barrie's crowing Peter Pan stories are perhaps just one example of such writing.

E. Nesbit's book *The Phoenix and the Carpet*, published in 1904, is another; the novel observes the introduction of an enchanted carpet to an Edwardian family in London, bought by the children's mother for 22 shillings and ninepence on the Kentish Town Road. Flying carpets expose a levity which was not only for kingly figures born with elemental powers: we find that the stories that surround them come possessed with a degree of chance and concern the most ordinary of persons. In fact, magic carpets appear to fall into the hands of the small and the lowly far more than they do the powerful. Of course, Disney's 1992 animation of the tale of Aladdin and the Lamp, *Aladdin*, turns a flying carpet into a device of male companionship, which the hero comes across in the Cave of Wonders; it soon becomes Aladdin's friend by helping him to escape. 'Carpet' is a moral compass and trusty friend, expressing embarrassment when Aladdin oversteps the mark, and shyness when praised. The magical carpet is also a metaphor for escape. Both the princess Jasmine and Aladdin are relinquished of their opposite roles – Aladdin the street urchin, and the princess resisting her royal duty to marry and presumably produce an heir to secure her family's monarchical dynasty. In flight, they discover a 'Whole New World' together, and sing about it. (The song won an Academy Award in 1993.)

Nesbit's tale sees the carpet growing to a larger size to accommodate the children – although not quite on the scale of Solomon's – and achieving a rigidity to make the rug more of a platform. These are common stories of childhood expansion. It takes them wherever they want to go, giving the children an autonomy of view and perspective they have not before experienced. The carpet is contrasted with the confinement of a train, where adults keep the windows shut and fog up the glass, concealing the children from the outside world. Meanwhile the train carriage lulls the adults quickly to sleep, leaving the children to sit in boredom.

In one startling illustration, two of the children, Cyril and Anthea, lie on the carpet face-down, hovering over London roof-tops. They beckon down to Robert and Jane; a hand is outstretched, imploring them to come up from the rooftops, onto which they had dropped after they fell through an un-darned hole in the carpet. Curiously, in 1998 five postage stamps were issued by Royal Mail on the theme of magical worlds for children. Nesbit's novel was captured in one of the stamps, showing four children riding the carpet above the countryside, the phoenix flying with them.

Jean Paul's advice was not universal, of course. If we look elsewhere, levity is to be enjoyed but also restrained and held back lest it become too excessive, or boil over to become too much. On the other hand, other adult levitations are accused of giving in to childlike whims. In Disney's version of *Mary Poppins* (1964), Bert and Uncle Albert are chastised by Mary in their levitated rendition of 'I Love to Laugh'. The scene is based on the chapter 'Laughing Gas' from the original book by P. L. Travers (1934); let us not forget that Travers was a regular contributor to the journal *Parabola*, whose articles were often peppered with Jungian psychoanalytical thinking. In the story, the children go to meet their uncle, Mr Albert Wigg,

'I Love to Laugh', in *Mary Poppins* (dir. Robert Stevenson, 1964).

who is found, after some searching, to be 'hanging on the air' above them, 'without holding on to anything', Albert appearing cross-legged and '*sitting* on the air'.[21] Mary immediately scolds him for his levity, before Albert explains to the children how his elevation is powered by laughter and cheerfulness; he bobs and shakes in correspondence to his mood: 'The first funny thought, and I'm up like a balloon,' he explains, his chuckles halted by a rebuking glance from Mary.[22]

In both versions of *Mary Poppins* Uncle Albert's levity could be compared to a balloon, as he is 'floundering in the air like a great human bubble'. Soon the children find themselves laughing, rolling on the floor and, just as suddenly, filled full of lightness before taking a bounding bounce into the air. In the film, Mary first holds them back, tugging them down with a 'come back down here' lest they be influenced by this adult expression of levity. 'Well, I must say', says Mary primly to Albert, 'that I have never in my life seen such a sight. And at your age, Uncle.'[23] But their mirth is contagious and Mary, albeit begrudgingly, soon gives in to the indulgence.

Mr Dawes Sr, in *Mary Poppins* (dir. Robert Stevenson, 1964).

Another kind of lightness enters the frame. When Mr Dawes Sr, chairman of the bank, finds gaiety in the punchline to a joke, which he repeats – 'a wooden leg' – his laughter pushes or pulls him into the air above the boardroom and he cannot be brought back down. His laugh is like a rasping exhaust pipe, and he lets himself be consumed by it. We might see it as a return to an earlier, more joyful stage of his life, an energy drained from him by the bank's weight of fiduciary responsibility and old age. Ultimately, for Dawes Sr, as for our saints in ecstatic bliss, he becomes utterly depleted through his laughter, which leads to a happy death. As the chairman bobs around like a trapped balloon – mirroring the later pay-off as Mr Banks flies a kite with his children during the film's finale – levitation can come as a form of redemption, allowing characters to atone for past sins. One can mend one's ways by returning from adult solemnity to a prior state, back to joy. It is the uplift of laughter that animates the bank's decision to reinstate Mr Banks Jr: 'Tuppence', Banks explains, is now not for the solemnity of capital investment as it was earlier in the film, but for 'paper and strings', for an investment in other sorts of values – which could provide 'your own set of wings'. And we know how the song goes.

Of course, Mary herself could be compared to the shaman, whose qualities resound with lightness.[24] Within the Travers books she is frequently found using clouds and rainbows for transit, climbing ladders to rearrange the stars, and, in the film, raising her umbrella to be caught upwards by the wind, which sends her floating across the London skyline.

Alternatively, levity can sometimes mean there is a price to pay. Lightness in some contexts means giving up innocence, resonating with a different set of moral codes to *Mary Poppins*. Such an economy is evident in *Santa Claus: The Movie* (1985), which features Dudley Moore as the elf Patch, who has left the North Pole to seek his own fortune in New York City. Patch is quickly enlisted for his technical and magical prowess by John Lithgow's ruthless capitalist B.Z. In this telling, the entanglement of levity and morality is captured in consumption. As the Cambridge-based cultural historian and critic Steven Connor suggests, the addiction to centrifugal lightness is best expressed in our love of the 'airy comestible' – drinks and sweets. In the movie, Patch synthesizes flying powder, usually given in the food of Santa Claus's reindeer to create new consumer products for B.Z. The powder is infused into the candy canes they give out for free at

Christmas, which causes those who consume them to magically float. This enables children to perform serious hang-time basketball dunks, while creating fervour for B.Z. and Patch's mass-produced yet entirely faulty products.

It is worth pausing here for a moment, because it is not uncommon for sportspersons, journalists and writers to attest to an athlete's uncanny ability to hang that bit longer in the air, to appear inhumanly airborne. Among the descriptions of zones, flow states, and other psychological and embodied peculiarities of movement and concentration, Michael Murphy and Rhea White explain that 'some athletes might, for a little while, remain up there in the air a bit longer than others.'[25] How peculiar that savant sportspersons seem to possess not only the powers of celebrity and wealth but the capacities of being lighter than air, if only for a moment. How apt that they seem inflated by ego or adoration, and inspired to perform the impossible.

Omri Amrany and Julie Rotblatt-Amrany, *The Spirit,* 1994, bronze.

Michael Jordan's renowned ability to display what became known as 'hang time' was of course refracted through corporate sponsorship. Jordan was famous for his basketball, but also his image in the form of Spike Lee-directed commercials that emphasized Jordan's ability to settle in the air and perform numerous tricks. Nike's 'Air' trainers and other clothing and equipment feature a logo of a silhouette of Jordan's splayed aerial figure. In the first of a series of adverts featuring Jordan, we see him beginning to run and a revving jet sound effect is scored over him. On take-off, the relative quiet of the jet – no longer in contact with the runway – times with the slow-motion lift-off as Jordan's feet leave the ground, careening over the camera, and he is captured dunking the ball. The commercial concludes with the slogan 'Man was never meant to fly.' Jordan is a superman.

The sheer visual feat of Jordan's many jumps comes from the seeming incongruity of his body. Other basketball players and commentators would identify Jordan's ability to continue to move his upper body (his neck, arms, hands, torso) upwards towards the hoop, even while his body was falling under the force of gravity. Not only did he leap high, but the visceral experience of a player near him was that he would unnaturally linger in the air. Jordan seemed to find some extra height or force to propel himself upwards, while others were on their way down. This is simple levitation, and the art of defence would lie in not letting Jordan ascend at all.

A *New York Times* feature on Jordan, 'Jordan Hovers Above the Rest', as well as other press and articles by sports writers, are probably as much responsible for this myth as Nike. In 1988, sports writer Ira Berkow repeated talk of Jordan's Christ-like abilities to walk on air, claiming, ironically, that many Americans 'believe they have actually seen Michael Jordan walk on air. Often. In a number of cities in America. With his size-13 sneakers. This they would testify to in a court of law.'[26] As with other levitators, appreciation of Jordan's aerial prowess combines the pathos of semi-religious belief with the measurement of scientific logic. Nike's campaign featured the explanation of Douglas Kirkpatrick: 'Michael has overcome acceleration of gravity by the application of his muscle power in the vertical plane, thus producing a low-altitude orbit,' reducing the total time he spent airborne in the NBA league to 'six hours – or four orbits of the earth', which he revised down to '1½ hours of hang time and one orbit'.[27] Or, as a formula, $\frac{1}{2}g \times t2 = v0 \times t$. Jordan's levity never looks light, though. Perhaps there is some sense here of a muscular levity – maybe even a manly levity – which does nothing to contain the bulging muscles and torquing tendons of the body that performs it. For Jason King, these cultural encodings of Jordan's vertical mobility are not out of kilter with the directionality of ascension in black popular culture.[28]

Patch and B.Z's story is more reminiscent of Robert-Houdin's 'ethereal suspension' trick. Robert-Houdin used a different magic substance, pretending to dose his son on stage with ether, allowing the boy to become 'as light as a balloon'.[29] Patch and B.Z see levity as something that can be chewed over and ultimately consumed, but in so doing something is lost. Levitation is really only a sheen or a veneer, and temporary. For all Patch's attempts to synthesize lightness, the outcome is more dangerous than authentic. His childlike innocence is corrupted, as are the greedy children and parents demanding B.Z.'s toys. At the end of *Santa Claus: The Movie*, having gorged himself fully on the candy, the crumbling mixture spewing from his bloated mouth as he tries to choke it down, B.Z. floats away and keeps on going, out of the Earth's atmosphere and into space, presumably for ever – or parts of him will. It is a sort of crash (chemical and moral too) in reverse.

Cities of the air

Adnan Morshed has compared the 1939 New York World's Fair and the figures of ascension that would ornament the 'World of Tomorrow' with the rise of the superhero. Morshed discovers an 'aesthetics of ascension' compatible with the modernist and Enlightenment association with the vertical, synoptic legibility and 'visual clarity' it provided.[30] Amateur footage of the fair shows patrons craning up towards the buildings and monuments, and the parachute ride that would allow the brave to ascend and descend from 250 ft (75 m) to the ground in around 10 to 20 seconds. The crowds would mimic James Thurber's cartoon sketch for the *New Yorker*, showing a mass of visitors – their heads atilt – below the canyonland of the fair's structures, the Trylon and Perisphere. Steel rings held the parachutes open. The ride would

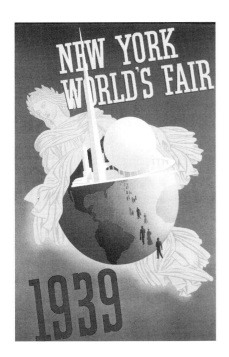

John Atherton, *New York World's Fair 1939*, 1939, offset lithograph.

later be purchased for Coney Island's Steeplechase Park.

As the first aviators were trotting the skies, new urban forms were accentuating ascension too. On and off the page was Superman, the *Übermensch* who was at once a modern, moral and spiritual point of view; 'the image of the New Man', writes Morshed, 'revolting against gravity by sheer physical prowess, with eyes fixed, as it were, on nothing but the future.' The World's Fair would even host the DC Comics-sponsored 'Superman Day'; the publisher had produced a special edition to be sold exclusively in the park. Superman as the 'Man of Tomorrow', played by Ray Middleton, was wheeled around on a stone plinth to an adoring public. The fair's structures dwarfed Superman, however, because they were all about height. Some even appeared to be floating, particularly the Perisphere, which was envisioned by Hugh Ferriss to be levitating above a fountain of water and light. John Atherton, the much employed Art Deco iconographer, designed a poster for the fair that shows the entire site floating away – a city on planet Earth carried off by a flying Lady Liberty. The fair would also show the extraordinary furniture of Gilbert Rohde in the form of the first Plexiglas chair, an emblem of lightness and repose, and his enigmatic rendering *Man Freed in Time and Space* in the Community Interests Focal Exhibit. His image is a vision of abstraction and uplift, the body freed by not only design but government, community and organization.

In the United States, illustrators such as Frank R. Paul would become well known for portraying levitating characters in the emerging landscape of science fiction comic books, such as *Amazing Stories* and *Wonders of the Air*. Paul's images would

The 1939 New York World's Fair Life Savers Parachute Jump.

combine incredible fantasy worlds of alien spacecraft, future technologies and fantasized, hypersexualized women occupying planets where men do not exist. On the cover of the 26 August 1938 edition of *Family Circle*, Paul, who was also interviewed by the magazine, describes a scantily clad fifth-millennium 'young lady', whom we see floating, shot out of an almost phallic-shaped tube to buy her groceries. Paul is almost saying, 'flying like this is so easy that even a girl could do it.' More bizarrely, Paul admits, the amulet worn by the woman features two plus signs, indicating 'that she is about average in attractiveness. The real beauties get four or five.' The editors comment, 'We can hardly wait for the Fifth Millennium.'

Many of Paul's images celebrate a future of levitating people and things, including somersaulting astronauts, flying brigades of soldiers floating in plastic exoskeletons, unknown spacecraft and, in many editions of *Air Wonder Stories*, islands and cities floating in the clouds. These sky cities anticipate future scientific imaginaries such as Lando Calrissian's floating cloud-city in the second instalment of *Star Wars*, *The Empire Strikes Back* (1980). Paul and others were repeating much earlier tropes of fantastic

Outside the Perisphere at the 1939 New York World's Fair.

An illustration by Roberto Nieto from 2016 inspired by Studio Ghibli's *Laputa: Castle in the Sky* (dir. Hayao Miyazaki, 1986).

writing and turn-of-the-century imaginaries from outside the United States.

The flying city is a familiar idea, most famously depicted in Jonathan Swift's *Gulliver's Travels* (1726). The flying island of Laputa begins, as contemporary representations have, with the surprise of a shape so massive it appears to be impossible. But of course, in Swift it is a city floating in the skies. Laputa surprises Gulliver when, as Alexander did with Diogenes, it shades him from the sun. This was a city or mountain over which the Laputians have complete autonomy, being 'inhabited by men, who were able (as it should seem) to raise, or sink, or put it into progressive motion, as they pleased'.[31] The Laputians achieve this horizontal and vertical mobility by magnetism, controlled by a lodestone at its centre, which enables the island to move in alternate risings and fallings over its dominion, the earth. In line with its height, Laputa is not really a place of or for femininity. Gulliver finds that its women are eager to take leave from their aerial confinement; many do not return upon venturing to the ground.

The lodestone is a useful narrative McGuffin for Swift, who would have been well aware of William Gilbert's *De magnete, magneticisque corporibus, et de magno magnete tellure* (On the Magnet and Magnetic Bodies, and on That Great Magnet the Earth, 1600), which set out the modern principles of magnetism, identifying the lodestone within earlier philosophic writings and religious architecture. Muhammad's coffin was purportedly levitated by magnetic force – as borrowed in John Clubbe's 1763 ideational contraption – above the Alcoran, while Christopher Marlowe dramatizes in *Tamburlaine* (1587–8) the peace treaty signed between Orcanes and Sigismond, King of Hungary, where Orcanes vows:

> By Sacred Mahomet, the friend of God,
> Whose holy Alcoran remains with us,
> Whose glorious body, when he left the world,
> Closed in a coffin, mounted up the air.

In the same play, Tamburlaine advises his son to 'Besiege a fort, to undermine a town; / And make whole cities caper in the air.'[32] Gilbert notices this trend elsewhere – even in Pliny, who records that the architect Chinocrates had attempted to use an arched roof or lodestone for the temple of Arsinoe in Alexandria, which would allow an iron statue to float above it. Gilbert is less sure of the possibilities of the equilibrium necessary for magnetic levity. He finds a proposition made by the Italian scholar Girolamo Fracastoro 'ridiculous'. Fracastoro had predicted that a piece of iron could be suspended in air 'by an attractive force on the iron equal to the force by which the iron tends downwards'.[33] Instead, Gilbert's magnetic treatise acts as an instruction manual for magnetic-derived mobility, going to great lengths to identify the spatial orientation of a lodestone's magnetic fields, and how to manipulate them.

Swift's Laputa is perfectly circular and 7,837 yards (4½ miles) in diameter, being 300 yards thick, its volume made up to a large degree of minerals, but also the waters that land on its surface. Determining Laputa's etymology is beyond Gulliver, but he ascertains its derivation from 'high' and 'governor' as fairly accurate, given that Laputa held the seat of the king, who would move the island over his state's great cities to hear their petitions. In some respects Laputa is a burgeoning form of airpower: the king would demonstrate Laputa's aerial prowess and use the city to crush his enemies. As a form of air power, Laputa projects power below to 'bring under his obedience whatever country lay within the attraction of that magnet'.[34] Laputa does this according to three distinct strategies. First, it may hover ominously above a rebel town, blocking out the sun and rain. Second, it may be used as a position from which to launch the dropping of stones. And finally, in extreme circumstances of rebellion, the king is able to order that Laputa be dropped gently onto the inhabitants and their dwellings, turning all to ruin.

Modern versions of urban levitation were not only Anglo-American. Swift's flying city would be reimagined by the Japanese animation house Studio Ghibli. Written and directed by Hayao Miyazaki, *Laputa: Castle in the Sky* (1986) features a flying city topped by a medieval castle, supposedly inspired by Pieter Bruegel the Elder's painting *The Tower of Babel*. A great tree has taken root through the city's core, the city a remnant of an earlier age of flying cities. The castle and a magical amulet get their levitating properties from 'sky crystals' known as 'volucite' in the original version, and 'Aetherium' in the dubbed American edition of the film. Various characters fight for control of Laputa, its riches and military possibilities.

We can look back to earlier in the twentieth century, when, as Richard Stites suggests, utopian science fiction works in Russia gathered a huge amount of energy. Those works of the 1920s documented 'an ascending surge in the revolutionary imagination'.[35] Science fiction's fascination with flight, levity and cosmic exploration was a liberatory metaphor outside the West, finding expression in 'a fear of not flying'. Yan Larri's novel *The Land of the Happy* (1931) probably marked the end of this tendency, imagining worlds of contraptions such as 'aeropters' permitting an Icarian civilization of personal flight.

Russian science fiction and literature boomed urban levitative energies, perhaps none more strongly than in Alexander Bogdanov's communist utopia on Mars in *Red Star*, published within the milieu of the failed revolution attempt of 1905.[36] Saturated in these energies, in Bogdanov's novel socialist Martians try to convince the protagonist that they are who they say they are through a demonstration of a levitating substance called 'minus-matter'. Bogdanov's central character ruminates on the existence of such a material, given that it would have been eliminated from the solar system long ago.

Minus-matter is a revolutionary analogue permitting 'free movement in the atmosphere and interplanetary travel'. The Martian society uses the substance to its advantage in flying machines, which they necessarily keep from the hands of earthly governments, lest they use them to 'enhance the power and might of the upper classes'. Flight is achieved by taking the strange liquid that the Martian character, Menni, offers, while being careful to ensure that the substance is counterbalanced by the weight of other objects. In *Red Star*, the monopoly over levity is well and truly held by the Martian proletariat.[37]

In this Russian utopian version of levitational material, the substance is something to be protected and kept safe from the exploitation of powerful interests. Published a few years before Bogdanov's novel, H. G. Wells's *The First Men in the Moon* (1901) is a different story – almost its opposite. Wells's tendency to normalize the extraordinary within the confines of Britain's existing political and social system envisions the capitalist temptation to exploit the profit-making opportunities of a substance opaque to the forces of gravity. This is known after its inventor, Cavor, as cavorite. Bedford, Wells's narrator, experiences the sensation of levity for the first time:

It was the strangest sensation conceivable, floating thus loosely in space, at first indeed horribly strange, and when the horror passed, not disagreeable at all, exceeding restful; indeed, the nearest thing in earthly experience to it that I know is lying on a very thick, soft feather bed. But the quality of utter detachment and independence! I had not reckoned on things like this. I had expected a violent jerk at starting, a giddy sense of speed. Instead I felt – as if I were disembodied. It was not like the beginning of a journey; it was like the beginning of a dream.

Compared to the socialist imagination of weightless materials discussed above, Bedford has rather different miracles and revolutions in mind. Wells draws the reader's attentions to the machinations of his character's imagination. His first impulse is to apply the substance to the machinery of war, to 'guns and ironclads, and all the material and methods of war'. From there he moves to the circuits of capitalist locomotion, shipping, building, 'every conceivable form of human industry'. Wells tells of an expansion that is not socialist or liberatory, but towed by the possibilities of wealth, unrolling and expanding in his imagination:

> I saw a parent company, and daughter companies, applications to right of us, applications to left, rings and trusts, privileges, and concessions spreading and spreading, until one vast, stupendous Cavorite company ran and ruled the world.[38]

Bedford convinces the inventor Cavor that such riches should not be used for equality or the progressive redistribution of wealth, but 'any sort of social revolution we fancied, we might own and order the whole world'. Cavor, Bedford believed, 'had got to be rich'.

Cosmopolitan serialized Wells's book first. In Britain it was published in *The Strand Magazine*. In the U.S., E. Hering's artwork illustrated the serialization and its publication into book form,

while in the British versions Claude Shepperson took drawing duties. Both capture levity differently. Shepperson manages to gather the violence Wells describes in the acceleration of forms, with movement and flight-lines to describe the motion. Hering makes their qualities of levitation perhaps more subtle but also more ordinary. Cavor achieves an odd comportment in Hering's images, while the everyday objects that would adorn late Victorian England appear drifting in weightlessness as their craft arrives at the Moon. Heavy-looking tasselled curtains flutter against the window. In both images Bedford stands masterfully, observing Cavor's levity in one image, and overseeing the Moon below in another.

Within Wells's writings we can see certain evolutionary notions of moral and social transcendence combining with biological advancement. This was represented in Wells's portrayal of two evolutionary extremes, the ape and the flying man, a curious

E. Hering's representation of weightlessness in the orbit of the moon, in *Cosmopolitan* (1901).

E. Hering's illustration capturing Cavor's levitation under the effects of cavorite, in *Cosmopolitan* (1901).

– aping – parallel we saw earlier with the тм-Sidhi evolutionary diagram showing the progress from primate to enlightenment. In Wells's imaginative picture of a future London, his first published piece in the *Pall Mall Gazette* of 1893 titled 'Advent of the Flying Man', he conceived of swarms of people making the evening commute in flight, 'homing to suburban "rookeries" from the dome of St Paul's'. This was a future expectancy felt in the present, Wells suggesting that 'even now the imaginative person may hear the beating of his wings.'[39]

English and Russian literature were not the only expressions of energies directed towards a future society. The Suprematist artist Kazimir Malevich had already proposed the concept of the aero-city, developing small structures for aerial living known as 'planits'. Indeed, Malevich would also display his works with verticality in mind, 'hanging his paintings so that they appeared to float at a distance from the walls', explains Eric Bunge.[40] As Peter Conrad notes, while Malevich was prophesying a future where 'not a single grounded structure will remain on earth. Nothing will be fastened or tied down,' his more terrestrial plans, such as the *Pilot's House* in Leningrad (1924), would prepare earthlings 'for levitation'.[41]

Malevich's collaborator and student Lazar Khidekel would work on his proposal further. Khidekel was a father of the Soviet avant-garde through the UNOVIS group, developing Suprematism in architecture as well as art. Khidekel was also connected to Marc Chagall, who was fond of depicting levitating *luftmenschen*, which we will explore in the final chapter. In 1919, Khidekel was admitted by Chagall to the Vitebsk school of art, where he would lead the Architecture and Technical Department.

Like the Suprematist floating artwork of abstract forms, adorned with cosmic feelings and textures, Khidekel and others developed architectural projects imagining levitating structures. These prefigured much later architectural renderings of future suspended cities such as Arata Isozaki's *Clusters in the Air* (1960–62), which would imagine enormous vertical structures creating overhanging apartments, as if branches from a tree, for modern Tokyo. Khidekel's buildings would have relied upon enormous cantilevers, while the young architect Georgii Krutikov's designs literally floated. El Lissitzky would capture some of these trends in Russian architecture directly:

> One of our utopian ideas is the desire to overcome the limitations of the substructure, the earthbound . . . the conquest of the substructure, the earthbound, can be extended even further and calls for the conquest of gravity as such. It demands floating structures, a physical-dynamic structure.[42]

Krutikov's work at the Higher State Artistic and Technical Institute, the Vkhutein in Moscow, culminated in his 1928 project which determined a vision of the city of the future. The future city would see levitating accommodation structures flying in the atmosphere high above other urban functions. The design was premised upon massive floating accommodation blocks, their organization rationally planned in a spiral. His plan was deliberately contrasted to what he perceived as the linear chaos of the earth's surface, which he saw as the expression of the 'anarchistic and individualistic world of capitalism'.[43] Little flying commuter pods would enable those living up high to commute down to earth to their workplaces and back.[44]

It is worth saying that Krutikov's invention of urban levitation was not intended to be purely technological but artistic and social. His Vkhutein teacher Nikolai Ladovsky had gone to some lengths to highlight the importance of utopian planning and distinguish it from futuristic technological forms, such as that proposed by Krutikov's predecessor, the Constructivist Anton Lavinsky. Lavinsky's project, which proposed to float housing blocks in *City on Springs* (1923), Ladovsky found problematic. He wondered whether it was even interesting to 'lift a house?' One could do it with balloons or electromagnets; 'Give me an artistic utopia,' he demanded.[45]

Krutikov's project featured an analytical component as well as extraordinary designs. Like many others who have considered levitation in a broader historical context, the levity of the future city in Krutikov's project was placed on a historical continuum. As with Wells, this timeline worked on a premise or *telos* of humanity's ever-increasing capacities to rise above the earth. This was a natural evolution from the 'hut to the house in the air'.[46] Several tables helped Krutikov represent this movement, with illustrations of improvements in transport technologies and building forms. The earth is shown from aerial perspectives, the stratosphere, a rocket, and cosmic space, represented with science fiction imagery – even a flying saucer. Importantly, the teleology at play in Krutikov's imagination was also political. His flying city was the natural successor to the evolution of society's political organization; out of terrestrially bound capitalist chaos could evolve a cosmic socialism. This would be marked in his design by a 'higher level of spatial organisation, corresponding to a higher level of social organisation'.[47]

Khan-Magomedov describes the electric atmosphere on the day of Krutikov's dissertation exam, suddenly quietened at the end of the verbal explanation for his project, which had been displayed on poster boards. Some of the judges and a journalist would seek to take the flying city down a peg or two – back down to the ground. Yakov Raikh, an architect and representative of the Moscow city authorities, asked how Krutikov's city could possibly resolve the problems of sanitation and waste removal from such a height. Worse came from the journalist N. Levochskii, writing for the newspaper *Postroika* (Building). His article was titled 'Soviet Jules Vernes: The Vkhutein [Vkhutemas] is Not Training Builders, but Day Dreamers'. Levochskii's article complained that Krutikov's designs were not fulfilling the Soviet needs of the day for good, cheap and comfortable housing. 'Nevertheless at this time', Levoschkii wrote, 'the Vkhutemas, instead of training competent, business-like young specialists for the building industry, has been occupied with fantastic visions.' Krutikov's was an example of the 'most glib, cheeky and stunning city designs', Levoschkii bemoaned. Most damningly, he suggested that if Soviet architects were allowed to build like novelists, 'the result is not really a building, but a bad adventure novel . . . with a criminal ending.'[48] For others, the design exemplified a manner of detachment common to levitators; the building plan was 'remote from practicality'.[49]

Superhero

Michel de Certeau's now famous elevation to the 110th floor of the World Trade Center unsurprisingly occupies the sentences of many

Illustration from Thomas Nachlik and Rich Johnston, *The Flying Friar* (2006).

writings on the vertical. But it is clear that Certeau was fulfilling the modernist fantasies we have been considering in among mystical and religious associations of flight and levity.[50] Certeau's rise is an 'elevation'. He is 'lifted to the summit'.[51] His ascension permits an 'ecstasy of reading' the cosmos of the city's form.[52] The ecstasy of his elevation marks a dispossession from the city's grasp; he is no longer clasped by the city's streets or the rumble of its nervousness. This is the kind of detachment we recognized among sovereigns earlier in the book, a quality also usually identified quite literally in superheroes, who are often bestowed with powers to hover and fly, or exude height in other forms. It is also something we find in common with our earlier flying saints, friars and mystics, and it is perhaps not surprising that St Joseph of Copertino's story has been told in black-and-white graphic novel form by Speakeasy comics in a story written by Rich Johnston and illustrated by Thomas Nachlik in 2006. We should not forget that Joseph's story was also told in *The Reluctant Saint* directed by Edward Dmytryk – one of the blacklisted Hollywood Ten – in 1962, starring Maximilian Schell and Ricardo Montalban. In the novella Joseph is a populist figure and misunderstood by the authorities. His levity signals a detachment (figural and literal) from the grounding institutional authority of the Church, which sees him pitted against several muscular 'bad guy' antagonists.

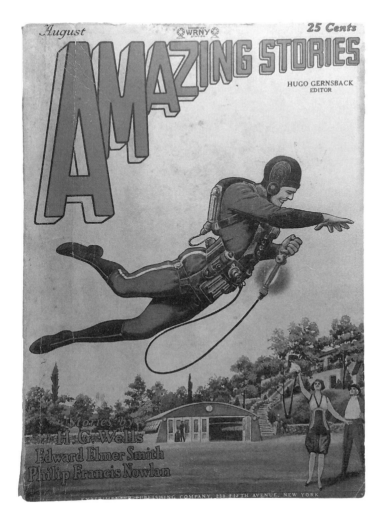

Frank R. Paul, *Amazing Stories* (August 1928).

The cultural and media theorist Scott Bukatman has argued that the comic-book superhero body holds together numerous contradictions: 'The body defies gravity space, and time; it divides and conquers, turns to fire, lives in water, is lighter than air . . . The superhero body is everything.'[53] This is one tendency of the lighter-than-air superhero, quick to levitate with whatever super-powers they have been given or exposed to. Not totally unlike the ballerinas of nineteenth-century Europe and Russia, the flying superhero would be adored. The context was the turmoil of the Second World War and frost of Cold War antagonisms. For adolescents in the United States, the superhero captured the kinds of dreams evident at the World's Fair, especially New York's in 1939.

One of the most famous levitational images Frank R. Paul would draw illustrates the collision of two dominant tropes in American aerial culture. The scene is a familiar pastoral landscape to American audiences: a lush garden or yard at the bottom of some steps that trail down from the main house. Paul's illustration was printed in the August 1928 edition of *Amazing Stories*, and was intended to depict not a levitating Buck Rogers – as featured in another story in the magazine – but *The Skylark of Space*, written by E. E. 'Doc' Smith between 1915 and 1921. The cover depicts a man levitating above a garden in a flying suit, much to the delight of a man and woman spectating on the ground; the woman waves her hat as he passes. What is perhaps so remarkable about the image can be found if we look closer at the background. Behind the waving couple is a garage; a man, perhaps a gardener maintaining the grounds, stands nearby. If one looks more closely, the garage begins to resemble a hangar, and just visible behind the ajar door can be seen the edge of an aircraft wing; its dark shape is silhouetted against the hangar's windows. Frank's illustration is an attunement of the cultures of science fiction to the already dominant myth of 'an airplane in every garage' so espoused by early boosters of aviation in the United States. The levitating superhero is merged with the aeroplane as a public and private technology of human and spiritual elevation.

A few decades later, the techno-scientific dreams of Paul's illustrations would evolve in a new wave of helicopter dreams that would excite Europe's urban planners, beleaguered by the demand for urban renewal.[54] Illustrator René Ravo's front cover of the April 1946 edition of *Science et Vie* is very similar to Paul's. In the wake of pre-war imaginations of flourishing post-war cities peppered with helipads, Ravo imagines a rural coastal scene. A house sits in the background, nestled in a crop of trees on the shores of a coastline. This time the woman gazing upwards is made to float, just a little. A helicopter hovers overhead, piloted by a man looking down, his arm outstretched to lift the woman into the air. She rises a few inches, ascending not to the future but an aerial life of the present.

The whirling, twirling ascent of the helicopter's prophecy was different to the aeroplane. As a technology it was more like levitation. It was smaller, lighter, more agile and not as fast, potentially more sedate and in other ways a more stripped-back experience. Equally, its flight seemed less serious than that of the aeroplane. The helicopter looked incongruent and not aerodynamic; it did not require the lift of a wing or aerofoil; it didn't seem ready to leave the ground. Satire and science fiction came together in the helicopter, and in the tendency to morph the human body with flying technologies – not anthropomorphizing the helicopter but making the body more like a machine.[55]

The post-war beanie hat would turn these concepts of levity into a consumer item. The helicopter had reoriented the propeller upwards and the beanie hat played on this. Invented for a science fiction convention by Ray Faraday Nelson, the 'propeller beanie' positioned a propeller at the apex of the child's cap. It was also known as the 'atomic propeller cap', or a 'fly boy'.[56] The hats quickly became a sensation and inspired a Disney-produced cartoon series titled *Beany and Cecil*. Beany's propeller cap allowed him to fly and go on various jaunts. It would also be shipped to the 1958 Brussels World's Fair for display at the u.s. pavilion 'How America Lives'. Artist Guy Pène du Bois' *Boy with a Propeller Hat* (1948) imagines an American boy hovering about.

What these figures begin to express are characteristics that would be commonly held by the superhero. Faster than a bullet, bird, or a plane. They literally performed their ascension through moral acts and virtuous deeds. Superman, as Morshed suggests, becomes the city's guardian angel, watching over its shoulder to spot injustice and to heal the urban plight. Even today, whether levitating or poised on skyscrapers and rooftops, superheroes in film or comic books frequently stand watch. The declared 'watchful guardian' hovers or stalks above city landscapes, almost always at night. To the superhero, attuned with their other capacities, such as super-hearing, super-sight or other preternatural powers, the night provides the best degrees of contrast between light and dark, the virtuous or innocent and the criminal.

The flight of superheroes such as Superman is to permit an almost omniscient, penetrating view; to see through buildings. Or, sight becomes the weapon of a red laser beam, able to cut through almost anything. This above-ness sets these heroes apart from others. In a scene of a stand-off from one of the latest filmic incarnations of Superman in *Man of Steel* (2013), Superman levitates above a desert location while the u.s. military points its various weaponry at him as he tries to begin diplomatic talks. This is an alien encounter. For Neal Curtis, superheroes are regularly represented as 'hovering just above the ground when speaking to mere mortals or those differently abled'. In other words, Superman and other superheroes regularly 'speak down' to the rest of us.[57]

Superman's omniscience is more complicated than this, however. His hover is undoubtedly biblically inspired. In various films Superman hovers with his arms outstretched, as if nailed to an invisible cross. His body bears the weight of the world in an angelic gesture signalling his responsibility to intervene in diplomatic and military affairs of nation states and with those off-planet. One might draw a more grotesque allegory, with the elevated and crucified forms of the prisoners photographed in Abu Ghraib, suffering in a complete inversion of power during the American occupation of Iraq.[58] In some respects, then, Superman's levitation is also a submission to earthly legalities and ethical responsibilities.

The genre of comic book and science fiction superheroes sees these powers embedded and embodied within the inhuman capacities of extraordinary people, as opposed to the lodestones of Swift's imagination. Magneto, the pseudonym of Max Eisenhardt or Erik Lehnsherr, depending on whether you take your lore from the comic books or the films about the X-Men, is perhaps the most powerful *luftmensch* we will come across given his ability to manipulate metals in almost any way possible. In the films, Magneto's parents infamously die in Auschwitz, where Magneto's powers are revealed. In the films, Erik/Max's separation from his mother on arrival in Auschwitz sees him warping the gates; several guards are dragged by him before one silences his powers with the butt of a rifle. Magneto is a 'mutant', his abilities derived from cellular changes in his body from rapid evolution. These are the outcome of the nuclear age, which charge other comic book characters with similar superhuman abilities.

Magneto first appeared in *X-Men* #1, in 1963. He is probably the most powerful character in Marvel's *X-Men* series of comic books and films and frequently levitates himself, others and other things, ranging from coins and desk toys to bullets, missiles, bridges, sports stadiums and nuclear submarines. Witness Magneto's escape from the plastic prison he is confined to at the end of Bryan Singer's film

Superman 'speaking down' in *Man of Steel* (dir. Zack Snyder, 2013).

X-Men (2000). In *x2* (2003), Magneto's partner Mystique embezzles a large amount of iron into the prison. She shoots it into an off-duty prison guard's buttocks – the very same guard who has been responsible for regular assaults on Magneto in order to soften him up for Stryker's interrogations.

Magneto's capacities to sense metal are shown to be more sensitive than the metal detectors that scan the guards as they enter the prison, picking up just a mere flickering of a ferrous metal signature. 'Ah, there it is. Too much iron in your blood,' Magneto utters wickedly, before levitating the guard and pulling the iron molecules out of his body, rupturing his skin, organs and blood vessels so that the guard, we assume, bleeds to death. Magneto manipulates the iron into a disc, upon which he floats out of the prison. The scene is striking because Magneto leaves his cell airborne, his arms folded, protected by the two ball-bearings he uses as weapons to puncture holes in the walls and the remaining guards.

Magneto's many levitations in comic book form or film play upon the body's comportment in various ways. As with other levitators, Magneto's control of his own body's flight is subtly

Superman as Jesus in *Man of Steel* (dir. Zack Snyder, 2013).

distinct from how he levitates others. In most cases his arms are by his side, bent at the elbows, palms faced up. His movements are graceful and controlled. Those he levitates he tends to fling around or hold up like a rag doll. The character Wolverine has been on the receiving end of these flights, controlled by his adamantium-grafted skeleton. Wolverine and others find their bodies absolutely rigid, their arms outstretched, almost crucified as Superman above, before being whipped back or flung about by Magneto's will. The films and comic books draw on Magneto as a protagonist moving against and occasionally with the X-Men as a purveyor of the rights of mutants against the will of governments seeking to suppress them. Interesting geopolitical contexts have set the scenes for Magneto's evolution. While the Nazi genocide sees the apparent birth of his powers, the Cold War and the Cuban Missile Crisis are the contexts for his radicalization, as the United States and the Soviet Union choose to bomb Magneto and his fellow mutants after nuclear war has been averted. National security surveillance and ID registration schemes of the early 2000s form the backdrop to the filmic representations of Magneto in the first *X-Men* movies.

Across various comic books and films, levitating requires something of the same posture in order to work, or just look cool. Alan Moore's Doctor Manhattan's emergence from vaporization, as his body had its intrinsic field removed, is his wilful coalescence from atomic dispersion to a corporeal, glowing, blue presence, several feet above the ground. His arms are outstretched, palms upwards, while spoons from the cafeteria float past his girlfriend Janey, who exclaims, 'Oh God, Jon. Is that you?'

Doctor Manhattan is actually Jon Osterman, encouraged by his watchmaker father to become an atomic scientist after realizing the effects of the nuclear weapons dropped on Hiroshima and Nagasaki. Jon's birth as the godlike Doctor Manhattan sees his incorporation into the U.S. military as a 'superman', his powers wielded by a desperate President Nixon to win the war in Vietnam. In one scene an onlooking military elite gazes upon him as he floats above, almost an apotheosis of the u.s. scientific and military complex that is expressed in his levitating body. Golden leaves flutter down from the autumnal sky.

We can see similar ideas of Eastern mysticism at play in Doctor Manhattan's levitations in *Watchmen*'s comic book and filmic incarnations through his increasing detachment from his loved ones and the human race. Able to manipulate matter, he also exists in a quantum-like existence, witnessing the pure simultaneity of past, present and future. Doctor Manhattan's detachment is more disillusionment, an apathy towards the course of events, and in fact extra-planetary, too, as he removes himself from planet Earth. He goes to Mars, whereupon he decides to build a palace of

Doctor Manhattan is born in *Watchmen* (dir. Zack Snyder, 2009).

solitude. There are no socialist utopian settlements of the
Bolshevik imagination here. *Watchmen* creators Alan Moore and
Dave Gibbons depict Doctor Manhattan sitting cross-legged,
almost in lotus position, pouring sparklingly pink Martian sand
through his fingers: 'Gone to Mars. Gone to a place without clocks,
without seasons, without hourglasses, to trap the shifting pink
sand.' Doctor Manhattan rises, still cross-legged, to bob above the
sand, the stars of space twinkling behind him. 'Below me, in the
sand, the secret shape of my creation is concealed, buried in the
sand's future. I rise into the thin air.'[59] He comes quite close here
to resembling the Hindu god Shiva.

In both Magneto and Doctor Manhattan we see protagonists
whose powers appear determined by radiation and the military-
industrial scientific calculus that surrounded it. It is perhaps no
surprise, as Jeffrey Kripal has argued, that the idea of radiation
accounts for almost the entire basis of modern comic book heroes
bestowed with superpowers, many of whom can levitate or fly. As
Kripal notes, the figure of the atomic bomb as *the* evental moment
in many storylines of comic book heroes has little to do with the
reality of the atomic bomb and nuclear radiation, and 'everything to
do with the history of animal magnetism, Mesmerism, Spiritualism,
psychical research, psychoanalysis, and now the mystical implica-
tions of quantum physics.'[60]

Coming of age

The detachment or disillusionment of the levitating superhero we
have just seen is in many ways completely different from earlier
versions of the superman, even in Cold War America. More recent
filmic portrayals tell of levitation and the attainment of superpowers
through a very different kind of visual style, which depicts not a
holding back but the movement of time and age, a coming of age,
a growing up with levity.

Adolescent levitation in *Chronicle* (dir. Joshua Trank, 2012).

In *Chronicle* (2012), levitation is made possible by the exposure of a group of teenage boys to a form of alien radiation, which gives the adolescents telekinetic powers. How the boys first deal with their new gifts is totally at odds with the responsibility of moral and civic duty that weighs down a figure like Superman.

The movie is told through a combination of *Jackass* aesthetics and found footage, once all the characters are dead. *Chronicle* finds considerable animation in a teenage levity of banter, friendship and wonder, as the characters begin to learn how to levitate and ultimately fly together. Interestingly, the video camera's point of view – our perspective through the film – is also levitated by the characters. So while Steven Connor remarks on the new phenomenology of the film body as being similarly light, 'weightless and placeless, allowing for an infinity of angles, elevations, cuts, pans and zooms', in *Chronicle*, the levitated camera constitutes a witness to the events that the levitators wish to record.[61] From the start, this witnessing view begins to move towards a perspective increasingly unhooked from the hand holding the camcorder.

A scene in a sawmill captures some of the wonder of other ascents. One of the teenage boys, Matt is looking down at his phone, wondering where his friend Steve is, while Andrew films. Matt receives a text from Steve, saying 'look up'; the camera and Matt's head crane upwards, and we see Steve floating above them. 'Hello boys!' he shouts. A resounding 'What!!?', 'Whoa!', 'No way!', from Andrew and Matt, as Steve spins in the air. Their efforts to get themselves airborne by a few feet result in roars of confusion and surprise, before Matt falls and then flips onto his ass. 'Eatin' dirt, man', Andrew quips, fulfilling the genre of candid camera 'fails' commonplace on television and in online videos today.

Andrew, the most talented of the group and the most advanced in his telekinesis, joins in and immediately finds more success than Matt. He rises up to meet Steve, his mouth agape. The camera operator shouts: 'Andrew, don't fart, we'll never find you again!' Matt's fail is particularly reminiscent of the conceptual artist Bruce Nauman's *Failing to Levitate in the Studio* (1966). Nauman helps us to realise how deflation, error and failure are part and parcel of the levitator, too. Kathryn Hixson suggests that Nauman's piece – where he documents his failed attempts to levitate, by lying, with a great deal of physical effort, between two chairs in his studio – is a means to upend the apparent high art of the saintly artist.[62] Levitators must eventually come back down to earth, and they rarely land all that gracefully.

6 Anti-gravity

IN 2014, THE SWIMSUIT MODEL and occasional actress Kate Upton floated on what have become known as zero-gravity aircraft for several minutes. A stunt to show off the model's seemingly gravity-defying body for a *Sports Illustrated* photo spread, the event continued the historic association of the levitator with a desiring and often hyper-exploitative gaze. And yet, for some, the weightlessness of the Space Age may inhibit desire, or at least sexual performance. Aaron Schuster reminds us that the psychoanalyst Jacques Lacan would characterize the sexual drive as that 'which usually manifests itself through transgression of the law of gravity'. 'How can the phallus properly "levitate" in a gravity-free environment?' Schuster asks.[1]

Other 'celebrities' have also enjoyed the experience of zero gravity. Levitators, as we have seen, draw and attract the eye like a magnetic or gravitational force. Some can be seen only through trickery, out of the corner of the eye; blink, and they might be gone. Other levitations are achieved by pushing at the limits of the levitator's association with other forces of attraction. In this chapter we explore the interplay of attempts to remove gravity in science, geopolitics and art since the first possibilities of space flight.

Zero-gravity

Upton's levity was achieved by a parabolic aircraft flight performed by the Zero Gravity Corporation, one of the companies that dominate the private market in this industry. Their flights usually perform fifteen or so parabolas, providing in each arc around 30 seconds of effectively weightless conditions. Since the 1950s, many of these flights have been performed by air forces and national space agencies attempting to simulate zero-gravitational environments.

To explore these flights we must examine what permits bodies to inhabit weightless conditions, ready to perform their own turns and tricks, bouncing around the cabins of aircraft. This form of levity requires an advanced technological apparatus to support it. But such a suspension is only relative, not absolute, because they are actually falling very fast indeed. Those who have achieved levity through the aircraft's performance of a high-altitude parabola are not necessarily without weight; their short-term lightness is not because gravity has been suddenly stopped. Levity instead might be understood as a relative phenomenon, as buoyancy and uplift are achieved in relation to another body in motion.[2] As with our earlier magicians and performers who have conjured levitation, this is another trick. The effect is actually a kind of acceleration understood as free fall.

Parabolic flights were initiated during the famous phases of high-altitude and fighter test piloting in the early years of the Cold War, manned by the men whom novelist Tom Wolfe raised to literary as well as public grandeur in *The Right Stuff* (1979).[3] Sub-, zero- or reduced gravity had been postulated as a potentially reproducible environment by various aeronautical scientists and engineers, who also worried about the potential effects on the human body, however charged, fit and manly, space travel might have.[4] Fritz and Heinz Haber, scientists at the United States Air

Force's School of Aviation Medicine, at Randolph Air Force Base in Texas, first began to consider the possible effects on people. A state of reduced gravity was considered incredibly unusual. Gravity, they conceded, 'has the outstanding property of being omnipresent and everlasting. Not a single individual has as yet been away from its influence for more than one to two seconds.'[5] With the development in rockets and the potential for space exploration in the imminent space race, the scientists would identify the growing importance of zero gravity as a new set of 'environmental factors of man'.[6] How though, they asked, could medical research be advanced? The answer they considered was the development of a means to simulate states of zero gravity by the elimination of its effect through other counteracting forces. The levitating, floating body they were after was not weightless in the sense of gravity having been removed, but rather its effect could be subjected to an equalization, a balancing of forces. After contemplating the possibility of using a vertically dropped missile, and a technique whereby an elevator would suddenly fall, they determined that the most probable solution was an aircraft achieving effective free fall by flying in the trajectory of a parabolic arc.

This approach effectively uses the body's inertia, motivated by the curve of the aircraft's flight, to cancel out the force of gravity. This works because bodies inside the aircraft would be undisturbed from the forces of air friction outside. The Habers predicted that it would be possible to achieve well over a minute and a half of zero gravity. As Wolfe notes, test pilots and early astronauts in F-100 jet fighters at the famous Muroc base (now Edwards Air Force Base) in California, and at Holloman in New Mexico at the Aeromedical Field Laboratory, would begin experimenting with the procedure. This included Scott Crossfield and the more famous Chuck Yeager. The tests subjected the body to intense speeds and gravitational forces. Joe Kittinger, who would later become famous for his involvement in high-altitude jumps from a balloon in the Excelsior project – and acted as capsule communicator for Felix Baumgartner's free fall from 128,000 ft (39 km) in 2012 – was one such pioneer of the technique. Kittinger recalls cats being used, to test their self-orienting powers, in some of the early flights.[7]

Tests began in earnest on the ground. John Paul Stapp – an air force doctor who would oversee the Manhigh project that sent Kittinger to 96,784 ft (29.5 km) in 1957 – developed a rocket-propelled cart or sled called 'Sonic Wind' along a 3,500-ft (1-km) track to deliver 40,000 lb (18,100 kg) of thrust and accelerate the body to simulate vast g-forces.[8] About the same time, v-2 rockets were being used to send animals, often monkeys and mice, to high altitudes, propelled from the rocket in an ejecting nose cone. A parachute descended the vessel to safety. The last Aerobee (a suborbital rocket) flights at Holloman in 1952 were successful in sending two mice and a monkey airborne and into temporary free fall. *Animals in Rocket Flight*, a u.s. Air Force public information film from 1953, saw the mice Patricia and Mike enjoying the effects of zero gravity in a confusingly rotating drum.[9] One of the mice sits poised on a shelf, while the other floats, flailing and spinning around helplessly. As the commentator explains, they move in and out of a sub-gravitational state.

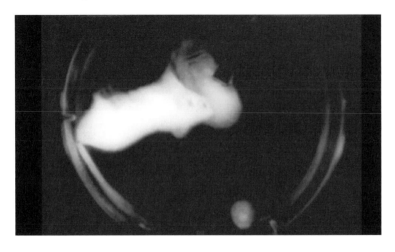

Patricia and Mike in the u.s. Air Force public information film *Animals in Rocket Flight* (1953).

The Soviet Union was advancing similar kinds of tests at the same time as the Americans, and they were also the first to send an animal into a form of levitation, floating above the earth in Sputnik 2 in 1957. The Russian scientists were impressed at the minimal effects of these conditions on the body of the dog Laika. Unfortunately, Laika would not make it back. Sputnik was never intended to return to earth, but the telemetry was. The scientists were interested in Laika's response to coming into an orbital path and settling on the orbit. The dog's electrocardiogram reading, blood circulation and breathing all intensified during the moments of increased stress preceding sub-gravitational flight. When the dog became weightless in orbit, these readings appeared to come down to a normal rate. The findings were presented by the Soviet scientist Dr Andrei Kouznetsov of the Institute of Aviation Medicine to the third European Congress of Aviation Medicine in 1958 in Louvain, Belgium. Holloman's John Stapp was in the audience, listening intently.

Lost in space

Weightlessness was believed to be confusing. In addition to the extreme sensory and physiological strain of achieving high-altitude or orbital flight, Cold War aviation and space medics were concerned with the sensory disorientation of zero gravity. Chuck Yeager is said to have described the experience of his high-altitude parabolas as like being 'lost in space'. It is ironic that the methods of achieving effective weightlessness – to enable the body to levitate – albeit 'artificially' and deliberately, occurred precisely through accelerating the body to extremes of speed and elevation in the upper atmosphere. Within the Mercury Project, the United States' first space programme, astronauts would take regular parabolas on the the Convair C-131 Samaritan, known as the 'Vomit Comet', although NASA preferred the nickname the 'Weightless Wonder'.

Project Mercury astronauts in weightless flight on a C-131 aircraft, 1958.

It is important to realize that sensory disorientation is a common experience in other almost-weightless environments. In water this is known as the 'breakaway phenomenon'. Learning to dive is learning to achieve a similarly levitated state of near-perfect buoyancy, where one is stable in the water, drifting neither up nor down. But just where up is, as with zero gravity, can be difficult to locate, especially in conditions so deep that sunlight does not provide a marker of orientation, or where debris obscures vision to near-whiteout. The need to simulate these conditions was one reason why the budding astronauts trained in water-filled tanks.

The Mercury Seven astronaut Alan Shepard had led the way. The stage of the rocket ascent just before the capsule is shorn from the depleted rocket is a transition into levity. Wolfe describes this as a smooth easing into, as if gravity had just 'slid off his body'.[10] These experiences would lead to other philosophical meditations wondering at the confusion of losing all fixed points. Others saw space flight as a transcendence to a more universal but less wedded position floating above the earth.

The philosopher Emmanuel Levinas pitted Yuri Gagarin's first orbit of the earth on 12 April 1961 in the Vostok against Martin Heidegger's thoroughly earthbound notion of being. For Levinas:

> What is admirable about Gagarin's feat is certainly not his magnificent Luna Park performance which impresses the crowds; it is not the sporting achievement of having gone further than the others and broken the world records for height and speed. What counts more is the probable opening up of new forms of knowledge and new technological possibilities, Gagarin's personal courage and virtues, the science that made the feat possible, and everything which that in turn assumes in the way of abnegation and sacrifice. But what perhaps counts most of all is that he left the Place. For one hour, man existed beyond any horizon – everything around him was sky or, more exactly, every-thing was geometrical space. A man existed in the absolute of homogeneous space.[11]

Similarly, the Algerian Jewish philosopher Jacques Derrida would characterize his own writing in his odd 'circumfessions' as a response to this new world of detachment. 'I have neither up nor down,' he wrote, 'like the squirrel climbing down horizontally, the form of my world, a literature that is apparently like the very look of my writing, cosmonautical, floating in weightlessness, marine and *high-tech*, more naked.'[12]

Hannah Arendt would comment in her prologue to *The Human Condition* (1958) on the significance of sending Sputnik into orbit in two related movements of modern life: political and religious freedom. This was the very 'first step', to lift off above the atmos-phere, to escape the imprisonment, as some commentators had put it, of the bounds of the Earth:

Should the emancipation and secularization of the modern age, which began with a turning-away, not necessarily from God, but from a god who was the Father of men in heaven, end with a more fateful repudiation of an Earth who was the Mother of all living creatures under the sky?[13]

For Levinas, the weightlessness of Gagarin's float around the planet was an exemplary rejection of Heidegger's rootedness in any sacred sense of place. Rather, it was an opportunity to see the world from the outside, from a position of alterity.

Levinas' writings on Gagarin can be placed within his wider thinking on cosmopolitan ethics.[14] But his appraisal of Gagarin was not one-sided. On his return to Earth, Gagarin is widely believed to have uttered, 'I flew into space but didn't see God.' Levinas would use the analogy of angelic omission and terrestrial weight elsewhere,[15] complaining that the cosmonaut, while emancipated from the planet, did not transcend the narrow ethical and moral strictures of modern science, and the geopolitical ambitions that sent them there. Otherness is actually not possible. His characterization of the cosmonaut in this instance becomes grounded to that of a 'space pedestrian'. In spite of the infinity of the cosmos, Levinas reduces the astronaut to a collector of rocks and soil: 'man – finds himself confined without being able to set foot outside.'[16] Gagarin's apparent disavowal of God disappoints Levinas, to the extent that 'the new condition of existence in the weightlessness of space "without sites"' that was promised by Gagarin's flight does not come true. Outer space, as opposed to the Earth, is still experienced 'by the first man to be launched into space, as a *here*, as the *same* without a veritable alterity'.[17]

In fact, Gagarin's supposed statement was created and promulgated by the Soviet leader Nikita Khrushchev, continuing the Soviet's pursuit of scientific atheism. And let us not forget aeronautics. Khrushchev's popularization of the idea that Gagarin

Alexey Akindinov,
Gagarin's Breakfast,
2011–12, oil on canvas.

had not, in fact, found God in space, continued a relationship between flight and the ongoing repression of religion in the Soviet Union.[18] While early Soviet aviation had been cast as its own religion, baptizing the air-minded in communist ideology, space flight marked its own distinctive 'assault on heaven'.[19] Such a phrasing, found in the reproduction of a propaganda poster representing Soviet aircraft eradicating heaven in the 1930s, was also a repurposing of Karl Marx's characterization of the Paris Commune of 1871 as 'storming heaven'. The Russian historian Walter Kolarz makes an oblique reference to the communards' use of balloons during the Siege of Paris against Prussian forces: mail and people were transported in and out of the besieged city by balloons.[20]

Gagarin's statements also hinted that a kind of domesticity could be found in space. His remarks about laying a table in orbit are responded to by artist Alexey Akindinov in *Gagarin's Breakfast* (2011–12), which pictures – in Palekh oil icon style – Gagarin enjoying breakfast in a chintzy interior with a floating coffee pot and other accoutrements.

Matter unleashed

While these accounts of space levity tend to focus on the physiological and medical registers of the floating body, they were in many ways preceded by other important oracles of space flight, who had prophesied the conditions and building structures necessary to live in and overcome weightless conditions.

Slovene engineer Herman Potočnik (Herman Noordung) wrote his *The Problem of Space Travel* in 1928. Potočnik was especially concerned with the dangers and problems of an environment of weightlessness. He considered the many problems a space traveller might experience, such as colliding with other objects should they push off from a surface too hard, hitting the edges and the corners of a room. His solution was almost to domesticate those spaces; sharp corners would need to be eradicated, cushioning might be necessary. Everything would need to be anchored in some way. Things and people could not be hung up or laid down any longer, but would need trapping, stowing or fixing in place. For the human to accomplish anything, their standards of comportment would be turned upside down, because, he argued, there is neither 'standing' nor 'sitting' or 'lying' down. In one sense, Potočnik's book indicated the vertiginous dangers of uncontrolled levity, should one push off too fast into oblivion. This was the counterpart, he argued, to the terrestrial danger of falling into the depths: 'The saying "man overboard" is also valid when gravity is missing, however in another sense.' Floating above the earth has been experienced in similar ways to vertigo, the sensation of being pulled down or out by the massiveness of space, or the chiasmic pull of the earth. These are common terms of the sublime. The disorientation of weightlessness in the immensity of space has been captured in few better ways than in Alfonso Cuarón's film *Gravity* (2013).

Gravity is well known for its innovations in weightlessness effects. To shoot the actors realistically, floating not only in a

Sandra Bullock in *Gravity* (dir. Alfonso Cuarón, 2013).

spacecraft or the International Space Station but untethered from objects, drifting uncontrollably – as Sandra Bullock's character does, spinning head over heels – was problematic. The usual art of hanging the actors by wires was deemed too torturous for the body, but also unrealistic. Gravity, it seems, pulls on our muscles and facial gestures in ways even an actor cannot control. Instead, the *Gravity* production team designed a camera rig that effectively suspended the actor, but instead of turning the actor, the camera could move around the actor's body in 360 degrees.

Unsecured objects, Potočnik proposed, would have infinite propensities should they be set moving. He imagined that if the velocity of an object was 'sufficiently large', things could bounce back again and again as if having an elasticity. The perpetual motion of things in levity he considered could occur over hours and even days, given the tiny forces needed to give objects propulsion. One contemporary astronaut even used a single strand of hair to push off from a wall. Potočnik warned that such motion would find no regularity. All objects, he argued, must be kept in a safe place: 'the ordering power of gravity now no longer exists: matter is "unleashed".'[21]

This is very different to our other levitants, which have been about singular, if sometimes privileged, spectacular performances. Banal things can levitate, too. Fluids behave differently, unwilling to obey the containers they are used to settling in under the force

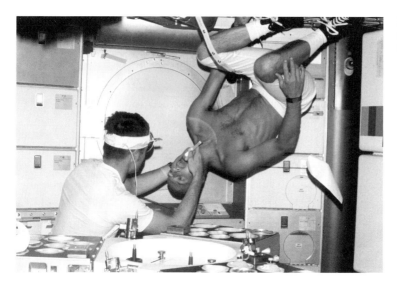

Dental testing of
Charles Conrad in
microgravity, 1973.

of gravity. Bananas, toothpaste, spanners, watches, syringes, hair, sweat and urine move about, their inertia lacking an opposing force like gravity to keep them down, or much wind resistance to slow them. These things ricochet and sometimes disaggregate in the confined spaces. Water breaks apart into tiny droplets. Detritus hides in the nooks and crannies of the now retired Russian space shuttle the Soyuz, or on the International Space Station. Nothing is at rest. Everyday objects placed for a while go missing, and are no longer where their owners thought they were.[22]

When floating astronauts lose an item, they tend to immediately look down. This reaction might seem strange. Before long, they realize that what they were looking for has actually floated up. But where is down in an environment lacking in gravitational coordinates? Since Russia's second orbital space flight of August 1961, cosmonauts and astronauts have described odd sensations of feeling upside down, a sense of phenomenal inversion even though there is no gravity to orient them, while weightless. Some scientists put these feelings down to some of the extreme experiences of acceleration that occur during the preceding stages of rocket flight, which can stimulate inversion in gravity because of the demands on the body's vestibular system. Other disorientating effects of levitational weightlessness are also recorded as 'visual reorientation illusions': sensations of ascension, being pulled or sucked downwards, or finding it difficult to recognize normal objects because they are viewed from different angles. Somehow, astronauts are able to maintain a 'subjective vertical' through visual cues, transforming walls into floors and floors into ceilings, imposing a top and a bottom when there effectively are none.[23]

In *Gravity*, the cataclysmic event that sets the drama of the film into motion, and the violent spinning of just about everything in or around the vicinity of the space shuttle, works on an interesting premise. That is, other things can be found in free fall, orbiting

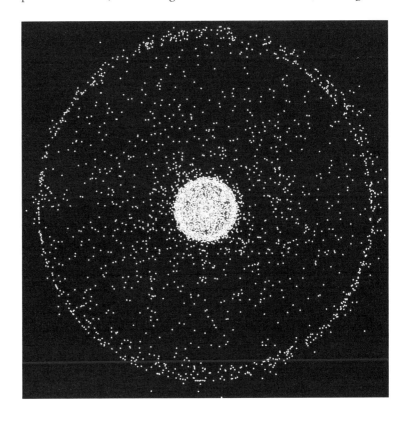

Space debris modelled by NASA.

around the planet – such is the problem
of space debris, which makes up reefs of
levitating waste. Made up of the bits and
pieces of old satellites and ejected rockets,
this floating waste is becoming hazardous
as objects hit one another and break up
into smaller parts. According to Donald J.
Kessler, a NASA scientist who worked on the
problem in the 1970s, the intensity of these collisions
could easily cascade into what has become known
as the Kessler syndrome: an event of impossibly
unpredictable collisions, in which each object
breaks into smaller parts. The cascade would work
exponentially, leading to millions of pieces of
debris hurtling through space, making travel
through low Earth and geosynchronous orbits
almost impossible through a so-called 'debris belt'.[24]
Kessler's warning is a magnification, on a massive
scale, of what Potočnik was suggesting could make
a vessel's internal spaces so dangerous.

Illustration from Herman
Potočnik's *The Problem
of Space Travel* (1928).

   Potočnik's solutions to the lack of gravitational force will seem
familiar because they were drawn upon by science fiction writers,
and notably Stanley Kubrick in *2001: A Space Odyssey*. The rotating
wheel space station, so ingeniously shot in the film as a rotating
set, built by Vickers-Armstrongs, sought to marshal the weightless
or free-fall internal conditions that would make space flight rather
difficult to embody. The idea was proposed to Kubrick by Arthur
C. Clarke, who had been inspired by Potočnik's work.

   Potočnik's plan was rather remarkable. A space station was
set out as if a large wheel, or 'habitat wheel', should spin around
its central axis, performing a complete rotation every 8 seconds.
This would create a centrifugal force that could emulate gravity
and nullify the inertia which would render an orbiting vessel a

Herman Potočnik's
design as portrayed
in *2001: A Space
Odyssey* (dir. Stanley
Kubrick, 1968).

place of weightlessness. But rather than gravity, which acts towards a centre, Potočnik's design, and indeed that used in *2001: A Space Odyssey*, means the force acts on the outer rim of the wheel. To orient oneself in this environment would mean that down was therefore found on the edge of the wheel, and up towards the centre.

Icons

In July 2014 the cosmonaut Oleg Artemyev blogged and tweeted a photograph from the International Space Station to celebrate the 700th anniversary of the birth of St Sergius of Radonezh, who was believed to have received an angelic visitation.[25] The cosmonaut is pictured with two colleagues, just keeping tiptoe contact with the space station floor, with several Christian icons floating with them.

The relationship between Soviet aeronautics and faith is an interesting but fraught one. Even while religious expression was repressed, those sent airborne in test planes and eventually rockets were idolized as if saintly, cosmic figures to be gilded and embellished as if icons made real. Fascinatingly, on the twentieth anniversary of the Russian inauguration of Cosmonautics Day, on 12 April 1981, a celebration of Gagarin's first ascent into space, the writer Albert Likhanov published a curiously illustrated book titled *Syn Rossii* (The Son of Russia). The book was illustrated by Kukulieva Kaleriya Vasilievna and Boris Kukuliev. Both artists worked closely in the traditions of icon painting which centred in the town of Palekh, in the Ivanovo region. Vasilievna was actually born in Palekh in 1937, while Boris studied at the Palekh art school and its workshops.

The *Syn Rossii* illustrations are extraordinary. They are not the rationalist or cold celebration of space flight in the stripped-back, abstract and utilitarian principles of some Soviet-era art. Gagarin has gone cosmic or celestial. He is reborn as a superhero, caped, able to master all the dimensions of space, driving his spacecraft as if a chariot on fire. Jed Mercurio's novel *Ascent* (2007) sketches a different kind of heroic personality to Gagarin's in the character Yevgeni Yeremin, loosely based on the Soviet pilot Yevgeny Pepelyaev, who secretly fought in the Korean War.[26] From his Chinese base in Manchuria, Pepelyaev would claim nineteen battle victories. The Yeremin of *Ascent* is not as decorated as Gagarin or Pepelyaev, or other pilots whom he finds dazzle like rising stars, or more like moons. Their shine does not come from the medals that decorate their chests, but the adoration of their peers.

Yeremin believes himself to be a dark moon and remains detached; a social space exists between him and others, even whenon the ground. When Gagarin finally reaches space, Yeremin is so jealous and indifferent to Gagarin's success that he allows himself to be literally blown off his feet, and gives himself to the freezing cold.

In the air things are different: flying his MIG-15 over Manchuria, Yeremin experiences the insights of levitative ecstasy; looking towards the airfield at Antung, he finds it 'shimmering' as if a mirage. Like Yeremin, the airfield appeared 'not to be part of the world', 'but to be hovering a few metres above it. No fighter pilot would wish to be anywhere else or to live in any other age.'[27] Mercurio's book tells us of Yeremin's ascent. Becoming the most deadly Soviet fighter during a career that takes place in secret, Yeremin is moved to a 'celestial plane'.

The race for a man in space

The race towards these first human suspensions in orbit above the Earth, within a wider geopolitical landscape of nuclear weaponry, would send other competing artistic responses into motion. Some artists would seek to express the propositions of space flight – the ability to inhabit an unsupported levitational space beyond Earth.

They would mix some of the most technologically sophisticated sciences with art practice. Like the clashing of space debris and the rivalry of nations during the space race, some artistic giants were brought into collision with each other.

One rivalry has become infamous. The French artist Yves Klein is renowned for his monochromatic artworks, his International Klein Blue, and wider interests in immaterial artwork, especially in his air architecture. The Greek sculptor Takis (Panagiotis Vassilakis) was his opponent. Gallery owner Iris Clert was in between the two. The parallels with the space race are not disingenuous: both artists were working in a time of artistic innovation in Paris, where pushing the envelope of technique and technology was all the rage. Takis's experimentation with light and magnetic technologies would see him invited to the Massachusetts Institute of Technology's Center for Advanced Visual Studies to work on the relations between art and science. Priority was also given to the originality of the work. According to Klein's girlfriend Bernadette Allain, this was an 'artistic milieu' that '*forced* people to do something new every time'. What mattered was to 'be the first'.[28] In Clert's gallery in Paris, Klein, Takis and another sculptor, Jean Tinguely, rancoured over their quite different artistic methods of creating levitating, floating artworks. Tinguely would call Klein a 'messenger of the age of space'.[29] In January 1959, at the opening of a Tinguely exhibition, Klein would make an unusual speech on collaboration and, among other things, the role of the artist and his ideas about levitation:

> Thus, we will become aerial men. We will know the force of attraction towards the high realms, towards space, toward nowhere and everywhere both at once. The force of terrestrial attraction thus mastered, we will literally levitate in total physical and spiritual freedom.[30]

At first, Klein and Tinguely argued over a collaborative piece they worked on in 1959, to float an aluminium tube that would be tethered to the ground by a small chain. Takis, meanwhile, was working on his own levitational projects. He was captivated by the possibility of magnetic fields and had begun demonstrating his 'telesculptures' in various parts of Paris. Later that year Klein would sketch plans and write to Clert presenting the idea for an 'aerosculpture', a floating sponge using helium and magnets to keep it aloft. The correspondence has become famous because it appears that Klein pre-dated his letter to Clert, as if to claim that his floating sponge concept occurred before Takis made his magnetic sculptures, earlier that year. Klein's registering of the aerosculpture with the patent office also continued this lie, claiming the invention to date from April, when it was actually formulated in June.

That the race for levitation in this artistic milieu was happening alongside frantic developments by the United States and Soviet Union to achieve human flight in outer space, while engaging in other proxy conflicts, was no accident. The gallerist Clert points to a wider atmosphere in her exasperation at the quarrelling artists, who appeared to blame her for passing on their secrets. Sarah Wilson has argued that this artistic milieu was also deeply implicated in the Jewish destruction and other moments of annihilation during the Second World War. Levity's inhabitation of the empty air, a 'void', was creatively possible because 'Nothing is made of nothing. To make *le vide*, *le plein* has to be forcibly evacuated, expelled, ejected, destroyed, rendered invisible.'[31]

Takis, *Electro-magnetic I*, 1962, sculpture.

In her autobiography Clert would deploy an aerial metaphor from which to make sense of the creative race between Klein and Takis. 'After all,' she argued, 'one invents nothing; ideas are in the air.' How could an idea ever be original? Originality in the suspension trick is a familiar one to levitation. Rather, Clert suggests, ideas 'are simultaneously seized upon by several people in the world; they belong to the one who is first to make them concrete.'[32] Klein was pro-American; Takis had pro-Soviet sympathies. Takis would nod to the imminent Soviet launch as a motivation to go beyond magnetically levitating objects to a work that would send the first man into space – the space a little closer to the Earth.

In November 1960 Klein and Takis launched similar projects, within weeks of one another. Takis's *L'Impossible* is perhaps the less well known, although it was subjected to a retrospective exhibition at the Palais de Tokyo in Paris in 2015: *Takis, Magnetic Fields*. Just six months before Gagarin's orbit, Takis would claim that he had sent the first man into space by using an elaborate apparatus of magnets and a net to temporarily levitate the South African poet Sinclair Beiles. Beiles had just enough time airborne to read out part of Takis's 'magnetic manifesto', declaring, 'I am a sculpture . . . I would like to see all nuclear bombs on Earth turned into sculptures,' before he fell into the net below.

Klein's photographic work *Leap into the Void* is far better known than Takis's piece. Publicized by a mock Sunday newspaper, *Dimanche*, on 27 November 1960, Klein used a series of photographs to create a fake one, showing himself leaping, apparently into thin air. Through transposition, the safety netting has been taken away and the photograph holds the leap still. Klein could almost be taking up the position of free fall, his body convex. The leap was a culmination of his more mystic interests in levitational ecstasy. Klein was influenced by philosopher Gaston Bachelard's writings on oneiric flight; judo was just as formative. As the art historian Sidra Stich suggests, 'He spoke about it continuously and did breathing exercises to enhance the body's ability to free itself – physically, mentally and emotionally – from the constraints of weight.'[33] Klein believed that levitation would allow him to understand the inhabitation of space better.

We could see Klein's leap into photographic levity, like the celestiality of the Russian aero- and cosmonauts, as a continuation of the medieval saintly levitators. The actual leap is not as important as the building of myth around it, the veracity assumed within the photographic image, and the use of the mock-newspaper write-up as the archival documentation of the event. Klein sought to create a parable of his self-levitation of 'the painter *of* space' as a 'man *in* space', and thus, argues Stich, the comparisons he made with Jesus we could see as 'consumate signifiers' to the mystical. He built a kind of hagiography of himself.[34]

Through Klein's interests in levitation and the cultivation of his own myth, he would make less convincing associations between himself and Yuri Gagarin. He was also ambivalent about the space programme's potential to truly make sense of the conquest of space – art was better positioned to do this. If the space race was a mirror of outmoded territorial expansion and positivist science, however, Gagarin's orbital space flight was simultaneously an inspiration for Klein, and an original event he sought to undermine. Seeing Gagarin describe the Earth as blue from space in 1961, Klein claimed that he had already declared the Earth to be entirely blue in 1957, making the Earth levitate in space without support. Indeed, Klein's scrapbook shows that he placed the photographer Harry Shunk's image of himself and his levitating blue globe next to a clipping from the front of a newspaper detailing Gagarin's orbit. Gagarin added the line to his photograph: 'Le globe est bleu.'

In *Leap*, Klein claimed a different, creative and phenomenal encounter with space: 'to go into space to paint, but he must go there without any faking, and . . . by his own means', 'and not in an airplane, parachute or rocket. He must go there by himself, an autonomous, individual force. In a word, he must be capable of levitating.'[35] Once more, Klein would announce himself as the pioneer of this modality of art, superior to the empiricism of space exploration, but equal to its conquest of apparent emptiness:

> I have felt myself volumetrically impregnated, outside of all proportions and dimensions, in the ALL. I have encountered or rather been seized by the presence of the inhabitants of space – and none of them was human: no one had gone before me.[36]

In a round-table discussion on Takis's work, and the relationship between art and science, philosophers Jean-François Lyotard and Christine Buci-Glucksmann found other creative energies in Takis, comparing him to Malevich.[37] Lyotard noticed that the emphasis in Takis's work is on non-human technology. Takis's wish to 'obtain grace of gravity' is to exempt mainly objects – balls, and other things – not people, from its force. Similarly, Klein would continue his pursuit of bodily levitation in a public space, producing other levitational photographs.

Cosmic dancers

It is well known that artwork has been taken into space since the Apollo 12 mission, when the Moon Museum was taken into orbit, featuring works by Andy Warhol, David Novros, Robert Rauschenberg, John Chamberlain, Claes Oldenburg and Forrest Myers. These were more acts of sending objects into space, rather than using space travel to investigate the capacities of levitation and weightlessness on the production and performance of art. Many others, however, have explored exactly this. For example, in Arthur Woods's *Cosmic Dancer* project, a many-angled form was taken aboard the Mir space station in 1993. Filmed by cosmonauts

Alexander Polishchuk and Gennadi Manakov, the dancer can be seen floating and ricocheting off the space station's different surfaces – just as Potočnik predicted – while the cosmonauts inhabit the same space, 'performing (rotating, hovering, flying) with the sculpture in the confines of Mir, where it was left'.[38] Eduardo Kac notes that *Cosmic Dancer*, along with the Mir station, would end their lives burning up in the atmosphere, the remnants plunging into the South Pacific in 2002.[39]

Perhaps one of the most sustained artistic elaborations of levitational weightlessness can be found in the work of Frank Pietronigro, who worked with NASA to develop what he has called 'drift paintings', explored within his 'creativity chamber', a semi-sealed plastic bag around 2 m high by 1.2 m wide and 1.3 m deep attached to a Boeing KC-135 turbo jet in 1998.[40] The artist filled several pastry bags with acrylic gel paint, which he would use to project the paint into the volume of the plastic chamber so that it would spatter on the walls of the bag. Some would also escape to the roof of the aeroplane. Notably, Pietronigro had originally given the chamber the name 'tabernacle', citing the ritualistic association of weightlessness.

For artists like Pietronigro, weightlessness releases authorship of an artwork to the inertia of the performance. While the creativity chamber and canvas – in this case the bag – would provide some record of the event, artists have valued a letting go to the momentum of paint, objects or performers let loose. Control and choreography are no longer what they were. For Pietronigro, the weightlessness he experienced can be compared to the mystical register we have explored. He gives an account of experiencing feelings of expansion, a literal inspiration as he senses the boundaries between his body and the environment being removed: 'I consciously crossed my legs and floated into a seated lotus position, shutting my eyes as I had planned to do from the moment I found out that I was going to fly.'[41]

The phenomenal experiences of expansion as levitation
sustain a bigger collaboration of the arts and sciences.⁴² Just
as Pietronigro and others ask how artists might 'harness such
experiences to create new works of art that respond and contribute to the evolution of cultural activities and creative expression'
in the new medium of weightlessness, the exploration of outer
space can be more than a scientific endeavour of collecting and
recording. How, Pietronigro asks, 'will new cultures, mythologies,
and creative methodologies unfold as our species learns to fly free
of gravity?'⁴³ The Zero Gravity Arts Consortium is one expression
of these sets of questions, just as the UK's Arts Catalyst would
send over twenty artists to explore zero-gravity conditions in
their collaboration with the Yuri Gagarin Cosmonaut Training
Centre in Star City, Russia.

Watching the many films of zero-gravity arts, however, estab-
lishes quite a different sense of levitation, unlike the constant
weightlessness of orbital space. The effect is more an oscillation,
an up and down, with a bit of sideways and lurching in between.
One actually sees the moment of becoming light, and it is
magical. The drag of gravity is apparent too, as things move
not smoothly but quite suddenly, falling back to earth, or the
bottom of the zero-gravity aircraft. So rather than a sustaining
levity over the long duration of a visit to the ISS, the artists
experience a rise and a resultant fall. We could wonder whether
this is the more authentic encounter with levitation, a similarly
tentative floatation.

Coming back down

Eventually, levitators do come back down, and mostly for
good. For our astronauts and cosmonauts inhabiting the ISS
for five months, however, returning to gravity is not achieved
so lightly. The levitator's body gets used to it, conditioned to

being without the downward pull of gravity. Many aspects of the body change under these conditions. The skeletons of astronauts get longer, the distance between each vertebra expanding the body's length. The end of weightless levity is an immediate shock and creates long-term pain. According to former Canadian astronaut Chris Hadfield, the best analogy he can find to describe it is

> like being a newborn, this sudden sensory overload of noise, color, smells and gravity after months of quietly floating, encased in relative calm and isolation. No wonder babies cry in protest when they're born.[44]

Hadfield's comparison of his terrestrial rebirth is resonant with wider cultural and philosophical understandings of being born from suspension, as psychoanalysis suggested. Stanley Kubrick's *2001: A Space Odyssey* ends with an allegory-rich set of images and sounds when the character David Bowman, subject of HAL's famous line 'I'm sorry Dave, I'm afraid I can't do that,' witnesses his life flashing before his eyes, only to be reborn as a foetus suspended in space, surrounded by an amniotic sack and looking back at Earth. While the meaning of the scene is ambiguous, according to Kubrick it offers the spirit of transcendence. Dave has become 'an enhanced being, a star child, an angel, a superman, if you like, and returns to earth prepared for the next leap forward of man's evolutionary destiny.'[45]

The Kubrickian allusions do not stop there. Hadfield would become increasingly well known as an educator through his shuttle flights and visits to the ISS, where he was commander during the second half of his five-month stay, from March 2013. As his Twitter feed grew in popularity, Hadfield, an amateur guitarist, made a cover music video of David Bowie's 1969 'Space Oddity', with his son acting as producer on Earth. Their production happened to be

the first ever music video shot in space. Bowie's song makes clear gestures to Kubrick's masterpiece, the lyrics anticipating the Apollo Moon landings. In Hadfield's version of the song, the modified lyrics are sung by Hadfield in various parts of the space station, gently drifting: ground control, he sings, calls the astronaut to 'Lock your Soyuz hatch and put your helmet on.'

    Other musical projects about space have also made their way there. Nelly Ben Hayoun's remarkable International Space Orchestra's *Ground Control: An Opera in Space* was blasted up to the International Space Station. The CD was set spinning in space

Canadian astronaut Chris Hadfield performs his rendition of David Bowie's 'Space Oddity' on board the International Space Station in 2015.

and broadcasted by two radio satellites, having been transported to the ISS by the Mitsubishi Heavy Industries and Japan Aerospace Exploration Agency's H-II Transfer Vehicle, Kounotori, in May 2013.

Hadfield's levitative free fall above the planet would not evade any obligation to terrestrial concerns such as those of law, especially when attempting to license Bowie's popular hit. As with the Klein and Takis rivalry in the late 1950s and early '60s, disputes over intellectual property and artistic originality make their way into levitation and sustain it – whether just above or several hundred kilometres away from the Earth. A piece in *The Economist* discussed the vagaries of outer space copyright law following Hadfield's success,[46] drawing on copyright lawyer J.A.L. Sterling's predictions

The International Space Orchestra on the International Space Station in 2013.

of intellectual property chaos in the future of space expansion, and the necessity for a Space Copyright Treaty. Hadfield and his son had requested a time-delimited licence from David Bowie in order to perform and release the song. Lawyers suggest that a Space Copyright Treaty would make the vagaries of this clear. At present, the conditions governing the performance, recording and distribution or publication of copyrighted material depend upon the location in which the activities take place, as well as their format. Determining where Hadfield and the video were located during the processes of production and distribution is not all that simple. For example, 'Space Oddity' was shot in numerous locations within the ISS, with each module owned by a different national or international entity, such as Japan, the United States or the European Space Agency. The covenants of the International Space Station used to govern intellectual property arising from research determine that the local rules of a country should shape intellectual property rights.

Too much levity of the free-fall kind can be demanding on the body. For once the human comes back down to Earth, as mentioned, sitting down or standing up become hard, painful activities.[47] Not only does the body's vestibular system play further tricks on the astronaut living back on the ground, but as well as muscle wastage the circulatory system struggles to cope with its reintroduction to gravity, having been used to pumping blood to the body's extremities without much of gravity's drag. Many astronauts complain of nausea, dizziness and light-headedness on their return, and are forced to don 'g-suits' to help exert the right pressure on the body's blood vessels. Hadfield and others describe learning to walk differently, tilting forwards, 'as though I was walking into gale-force winds'.[48]

Cabinets of levity

Just a year before Potočnik's writings, and two years before his death, the *Trieste Constructivist Cabinet* of 1927 was created by Slovene artists Edvard Stepančič, Avgust Černigoj, Giorgio Carmelich and Josip Vlah. The cabinet installation they designed used extremely fine threads to 'levitate' several objects on the edges and in the middle of the room. The project sought to capture the possibilities of the emerging Space Age that figures like Potočnik would come to usher in. But the cabinet was more than a suggestion and was a manifesto for art, in what more recent artists in the former Yugoslavian state have called 'post-gravity'.

Other artists since have taken some inspiration from the *Constructivist Cabinet*. If we turn to the work of the artist Ilya Kabakov, who has established a notable partnership with his wife Emilia since they left the Soviet Union in the late 1980s, our attention is drawn to the most banal of spaces, miles apart from space orbit: a domestic apartment. Yet it is here that Kabakov's installation *The Man who Flew into Space from his Apartment* (1981–8) is located. Levitation had featured in much of Kabakov's earlier illustrative work, especially for children's literature. His 'The Flying Komarov', the sixth album in his series *Ten Characters*, features numerous hovering bodies and even furniture, flying, sitting, drinking above cities, countryside and other landscapes. Each image builds on the previous to make a story. The 'Flying Komarov' illustrations would also take form in the medium of three large woven carpets – highly appropriate to the theme of levitation, as we have seen – shown at the Deweer Gallery in Belgium in 2005–6, entitled *The Flying*.

The installation of *The Man who Flew into Space from his Apartment* sets an odd scene – perhaps even a crime scene – encouraging us to reconstruct the life and passions of whoever it was who used a slingshot to catapult themselves into space.

The gaping hole in the ceiling bears testimony to that. By setting the work in or as an apartment (the installation is really a room, only a metre and a half square), Kabakov builds on a familiar trope of life in the former Soviet Ukraine: the room is the only private space someone could hope for in a communal and spartan home. The room is demonstrative of this simplicity. A bed in one corner looks like a converted sun lounger, with just a blanket to cover the springs. The slingshot itself is also rudimentary: thick elastic straps, coils of wire and rope, a plank of wood spanning two chairs. Two shoes are left behind, perhaps where the astronaut left them. Curiously, and perhaps most fittingly, the room is adorned not only with sketches and plans for the apparatus that would launch the man's exit, but with the icons of Russian space flight.

In Boris Groys's delightful book-length excursus on the installation, he explains that there are several contradictory moves at play here. At first we could see the man's ascent into levity as a continuation of the Soviet policy of scientific and space atheism, but of a different kind. Even if the room denotes a practical and technical apprehension of how to get to outer space, there is no moral, ethical or spiritual rocket fuel needed here. As Groys notes, 'He only believes in the material, the physical, the real world. He doesn't dream. And he doesn't pray.'[49] And yet, the man has surrounded himself with the myths of cosmic mysticism that were associated with the heroes of the Soviet space programme, and the collective, affective, utopian energies that space exploration under communism fostered. The room is a shrine to the worship of a Soviet mysticism that would bound the gods of space flight and scientific progress to a cosmic myth of weightlessness, to leave the earth's gravity, the pull of history. Of course, the Palekh icons of Gagarin are hung on the room's walls.

For Groys, however, as well as reconciling the collective myth into a personal one, something else is going on. Groys sees the Soviet propagandist promotion of the spectacle of space travel as a misuse of collective myth, to the extent that the 'dream of unconstrained flight, of weightlessness, of the ecstasy that can overcome any gravitational pull' had been jettisoned.[50] In other words, the transformation of the cosmic myth by communism and the Soviet space programme has eroded the desire for the anti-gravitational, political and economic weightlessness we have seen. In many respects, communism becomes an enclosing, controlling and gravitational drag, to the extent that we could see Kabakov's man as a radical figure redeploying the liberatory potential of socialism's original ideals.

In the milieu of other artistic movements, such as Malevich's Suprematism and Potočnik's science, the 1927 *Constructivist Cabinet* has been rediscovered within a rather different ambience of art in post-socialist Slovenia. Levitational or post-gravitational art has also become an intrinsic part of former Eastern Bloc countries, especially in Potočnik's home town of Vitanje. It is there that the *Constructivist Cabinet* has inspired a museum dedicated to space flight, with significant parts of it dedicated to Potočnik's leadership in the Slovenian contribution to the inhabitation of space. The KSEVT (Kulturno središče evropskih vesoljskih tehnologij) takes inspiration from the *Constructivist Cabinet*, so that the building and its exhibitions would be 'all frozen in the moment between levitation and descent, at the exact juncture when a new paradigm of art in zero-gravity made its original appearance'. In other words, the building itself is a celebration and an echo of the social milieu and artistic ambitions of 1927, and the year of Potočnik's publication in 1928.

7 Exorcize the Pentagon

To walk among the clouds

IN DIRECT CONTRAST TO SOME other feet or legs dangling down from the heavens, Philippe Petit's – like those of Marie Taglioni earlier – are torqued and put under strain. They press incredible force into the bouncing, wobbling and twisting wire that was strung between the towers of the World Trade Center in 1974. Let us say quickly that Petit was not levitating quite like the other figures explored in this book. Stepping out into the void above the Sydney Harbour Bridge, between the towers of Notre-Dame Cathedral or the Twin Towers, Petit appears from a distance to be hovering in the sky.

Petit's story is not one of visual omniscience. His view from the World Trade Center was frequently blurred by clouds. He was almost knocked off the wire by the downdraft caused by the buffeting blades of a helicopter. His walk was a surprising and excessive moment. James Marsh's 2008 documentary film on Petit, *Man on Wire*, sees Petit's stunt as a caper – as does Robert Zemeckis's more recent dramatization *The Walk* (2015). Of course, Zemeckis was also responsible for the cult levitational device the 'hoverboard', made famous in *Back to the Future Part II* (1989) by Michael J. Fox's character Marty McFly. The film was also responsible for many teenagers believing the board was real,

Badge worn by anti-Vietnam War protestors at the Pentagon in October 1967.

and begging their parents to deliver the product in wrapping paper for Christmas.

Petit's mid-air walk in *Man on Wire* has the qualities of a heist movie, so cinematic is his story. Petit and a set of his close friends, with quite inappropriate skill sets for pulling off his aerial traverse (one did not even like heights!), perform their own reconnaissance of the World Trade Center. Petit must imagine that he can make the walk before he does it. They gain access to inaccessible floors. They spend the night on the floor with access to the roof. The wire is strung across the divide between the two buildings by firing an arrow from one tower to the other; to the arrow was tied a string, in turn attached to the cable, which was then pulled across.

Petit's walk-dance is highly ambiguous; the public on the ground are not sure what they are watching. Others simply cannot see him, because he is too far away or shrouded by clouds. It is the impossibility of his lightness – 'how could he do that?' – that is questioned over and over again by his witnesses. Ecstasy is an apt word to describe the experience of his close friends, girlfriend and witnesses to his act. The moment comes when Petit decides to lie down on the wire. Prostrate, with his balancing pole resting on his stomach, Petit is almost staked like St Teresa impaled with the angel's spear. In Marsh's film, Petit's girlfriend becomes speechless

The levitational 'hoverboard' in *Back to the Future Part II* (dir. Robert Zemeckis, 1989).

even when recounting the moment. From the ground, Petit is a speck in the sky; all that is visible is his levitating horizontality against the shape of the clouds and in the face of the vertical. The police officers tasked with coaxing him down are just as dumbfounded by the magnitude of the act. Petit's walk is so sublime, it seems, that they find it inexpressible during the subsequent press conference. How does one give voice in the face of the immensity of such a moment? When Petit lies down, his spectators are overcome with a mixture of emotions.

In lots of ways, Petit's story is one of delight, of incredible skill and unsurpassable mastery – especially given that his walk can never be repeated. He was also trespassing on the skies and a private construction site, and thus subjected to numerous claims of legal and public order misdemeanours, and not only accusations of the moral kind levelled at our earlier funambulists. Charged with disorderly conduct and criminal trespass, Petit was arrested immediately, although the charges were dropped when he agreed to give a free, and much lower, performance in New York's Central Park. The ecstasy of his walk – and its release when he descends – as Marsh's version of Petit's story explores, is also an act of egoism. Following his arrest, Petit sleeps with a woman who propositioned him immediately after leaving the courthouse.

As we have already seen, our levitators might actually be quite radical. So argues Scott Bukatman, who contemplates Fat Boy Slim's music video for 'Weapon of Choice' (2001), directed by Spike Jonze. The video depicts Christopher Walken as an alienated business type, sitting exhausted or perhaps just impassive in the lobby of a hotel. We don't know where this is exactly, but the feeling is probably LA, an iconic setting for American dreams and their disillusionment.[1] The video slowly but surely accelerates Walken as his movements pick up speed, his burgeoning animation combined with a 'bricolage of sampled tracks'.[2] Some of the odd lyrics in the song are taken from lines spoken in David Lynch's movie *Dune* (1984), based on Frank Herbert's sci-fi novel: 'walk without rhythm, and we won't attract the worm.'

Walken's movements start slowly but surely with taps and rhythm. They excite towards dancing, which soon sends him airborne, gliding and pushing off from walls. Walken's acts are ones 'of fantastic mobility, and perceptual surprise (with the merest touch of shock)'.[3] For Bukatman, the video is a not-so-subtle performance of resistance or transgression – what he describes as a 'musical tactics of inhabitation and trespassing, a fantasy of repossessing both one's space and one's body, almost a jumping out of one's skin'. This is an 'embodied kinetic incursion, a means of remapping the subject' by what we might consider the levity of weightless escape.[4] It is, of course, also a satirical take on the suited and contemporary businessman or -woman. Walken turns all assumptions of propriety in the space of what we assume is a global corporate chain topsy-turvy.

This manner of corporate and symbolic subterfuge is not uncommon to the levitator, as we saw in 1974. Some levitations do not work so spectacularly or not nearly as high. In fact, some fail spectacularly. We could also learn from a counter-current of work incommensurable with Petit's funambulism above New York. In Bruce Nauman's failed levitation piece, mentioned in a previous chapter, the artist provides, or provokes calls for, 'a respite from an entire system of seeing and space that is bound up with mastery and identity'.[5] Once again, the levitator, and its deployment in critical artistic practice, seeks to upend the association of the aerial with mastery and power. It suggests ways one might work against these structures.

This sending up or down by the failure of a work is celebrated as a rather uncelebratory agenda to debunk the mystical status of the artist, or the kinds of vertical trespass the mythologized Petit was to perform eight times above Manhattan, all forever repeated in images, documentaries and movies. As Chicagoan art critic Kathryn

Hixson writes of Nauman, the 'quasi-religious high-falutin'' tendencies of the artist as a mystic or having 'inordinately saintly' status are underwritten by Nauman's fall/failure to levitate as he unceremoniously slumps to the floor.[6]

We see an echo of Nauman's failure in the artist Susan Hiller's little blue book *Homage to Yves Klein: Levitations*. The cover is in Klein's International Klein Blue. Hiller's book presents an odd parallel to Olivier Leroy's pseudoscientific classification of levitational phenomena. Yet while Hiller invents other categories with which to order and frame levitants, through photos she has drawn from popular culture, the Internet, and a recent trend of levitating oneself through Photoshop, her book also illustrates the strong relationship between levitation and humour. Levitation, we must conclude by now, can obviously be hilarious. And it is the relation between humour and aspiration which Hiller acknowledges in an interview in which she was asked what attracted her to the topic, suggesting: 'for the most part: "This is me, I'm levitating. (You know, I'm not really levitating but, hey.)"'[7] In this sense, we see qualities in Hiller's gathering of levitations that, in a way similar to Nauman, refute aspects of the levitator's seriousness by recovering its levity. Aware of the fakery of the many levitation photos, Hiller's homage does not simply see levitation as funny in and of itself, but deploys humour at other vestiges of power which may rely on the seriousness of levitation, or merely its existence, from organized religion to spirituality. In its potential for failure, levitation offers a tactics of resistance.

The Pentagon is rising

It was a simple badge. It was coloured orange-red, with a silhouette of a pentagon, hanging askew above grass. It was designed for a peace rally that culminated with a stand-off at the Pentagon, the U.S. Department of Defense's headquarters. Organized in October

1967 by the National Mobilization Committee to End the War in Vietnam ('the Mobe'), estimates of the number of protestors have varied considerably, from 25,000 to 100,000. It is clear that the scale of the movement was in the tens of thousands. Protestors made their way from a rally at the Lincoln Memorial, before moving to crowd the Arlington Memorial Bridge, crossing the Potomac on their way to the five-sided building of American military power.

The aim was to perform a ritual, an exorcism, that could play on the myth of the Pentagon as the face of the then United States Department of War – a familiar Washington symbol. The building was designed by George Bergstrom in the midst of the Second World War, but it was not really intended as a symbolic gesture. The building's design is geometric and lacking in ornamentation. Its fittings and fixtures are hardly ornamental – a luxurious finish was impossible during wartime and its scarcity of valuable metals and materials. The shape of the building was dictated by the site at Arlington Farms, where the landscape and existing infrastructure had suggested an irregular five-sided shape. It is a rather imposing form, the building seeming to possess mythic and military force. Michael Bowen, a friend of the rally's organizers and who had organised the San Francisco 'Human Be-in' a few months earlier, was interested in occult and shamanic practices. Bowen reportedly believed that the five-sided shape, which pointed north, could be resisted, its symbolic power disrupted in some way. A blanket of protestors might blunt its sharp points, Bowen suggested. By surrounding the structure, the Pentagon could be 'wounded'.

The main instigators of the march were Abbie Hoffman, Jerry Rubin, the project director, and David Dellinger, an organizer of the Mobe. Rubin and Bowen were part of the West Coast hippy scene. Bowen, with Allen Cohen, was a co-editor of *Oracle*, which originated in the San Francisco neighbourhood Haight-Ashbury. Cohen and Bowen claimed inspiration from Lewis Mumford's description of the Pentagon. For Mumford, the building was a monstrosity, an 'effete and worthless baroque conceit, resurrected in the nineteen-thirties by the United States military engineers and magnified into an architectural catastrophe'.[8] The building signalled the 'priestly monopoly of secret knowledge', which, he warned, would be catastrophic for politics, nullifying 'public reactions' and making 'rational dissent the equivalent of patriotic disaffection, if not treason'.[9]

Mumford's essay was reprinted in *Oracle*. Richard Honigman, a key member of the Haight-Ashbury scene, would follow Mumford's lead in his anticipation of the march, seeing the building 'as a citadel of propaganda, corruption and mistrust. A totalitarian, drab crypt ironically configured in a symbol which appears in many religions and cultures as the symbol of evil.'[10] Somehow bringing the building to its knees could strike the greatest chord for the peace movement, they thought.

The point of the march was to create spectacle, with the aim of political change, and levitation by a staged public exorcism became the ritualistic mechanism to do it. The media was the conduit. On the eve of the march, at a press conference, Hoffman explained the process of the exorcism:

> we're going to assemble a mass of holy men to surround the Pentagon. And they're going to surround it with chanting, and love and drum beating. And the Pentagon is going to rise into the air on October 21st. And when it gets about 300 feet in the air . . .

At this moment Hoffman looked up at the ceiling in the press room and announced, 'it's going to start to vibrate. Slowly at first and then a little quicker. And all the evil spirits are going to pour out.' Elsewhere he would declare, 'There are seven million laws in this country. And we aim to break every single one of them, including the law of gravity.'[11]

There is something hallucinatory about the idea of peace march attempting to levitate the Pentagon. But it follows: you'd probably have to be high to think up such an idea – but, given the culture of acid-taking (LSD) in the peace and anti-war movement of the time, it makes some sense. Several of the organizers were well known for their experiments in drug-induced trips, and the potential clarity these gave them. Bowen, who had an existing interest in Mexican spiritualism, is reported to have investigated indigenous levitation practices and smoked large quantities of peyote.

Throughout this book the interaction of authority and levitation has been crucial. In some instances levitation defies it, in other instances levitation requires it, and in some instances levitation embraces it. According to various accounts, Hoffman and others embarked on a two-and-a-half-hour meeting with Pentagon officials in order to request a permit for the planned levitation. Bizarrely, the Pentagon acquiesced to their demand. Whether this makes a mockery of the department's bureaucracy, or shows some degree of humour, is unclear. It probably does both. Paul Krassner recalls that the original height the Pentagon officials permitted the building to reach was 22 ft (6.5 m). This was the height of their tallest ladders – and so would allow officials to pull the building down should it remain airborne following the ceremony.[12] In the end, the general services administrator permitted a rise of just 3 ft (1 m), and asked the building be returned to the ground once the ceremony was over.

Wings, rays and auras

The artist Martin Carey would create one of the posters for the campaign. His psychedelic image was no accident. Inspired by his acid trips and the Yippee political philosophy, Carey played an active role in the march as well as the San Francisco Diggers activist group. Carey would live communally with his family near

Woodstock, according to a *Life* article that featured Carey as part of its review of the rise of new spiritualism at the turn of the 1970s.[13] Carey's aesthetic was in many ways symptomatic of wider hippy expression. A combination of Tibetan and Byzantine art, of a kind that could regularly be found in *Oracle*, the illustrations were intended to raise or 'elevate' their readers. As Allen Cohen, one of the editors, explained, actually reading *Oracle*'s pages could induce some form of 'elevated' state: 'looking at *Oracle* could be a sort of occult trance experience communicated across the dimensions of space and time through the tabloid medium.'[14]

The magazine celebrated a variety of influences common to levitation, ranging from ancient China to science fiction. The printing of *Oracle* avoided the usual conventions, veering away from regular columns into odd and irregular shapes of text and image. Split fountain colour inking, Rubylith overlays and double burns were achieved in the newspaper's offices above the Print Mint on Haight Street. Cohen particularly emphasizes the magazine's expression of broad spiritualist energies, in 'soaring experiences' and 'rising vital energies' found in the occult philosophies of the West and the 'the meditative philosophies of the East'. They would also connect to the 'improvised jazz and marijuana high' from African American culture, and the 'ancient tribalism of oppressed American Indians'. And all were brought together in graphic form, through collages, used to display 'pattern, and flow; wings, rays, auras, arabesques, swirls, unicorns, and centaurs, mandalas, collages, flying saucers and their inhabitants'.[15] Such forms, common to religion and mysticism, made up the visual grammar of *Oracle*, and would collide or collude with the mind-bending and hallucinatory effects of LSD, the so-called 'rocket engine' of the movement. Chemical consumption was a way to address the experiences of mystics, saints, visionaries, artists and others.

Reminiscent of the evolutionary allegories mentioned in the book so far, the hippy movement also drew on the levitational and the vertiginous. Levity was a critique of what Stephen Levine would see as civilization's perceptible imprisonment as populations locked into vast, urban, industrial societies performing environmental and spiritual degradation. Horizontal populations, as he saw it, needed liberating from their lateral lives, as if stuck in heavy geological layers.

> Citied in flat stone and moved by machine, Man is an alien; suspended in that which has ceased to grow. Wombed in plastic. Seedless. In his megalopolis compressed by false horizons and bisected by the motion of machines to either side of him, Man is a superimposure, imbalanced by the predominance of lateral energies. Flanked by gliding herds of stamped metal, curbed by the intersection of the cross: Out of order. Substrata to the birdless chasms lined in glass that reflect the horizontal riot of energy.[16]

Written one year after the march, Allen Cohen's poem 'Returning from Mexico' emphasizes these themes, accompanied by a strange sketch of hovering UFOs drawing one into the centre of a pastoral scene, decorated by a radial pattern of symbols floating in the air in the foreground. Cohen's vantage point is from an aeroplane, which gives him perspective on the mechanistic and 'ascending desires' of the landscape and settlements below. The elevation his flight provides is not the same as that lauded by early twentieth-century modernist planners or utopian urbanists captured in the aeroplane or skyscraper:

> Monuments to your impoverished spirit – your energy externalized
> to skeletal & rusted cars tractors, chimneys & planes
> testimony of your ascending desires[17]

A similar image was presented by Lawrence Ferlinghetti in 1966 in the poem 'Temporary Flight', also published in *Oracle*. This time, flight is an ecstatic escape from the illusion of the world below:

> Hum of Elektra winging down
> wigging down
> Seatbelts on
> flaps down
> . . .
> Temporary flight
> of ecstatic insanity

If these accounts of levity continue in the genre of *Oracle*'s very active critique, they also fall into the tendency of sexism and misogyny common to the levitator and, of course, the surrealism of the time. Two horizontal, half-naked women, one bonded to a floating plank being pulled up by a similarly semi-naked but unexposed and vertical man, accompany Ferlinghetti's poetry. Cohen's narration of his flight from Mexico also revels in the short-skirted sexuality of the flight stewardess who serves him.

Ritual

Back to the Pentagon, and the organizers turned political performance into a mythical and religious ceremony or ritual. This was an explicit combination of older liberal politics: speeches and talks, wedded to the self-consciously performed 'guerrilla theatre and a religious exorcism ritual'. It was a 'spontaneous happening and religious rite', composed of actors unfamiliar to the Washington political or military elite, from shamans, wizards – Gandalf was shown meditating outside the Pentagon in a later edition of *Oracle* – rabbis and other religious leaders, to the Black Power movement and a range of other protest and alternative communities, such as SANE and the Diggers. Hoffman would compare the event to the Battle of Jericho, relying on the Judaeo-Christian narratives of the power of collective action.[18] Here the rituals of exorcism drew on other traditions for razing the walls of power to the ground. As Honigman explained in *Oracle*, 'To ring a Pentagon is to render it impotent. We will ring it many times over with thousands of people celebrating, defying, dancing and praying . . . The Pentagon is rising. Join us. The Pentagon is rising.'[19]

But where the Israelites circled Jericho, the protestors were only permitted to assemble at the front of the building. In a further sacralization of the protest, a model of the Pentagon was lifted by piano wires up into the air, as a circle of protestors held hands and chanted 'Up, demon!, Up, demon!'[20] Norman Mailer, who was invited to take part in the march and to give several addresses to the movement, would write extensively about his experience. Apparently inured to resist this kind of act of togetherness, Mailer quickly found himself taken up by the rhythm, brought along in the tide or the flow of things: 'Out, demons, out,' he began to whisper, 'Out, demons, out.' And, like Christopher Walken's businessman character seen earlier in this chapter, Mailer's composure shifted, starting with his voice and moving down to his foot, his 'simple American foot – was, of course, tapping. "Out demons out."'

Making a little bit of a detour from the Pentagon peace rally, we might consider the *longue durée* of levity, of a raising. Some levitational sculptures positioned elsewhere tell a similar story of a long durational raising of something massive, which, like the march, is more horizontal in its nature than vertical. Levitation is not always a quick ascension, but sometimes more of a slow crawl.

The artist Michael Heizer's *Levitated Mass* (2012) is one example. A mammoth sculpture in the genre of land art, it was conceived as both an object and an event. The piece is a 340-ton megalith of granite rock, now suspended on the grounds of the Los Angeles County Museum of Art (LACMA) campus atop a 456-ft (140-m)

Michael Heizer, *Levitated Mass*, 2012, sculpture.

concrete gash in the ground, amid the museum's grassy surroundings. The rock's levitation is no mystery. There's no real puzzle as to how it got there. And yet the raising of the rock is utterly spectacular. The slot functions as a passageway for pedestrians to pass underneath it. This is how the cultural geographer Harriet Hawkins describes coming across Heizer's sculpture:

> We walk across the grass, frayed looking in the drought, towards Heizer's site-specific sculpture sitting amidst its own miniature desert. Look in the other direction and this ancient rock is framed by a banal backdrop formed from lorry cabs crowding the parking lot, advertisement hoardings marching across the skyline 'against anarchy,' and a faded 99 cent store sign. From here *Levitated Mass* looks rather more domesticated than its transcendental name implies. Move below the surface though, walk down into the concrete trench, passing out of the glare of the sun beneath the rock and then back out into the light, and something happens; Heizer's perfect geological specimen appears to levitate.[21]

The rock, taken from Stone Valley Quarry in Riverside, California, took eleven days to reach the campus. The installation has had critical responses. Some have seen the work as a muscular, imperial-like product, the rock an emphasis of the domination of nature by technology and human will. Making the rock levitate, critics argue, is about Heizer's mastery, or the culmination of a world in suspension of the kind many levitations seem to undermine.

But let us focus on its raising along that eleven-day journey to its resting place 105 miles (170 km) from the quarry. Documented by members of the public and a documentary film directed by Doug Pray, the rock was suspended in the transport vehicle, which was 300 ft (91 m) long, on 22 axles and 200 tyres – which crawled along at a maximum speed of 8 mp/h (13 km/h). This heavy thing was

intensely illuminated but veiled in white cloth, the lights lining
the special transporter spotlighting the shape. In the film, the
rock's movement appears more like a procession, with people
shouting 'it's a parade!' as the vehicle passes. The documentary
seeks out the visual spectacle, and the rock's displacement of the
many impediments that stood in its way, from street signs, wiring
and cabling to advertising and even fifty sets of traffic lights. It is
an arrival that seems never to happen: the suspense of the mass
that is so exceptionally slow to get there. Despite the excitement
Pray's movie gives the levitation, it is really a thoroughly slow and
boring event punctuated by occasional moments of elation. In fact,
writes LA critic and peripatetic thinker David L. Ulin, coming across
the rock *in situ* is rather anticlimactic.[22] It is not even as big as one
imagines; Ulin expects enormity, an ecstatic moment reliving the
Pharaonic and monumental movement of the megaliths of the past,
embodying the sovereign's levitative capacity to block out the sun.
He makes comparisons to Cleopatra's Needle in Washington,

Michael Heizer's
Levitated Mass moves
towards the LACMA.

writing, 'I wanted to be awed, to be pulled outside myself, to consider this place not only on human but also geologic terms,' aping Heizer's claim that people demand a 'religious object'.[23]

The ecstasy Ulin demanded was probably more available in the process of the rock's raising. The LACMA provided tips 'for gawkers': make a day of it!, they suggest. Their guides make other recommendations for nearby food and other activities. And so we must conclude that the levitation, like artworks Heizer has also completed in the Moapa Valley in *Double Negative* (1970), was successful in terms of its brute spectacle by the way it was displaced. The levitation, the mobility, and the spaces it evacuated along the way, writes Char Miller, 'where mobility is so important, the idea of movement, and closing down streets, may have been more impressive than the art installation itself, which is static.'[24]

Heizer's sculpture for some is a levitation failure, and the more interesting for it. It actually disappoints on the level of its anti-gravitational feat, as well as its mass. Perhaps this is in tune with the waning excitement for the earlier types of levity or ascension. But we might also consider that Heizer's and his team's feat was accompanied by a parallel movement. In France, the artist Régis Perray performed Heizer's levitation synchronously and on a smaller scale.

Perray is an almost anti-aerial artist. His works refuse the verticality of many of our levitators, finding that transcendence can be found in the below, what is at our feet, as expressed in his fascination with groundedness, dirt and rubble. Explained in his growing dictionary *Les Mots propres*, Perray finds that the pull of the earth does not constrain or deaden but 'soothes my body. Sitting, contemplating the horizon. Giving oneself time, resting time. Forgetting neglected ground, forgetting the earth that covers buried loved ones. Grounded, at rest.'[25]

Perray's raising was a suitably less vertiginous one than Heizer's: the movement not of 340 tons, but 340 g – and of

Régis Perray, *6th Day of Displacement*, 2012.

dust, which would be gathered and transported from the roof of Chartres Cathedral to Nantes by a miniature dump truck. Following the movement of Heizer's sculpture, Perray made synchronous moves with his miniature dump truck, carrying the 340 g of Chartres dust to his home town in Nantes. Even if Perray's raising was nowhere near as well documented or mammoth as Heizer's, it might provoke us to consider the doubling of the levitator with a mocking and more cynical copy; Perray is more ready to poke fun at the original, but, and probably more importantly, even while his practice accomplishes the same extractive moves as Heizer's, the work eludes levitation and ascension as the favoured disposition of art.[26]

Fascinatingly, another artist connects the Pentagon's exorcism with Heizer's artwork. Mungo Thomson, who had previously portrayed the protestor's vision in his 2004 *Levitating Pentagon*, would create an inflatable float for the Aspen Art Museum's 2012 Fourth of July celebration parade on Aspen's Main Street. Thomson created a half-size inflatable copy of Heizer's massive lump of

Mungo Thomson,
Levitating Pentagon, 2004,
coloured pencil on paper.

Mungo Thomson,
Levitating Mass, 2012,
inflatable float.

granite. The float was then pulled down Main Street by six people tethered to the rock.

Mantra

Back to Washington, and the march on the Pentagon. Allen Ginsberg topped off the show with a reading of poetry, set in the context of his wider poetic resistance to what he described as the 'coldwar subjectivity' that had enabled so many to submit to the atmosphere of conflict at a distance in Southeast Asia. As Ginsberg would write in *Oracle*, the metallic and political machinery surrounding us 'conditions our "thoughts feelings and apparent sensory impressions" and reinforces our mental slavery to the material universe we've invested in'.[27] For Ginsberg, LSD would help transcend the political Cold War and its 'mental dictatorship'.

Ginsberg had made a habit of taking inspiration from mystic forms of prayer. Automating, via tape recorder and his Volkswagen camper van, the pace and rhythm of mantras, Ginsberg had mobilized mantra at other political events, notably breaking up tension at another anti-war protest.[28] Ginsberg would even be quite explicit about Antonin Artaud's influence on his poetry in this regard. In an interview, Ginsberg described his employment of Artaudian mantra as breath made solid, pouring out of the body. He was keen, however, that to emulate Artaud would not be to become him: 'Get hysterical? – I don't know if you can practice this. You've really got to be it. It's not something you can practice on. You can modify it. I mean, you wouldn't want to be Artaud.'[29]

It is possible to align Ginsberg's poetry with other forms of repetitious political voice, especially in light of voice technologies such as the human microphone wielded by movements like Occupy. Alex Houen has suggested that what Ginsberg was really interested in was how the act of chanting could have radical potential for the bodies that took part. It could short-circuit media indoctrination by welling up passions among people at a visceral level. In other words, the act of speech or a chant could be as powerful as its content.[30] This is how Ginsberg's chant went:

> Om Raksa Raksa Raksa Hum Hum Hum Phat Svaha! Anger
> Control your Self feared Chaos, suffocation Body-death in
> Capitols caved with stone radar sentinels! Back! Back! Back!
> Central Mind-machine Pentagon reverse Consciousness!
> Hallucination manifest![31]

Ginsberg's protégé Ed Sanders would join in to lead the chanting. Calling out the Pentagon's source of evil power and magic, Sanders's words were accompanied by further chanting and wild cries.

It is worth remembering that the relationship between levitation and rhythm is a strong one, common to musical performance and the shared vibes of moving, singing or playing in time. The Rolling Stones guitarist Keith Richards has frequently described the inexpressible sensation of feeling during a performance as being closest to levitation, 'whether it's "Jumping Jack Flash" or "Satisfaction" or "All Down the Line" – when you realize you've hit the right tempo and the band's behind you', Richards suggests, 'It's like taking off in a Lear Jet.' There is a sense of togetherness, he continues: 'I have no sense that my feet are touching the ground. I'm elevated to this other place.'[32] Other music acts of the late 1960s and '70s would perform levitational tricks as ways to enhance their stage performances. Earth, Wind and Fire, described by the magazine *Jet* as an 'ethereal mixture of spiritual, astro urgings', drew on the expertise of television magicians. Curiously, they employed none other than Doug Henning – our yogic flyer and vote seeker for Transcendental Meditation – and David Copperfield.[33] Maurice and Verdine White were both interested in astrology, occult science and Egyptology.[34] Levitating the guitarist Verdine – despite his fear of heights – along with flying drums, a floating gold pyramid and a hovering spaceship, became common events during their 1978 tour.[35]

If the chanting on the way to and at the Pentagon may not eventually have moved the building very much, it may have been more effective at elevating the crowd to another place. Imagine the atmosphere, with the crowd all chanting 'End the fire and war, and war, end the plague of death. End the fire and war, and war, end the plague of death.' In the background were the sounds of a long sustained 'Ommmm'. Mailer remembers being immersed in the throng, among a kaleidoscope of smells and most potently the sounds of the marchers. An Indian triangle being repeatedly struck. A cymbal being clanged. A trumpet. Drums beating. Finger bells tinkled like 'sour groans from hell's dungeon', Mailer narrates.[36] It is as if the levitation/exorcism created a visual and audible challenge not merely to the military arm of the U.S. government, foreign policy, and its subjectifying powers as critiqued by Ginsberg, but what Mailer located as the Pentagon's mood, its atmosphere over Washington, DC. The event could serve, in some way, to combat the gaseous feeling that the Pentagon was spreading, spewing forth. As Mailer puts it, perhaps the levitation combatted the Pentagon's 'deodorant', its atmospheric 'presence all over the fields of Virginia'.[37]

Hover

Mailer imagines a bizarre fight between the press and police helicopters that are hovering in the air to monitor and report on the passage of the marchers across the bridge from the Capitol building. They buzz about and hang above them, 'chop-chop'. Their view of the march, Mailer concedes, as others have in wider contemplations of the aerial perspective, would reduce the mass of marchers, as aggregated individuals, personalities and motivations for being there, to the 'pulsations in the progression of a caterpillar'.[38] While the allusion is not his, we could assign to the helicopters the deodorizing force Mailer identified in the Pentagon's presence or mood in Washington, a metaphor the British poet Paul Farley uses when he describes the contemporary police helicopter as 'the devil's hairdryer'.

To the helicopters Mailer pitches his anger; they become his target and legitimise his presence at the event. The machines, he contemplates, are as out of place as he is given that their home has been the ruined landscapes of Vietnam:

> yes the helicopters, ugliest flying bird of them all, dragon in the shape of an insect, new vanity of combat, unutterable conceit, holy hunting pleasure, spills and thrills of combat on a quick hump and kump from the down-home Vietnam country club symbol of tyranny to a city man, for only high officials and generals and police officers flitted into cities on helicopters this small in size.

The fight Mailer imagines is from a potential 'Rebel Chopper', one driven by the peace marchers that could disrupt the 'insufferable arrogance' of the acronym-adorned helicopters – 'CIA', 'FBI' – by dropping cans of paint on them. Until suddenly he realizes that the 'swinging and wheeling overhead' will simply act to 'remind everyone below of their sufferance, their possession, and the secret of who owned the air – corporation land'.[39]

Several hundred protestors were arrested – several temporarily elevated from the ground, kicking and screaming – and many deliberately. Mailer embarks on the ritual of arrest, the march to a queue, to be placed on a van, sent to the prison. The experience was as powerful for him as the attempted exorcism. At one point the army decided to use tear gas to control the crowd. Rupert Fike's poem 'Levitation Gone Wrong' draws on this moment to compare

his experience with Allen Ginsberg, and Wilfred Owen's poem on
being gassed in the trenches during the First World War:

> Chanting, 'Ho, Ho, Ho . . . Chi Minh.' Nobody laughs . . .
> because he doesn't, and I get the message to just . . . shut . . .
> up.
> . . .
> An *ecstasy of fumbling*? Perhaps . . .

How might one connect the gassing of the marchers in
Washington in 1967, taking part in their exorcism–levitation
of the headquarters of the military administration of the world's

greatest power, to the immersed, wounded, mud- and blood-soaked pathetic bodies, spluttering for breath in the horrors of the Great War? Ecstasy might seem incongruous to this moment, but perhaps we should recall Jung's investigation of the experiences of levitation during moments of trauma.

It is not as if there were not other levitative responses to the First World War. In 1920 the Dadaist *Preussischer Erzengel* (Prussian Archangel) was completed for the First International Dada Fair in Berlin by John Heartfield and Rudolf Schlichter. Heartfield is pictured in the image of the fair with Raoul Hausmann, Hannah Hoch, Otto Burchard, Johannes Baader, Wieland Herzfelde, Margaret Herzfeld and George Grosz. The members of the group are found standing or sitting below a levitating soldier, who is suspended from the roof. The soldier is topped by a pig's head. Berlin Dadaists presented an explicit rejection of the almost levitating, 'holy' view of art, a 'floating', 'head-in-the-clouds' point of view that barely perceived the violence of war. Only here, the Dadaist manipulated both up and down. 'Down with art, down with fighting bourgeois intellectualism,' the slogans in the room read. The banner on the body states: 'I come from heaven; from heaven up high.'

The Dadaists deploy levitative ecstasy as critical response – just as the peace marchers did in Washington – to the violent ecstasies driven by the trauma of war. Perhaps we could consider the tear-gassed confusion imposed on the peace rally as an attempt to suppress the liberation or expansion of their ritual ecstasy of ascent with another, replacing it with a falling. Santanu Das recalls Wilfred Owen's comparison of going over the top of the trenches of the Western Front to what Owen identifies as 'those dreams of falling over a precipice'.[40] As Vincent Sherry comments on Owen's poem, the ecstasy of the events expresses the extension of self into the wider space of the battle or war. The dream of the freedom of ecstasy is 'diminished into the vertigo of "fumbling"'.[41]

The protestors in Washington actually did try to use their own airborne means of demonstration. Michael Bowen had ordered several thousand daisies, with which he planned to sky-bomb the city. The plan was to drop the flowers from an aeroplane, so that they would float down over the Pentagon during the protest, as if a rain of daisies. Whether it was the FBI who foiled his plan, or bad luck, Bowen was unable to get the daisies airborne, so instead drove them to the rally and passed them among the protestors. The Pulitzer Prize-nominated photo, by Bernie Boston, of a flower placed in the barrel of an MP's (Military Police Corps) rifle, has become a classic example of the asymmetry of force during the protest. Zack Snyder's film *Watchmen* (2009) would draw on this image in an alternative telling of history. In Snyder's version the MPs open fire on the protestors.

Ginsberg would conclude that the march was a success: 'I think we demystified the authority of the Pentagon, and in that sense we did levitate it.'[42] Jerry Rubin suggests that they had 'symbolically destroyed the Pentagon, the war-machine'.[43] In the sense that levitation, or attempts at it – practical, spiritual, magical – could be political, we find that other protest movements have attempted to follow the example of the Pentagon marchers. The 1967 exorcism is a ritual or rite to be rehearsed over and over again, in different settings and contexts. Inspired by the protest, in October 1968, in Staffordshire, UK, Keele University's students, in a protest at tuition fees, proposed to levitate the university's clock-tower building. The building was then the vice chancellor's residence, which they proposed to raise by 300 ft (90 m). The students undertook to surround the building while chanting along to the lines of The Fugs, 'Out, demons, out!' along with the lines of The Fugs' song 'Exorcising the Evil Spirits from the Pentagon October 21, 1967'. The students had also been influenced by the underground Edgar Broughton Band, who had released the song as a single and played a gig on campus.

Underground Zerø chose Bastille Day (14 July) 2014 to perform a levitation ritual of the News Corp building in New York; adapting the original Fugs song, the crowd chanted, 'Demon Glen Beck, Out!' 'Demon Roger Ayles, Out!' 'Demon Rupert Murdoch, Out!', 'Demon Shaun Hannity, Out!' Meanwhile, Tim Franzen, one of the mouthpieces for the Occupy movement, would attend the attempt to exorcise–levitate the Koch brothers' headquarters in Atlanta. During their preparation outside the Georgia-Pacific Tower Franzen advised the crowd to 'visualize' – although it's not clear what – before telling them to 'take a deep breath'. The crowd performed a version of the human microphone: 'Breathe in levitation, breathe out Koch Brothers. Breathe in levitation, breathe out Koch Brothers,' he directed, just 'getting in that space'. Even a fundraising arm of Students for Bhopal recommend that, among other 'creative' ways of raising monies for the campaign to award reparations to the victims of the Bhopal disaster in 1984, 'levitation' is a possible political strategy of dissent.

8 Luftmenschen

THROUGHOUT this book the levitator has been explored as a common figure of suppression and derogation. The levitator is really quite *other*. There are moments when we might see levitation as a product of pernicious and even racist discourse and tensions that are somehow absorbed and turned back upon the very subject of its discourse. To help us make sense of this, let us explore our final levitator, the Jewish myth or figure of the *luftmensch*.

The *luftmensch* was a figure the Washington peace marchers would have been aware of. Steve Levine's story 'Lovebeast', which was published in *Oracle* in 1967, characterized the awakening of the modern hippy into psychedelic culture. His 'lovebeast' – like Mailer's moment of helicopter daydreaming – 'looks up at the sky while wheeled machines gronk and klatter to either side'. The lovebeast 'ascends the pentatonic scale of sanity' and, in a nod to Nietzsche, 'recognizes the übermensch, the Nietzschean superman, to be a handsome cripple'. The lovebeast has more in common with the *luftmensch*, argues Levine; he is 'the man of flight, is messenger of the gods'.[1]

The *luftmensch* characterizes a more general designation, which holds that to be Jewish is to be different. Exposed to post-Darwinian forms of racial purity in Europe, the *luftmensch* would be a source of denigration within both Nazi and Zionist discourse.[2] In more modern contexts, *luftmensch* also internalizes prejudicial celebrations of the Jew as a neurotic type of character, such as that embodied in a figure like Woody Allen and who flits about nervously.[3] Sander Gilman's reading of the Martinique-born writer Franz Fanon sees the *luftmensch* almost in the same vein as other kinds of racial persecution. While racism against blacks, Fanon argues, is directed towards the black body, the Jew is often decorporealized, denigrated, as if without flesh or body.[4] Hence some configurations of the *luftmensch* would be poetically compared to the chimneys in which the Jewish body was incinerated during the Holocaust.

And yet the *luftmensch* is not simply a figure articulated from afar, from outside Jewish culture, literature and other political writings. In fact, these mediums have sustained the idea. In this tradition, the *luftmensch*, as with other figures of literature and Jewish storytelling such as the *shtetl* – the former Central and Eastern European Jewish settlements – could be a figure of comedy and satire as a manner of light self-criticism, as a figure of romanticism and nostalgia and, in some extremes, a form of political exclusion and divisiveness. The *luftmensch* is a site of reflection, redemption and resistance to narrative; even when outward aggression towards Jewishness has been turned inwards, the *luftmensch* emerges as an ambiguous form of 'self-critical witticism'.[5]

Exiled in air

Compared to the artists of the Soviet avant-garde, of whom Marc Chagall was one of the most notable, the *luftmensch* was a more ambiguous and ambivalent figure, subjected to pictorial representation and constant narrative renewal in painting and contemporary literature. Socialist realism and an avant-garde of Jewish artistic talent saw other levitation themes cultivated that were less obviously rooted in Jewish motifs. This was a key period, before Socialist realism became enshrined in law as the only artistic method permissible. Preceding the Soviet obsession with space flight, and the celestialism of Yuri Gagarin, artists and painters worked hard to capture flight's exhilaration. Flight was a promise articulated through abstraction, religious imagery and older Russian legends.

Strange as it might first seem, within this milieu the footballer was drawn and imagined in the same space as the celestial and aerial expressions of levity we have discussed. Kazimir Malevich's *Aeroplane Flying* could be compared with his *Painterly Realism of a Football Player* (both 1915), both pushing and pulling at the force of gravity through abstract and floating shapes. El Lissitzky, whom we discussed in the context of levitating architecture, was one of Malevich's students, and had been appointed by Chagall to the Vitebsk Popular Art Institute. Lissitzky produced an array of images of footballers and other athletes in *Footballer* (1922), *New Man from the Victory Over the Sun* (1923), and in *Record* (1926) – a photograph of a hurdler in flight, set against a double exposure of New York's theatre district. *Footballer* (1926) showed a floating figure through abstracting photographic images as 'football-aviators' to an abstract background. Similarly, Aleksandr Deyneka's *The Football Player* (1932) shows a rising, flying footballer with the backdrop of the Kremlin. Lissitzky and other Jewish artists of the time were seemingly moving away from their interests in Yiddish culture to a universal kind of being of the future, hence the emphasis on the 'new man'. Here, the footballer becomes the 'steadfast anonymous superman who crosses time and space with his ability to fly'.[6]

The Ukrainian painter Solomon Nikritin's excursions into Socialist realism would enhance rather than negate some aspects of the avant-garde.[7] Nikritin's *The Old and the New* (1935), alongside other levitational paintings, shows four figures, between them a floating blue orb – perhaps a globe, the world captured or saved like a football by a crouching, grasping figure. An aviator stands behind them. While ambiguous, the figure could be a goalkeeper, floating 'into the cosmic dimension', argues Polish art historian Przemysław Strożek, refiguring a tendency for Soviet art to depict levitating footballers.[8]

A more imaginative rendering can be found in *People of the Future* (1929) by the Russian Konstantin Yuon, showing winged figures – who look like football players – flying above a countryside landscape. Deyneka would paint *Nikita – The First Russian Flyer* in 1940.[9] Nikita is in the same vein as Klein's jump, leaping from the bell tower.

Indifferent to these movements, Chagall's magical worlds go some way to expressing the *luftmensch* as a version of the idiom of the wandering Jew. Painted a year after Chagall's fall-out with Malevich and the disbanding of the Vitebsk institute, *Over Vitebsk* (1922) is easy to situate within the idiom, despite the strange levitation that befalls the figure's walk over the town. As Benjamin Harshav shows in a genealogy of the *luftmensch* through Chagall, the bearded figure in *Over Vitebsk* collapses the notion of the wandering Jew as the 'unproductive' expression of the Jewish pedlar who is an essentially 'parasitic' figure.[10] This figure of Jewish self-understanding adorns Chagall's old man with a beard, hat and a cane, with a sack slung over his shoulder. Notably, the old man's walk in the air corresponds to the eternal walk Morris Rosenfeld would characterize in his poem 'A Goles Marsh' ('March of Exile'): 'Always walk, walk, walk; / Always stride, stride, stride; / While your strength can still abide.'

Not all of Chagall's levitating figures would capture this idiom so clearly, even if they deploy other tropes of Jewish and Yiddish culture. The similar *Over the Town* (1918), for example, shows a couple holding each other tightly and flying over a similar town with an Orthodox church in the far distance just visible. The painting, Harshav argues, is clearly not a celebration of the wandering Jewish figure; instead it captures the ecstasy of love,

Marc Chagall, *The Stroll*, 1917–18, oil on canvas.

but also a series of Yiddish expressions associating levitation with fantasy. As Harshav explains, *er flit in di himlen*, meaning 'he is soaring in the heavens', relates to elation but also delusion. Equally, *zayn kop flit in himl*, 'his head is flying in the sky', for Harshav 'implies unsubstantiated fantasy'. We will come back to the levitative in language in a moment. Interestingly, Lakov Tugendhol'd suggests that all this history of idioms, mysticism and language 'weighs' down on Chagall's work.[11] But it also enables precisely Chagall's resistance to the conditions of Russian and Eastern European Jews, in 'a burning thirst for the mysterious, a tortured renunciation of the life of the contemporary ghetto, "rancid, swampy, and dirty"'.[12]

Franz Kafka, a contemporary of Chagall, would respond to Jewish folklore too. His 'Investigations of a Dog' (1922) takes the idea of the *luftmensch* as an air person to an even more playful and less grounded sense through animal allegory and metaphor, not unlike Chagall. We will see Zionists resisting this later, while Kafka's piece works from the perspective of a narrator as a young pup investigating the properties of several remarkable dogs. He comes across seven dogs that are able to sing. As incredible as this seems, it sets the groundwork for the narrator's consideration of a particular brand of the light and the 'soaring dog', which Kafka uses to satirize both the demands of Zionism and the erroneous conception of the life of the wandering Jew as a 'dog's life'.[13]

Iris Bruce has traced Kafka's interest in Judaism to 1911, when he became fascinated with a Yiddish theatre group in Galicia, a region on the border of modern Poland and Ukraine, while in Moscow Chagall's work would feature in murals, stage design and costume. Indeed, Kafka's interests in metamorphosis were not particularly at odds with aspects of Jewish moralistic folklore. But, back to 'Investigations of a Dog': let us pick up with how the narrator describes hearing about the idea of the 'soaring' canines:

The first time I heard of one I laughed and simply refused
to believe it. What? One was asked to believe that there was
a very tiny species of dog, not much bigger than my head even
when it was full grown, and this dog, who must of course be
a feeble creature, an artificial, weedy, brushed and curled fop by
all accounts, incapable of making an honest jump, this dog was
supposed, according to people's stories, to remain for the most
part high up in the air, apparently doing nothing at all but simply
resting there?[14]

Like other accounts of levity, Kafka's narrator puts into play
notions of truth and testimony. He believes the dogs or *lufthunden*
exist, without ever having set eyes on them. They are also a superfluity because the narrator can find no reason for their existence.
He finds them 'senseless' and can identify no reason or cause for
their particular brand of aerial life. 'Why, my good dogs, why on
earth do these dogs float in the air? What sense is there in their
occupation?' he asks. 'Why can one get no word of explanation
regarding them? Why do they hover up there, letting their legs,
the pride of dogs, fall into desuetude?'

The dogs perform a manner of detachment, too, existing
quite apart from their canine community, perhaps at a cost to
themselves, not having the 'nourishment' of the earth and their
fellow dogs. In all, Kafka's narrator repeats the wider criticisms
of the tropes of the *luftmenschen* as airy intellectuals. As with
the maligning of other Jewish writers, the *lufthunden* occupy a
'lazy existence', which they disguise through their 'unendurable
volubility', their incessant chatter and nervous dialogue, having
'completely renounced bodily exertion' – another deep difference
from the body cultures of Zionism but an expression John Clubbe
levelled at women in the beginning of this book. Kafka goes even
further to suggest that their thoughts are just as useless, for
'they are not much distinguished for intellectual power, and their

philosophy is as worthless as their observations, and science can make hardly any use of their utterances.'[15]

In the worst terms made yet, the narrator suggests that he may 'yield to public sentiment, to accept the extant soaring dogs, and without recognizing their right to existence, which cannot be done, yet to tolerate them'. He even questions their ability to reproduce because how could they have time to, and when and where? Their only exertion appears limited to a few 'mincing struts'.[16]

Soil

It is evident that the *luftmensch* was the enemy of a more earthy kind of imagination of Jewishness. If it was partly pejorative, used to describe the wandering and exiled Jew, it also pushed against the Zionist cause that became inextricably tied to the ground in the territory of the map and soil. In fact, it really was a tying down, a sinking or burrowing to establish roots in the bowels of the earth. It is obvious that Kafka was following exactly this tendency in his 'Investigations of a Dog', allegorizing the dog's (or Zionist's) preoccupation with the ground. It is the ground from which the dog expects nourishment, 'it is the soil that the incantations must be whispered to, the soil that must be danced to. And to the best of my knowledge science ordains nothing else than this.' He cannot quite understand why rituals look skywards, 'chant their incantations with their faces turned upwards, wail our ancient folk songs into the air, and spring high in their dances as though, forgetting the ground, they wished to take flight from it forever'.[17]

The *luftmensch* would do an awful amount of political work. Chaim Weizmann, the first President of Israel, was quite explicit in his efforts to reject the stereotypes of the *luftmensch* image. In his autobiography he compares himself to those Jews whom he identifies as 'gifted, rootless, aimless, untrained and well-meaning'. This was, for Weizmann, 'that type of lost soul which haunted me, filled me with dread for myself, and served as a terrifying example'.[18] Why would Weizmann have such a reaction to avoid becoming a *luftmensch*?

Max Nordau, father of the World Zionist Organization and so-called Muscular Judaism, would contribute to Weizmann's perspective. Nordau's influential *Degeneration* (1892) had its own troubles with lightness, finding the mind of the 'mystic imbecile' to contain a 'figurative ideation' and be 'filled with evanescent, floating, cloudy ideas'.[19] Nordau's tract rebels against the undulating, 'nebulous or amorphous' – what he calls 'the flightiness of thought'.[20] In fact, there is a more direct relationship between Nordau and our levitators than might be obvious. Nordau was the student of Cesare Lombroso, who was particularly taken in by Eusapia Palladino, the nineteenth-century medium whom we explored in Chapter Three. Nordau, presumably unaware of this relationship, dedicated *Degeneration* to Lombroso, his 'master'.

The kind of wandering, aimless *luftmensch* Nordau and Weizmann are drawing upon emerges in a context of economic, social and cultural change which afflicted Eastern European Jews suffering at the hands of anti-Semitic policies and exclusionary practices in the middle of the nineteenth century. The 'wandering Jew' was the literary and artistic expression of this struggle. Several authors have located its origins in Poland, and the agricultural and urban tensions that were restructuring the relationship between the Jewish population, the Prussian nobles and the peasantry. Legislative measures excluded Jews from engaging in many trades, from inn-keeping to distillery, driving Jews from the land. A small number of those engaged in financial services became the model for what some have called the 'Jewish capitalist', while specialist and skilled workers under industrialization were no longer in demand.

Within this context, the *luftmensch* quickly became a satirical figure to extend or amplify the Jew's rootlessness. It was deployed by Sholem Aleichem and the Hebrew writer Mendele Moykher

Sforim, enabling the *luftmensch* to resonate with the mobility and exile of these figures within Christian and Yiddish literature. Exile also came from the notion of the *shtetl* – the Yiddish term for the small Jewish towns in the demarcated area of Eastern Europe governed by Imperial Russia – known as the Pale of Settlement – within which Jews had rights to permanent residency. Leaving the native ground of the *shtetl* towards alienation and rootlessness, the *luftmensch* captured this sense of detachment and unbelonging. In this sense, the *luftmensch* expressed a moralistic but also peculiarly economic sense of waste and inefficiency; he was a 'person inclined to speculative, economically unproductive occupations, but also in the sense of weightlessness, lacking a centre of gravity'.[21] Brian Swann's poem 'The Luftmensch' (1977) depicts a Jew at a market, standing outside it in the mud, 'Selling what he doesn't own' to people who 'can't pay'. The *luftmensch* trades with breezes and breaths; they are excessive.[22]

Luftgesheft is a Yiddish term invoked to describe the businesses and occupations of the rootless Jews that were frequently invoked by Zionists as bad examples. The Marxist Zionist Ber Borochov's diagnosis of the tendencies of the Jewish population was to see Jewish economics as a *luft*, and thus *luftgescheft* – meaning 'air industries' or 'air business' – a business based on nothing substantial. As Borochov concludes, the 'natural gravitation of the Jew' is directed 'toward the occupations that require mental labor'.[23] These ideas even survive today. Israeli economist Ariel Rubinstein invokes *luftgesheft* in the context of a Darwinian characterization of the market. For Rubinstein, emphasis on contemporary Israeli economics deliberately renders quite un-*luftmenschen*-like behaviour in favour of a muscular kind of Jewish competitiveness:

Our economic system encourages people not to be weaklings. The School of Economics is named after mighty Samson. Our business school awards the MBA degrees to those who have specialised in taking over the assets of others in elegant and original ways. Our best people devote themselves to the army, security, and the construction of walls and fences, and do not waste their talents on luftgeschaft, pie in the sky ideas.²⁴

During the Holocaust the idea of the insubstantial Jew would reach its highest degree, but the *luftmensch*'s exile was partly self-imposed. Max Mohr was a German-Jewish playwright and author, who featured as the subject of Frederick Reuss's extraordinary reconstruction of his life from diaries and photos. Mohr does not stay true to the *luftmensch* course, because it is so one-dimensional. Moreover, Mohr's exile to the International Settlement – a blip of sovereign territory following the opium wars in war-torn Shanghai during the Second World War – is a story of a certain kind of unburdening of attachments, from Nazi anti-Semitism, from his marriage, his daughter and from his literary career. However, Mohr's mobility is not superfluous wandering. He exhausts himself working as a doctor at a Shanghai hospital when the situation turns desperate as the Japanese bomb the city. Despite his Chinese exile, Mohr only experiences little glimpses of lightness as his past, his commitments and his betrayal of his wife and daughter weigh on him heavily.

Unsurprisingly, then, the idea of the resettlement of Israel and the allegiance to working the land were at complete odds with our levitating figures, who seemed to work against this yearning for a homeland, and the submersion of body and language within the soil. As Boaz Neumann argues, because 'the exilic Jewish body was not part of a territory, it lacked solid existence.' The Jewish people were an 'air people' (*am avir*), or 'airy jew' (*yehudi avriri*).²⁵ Of course, *Yehudi* is a Hebrew endonym for Jew and notably the name of Paul Auster's master in *Mr Vertigo*.

In other contexts, language and levity are tied up even further than in Yiddish or Hebrew. The towering forms of Chinese writing,

Michel Serres argues in a peculiar book, *Detachment* (1989), mark the strange associations he draws between Chinese agriculture and other vertical tendencies, found in the sky-writing of kite festivals and the architecture of the pagoda. China, for Serres, is levitating:

> The plain towers. Dragons and pagodas are in the sky. Roof corners are ramps for lifting off. Culture contemplates a land filled to capacity. Farmers are in the sky, their heads in the clouds above the plain with no place where to rest their heads, no roads allow them to get away, kite-like farmers, sons of the land and fathers of the sky. Left in the wind and the wide open space, they are the sailors of the loamy sands and muddy loess, they become masters of the sky, or Levites.[26]

Neumann, a remarkable Israeli academic who died at the age of 43 in 2015, has written an amazing book that explores the body culture of early settler pioneers in Palestine during the different stages of the 'Aliyah', or return. Of course, Aliyah meant 'ascent' (emigration meant descent) from an already floating exile. Neumann explores the derogation of the exilic *luftmensch* Jew, whose itinerancy lacks a connection to the land and or soil:

> The space of exile is a . . . space where the 'eternal', wandering *luftmensch*, or airhead, Jew exists. It is a utopian space in the original meaning of the word – a nonexistent place (*ou-topos*) that does not allow the Jew 'to be' within it.[27]

As we have seen, here we can see a relationship between levitation and language, words hardening to float in the air, like crystallized bodies stored in a block of ice. The *luftmensch* is related to the earthening of the Jewish language within Hebrew, and a celebration not of the weightless skies but the labouring of resettlement, work and also language.

The jump artists

While the *luftmenschen* could be derided for their superfluity, their excessiveness, in other mediums their lightness could be celebrated. Philippe Halsman was a Latvian Jewish émigré with whom Dalí would collaborate to produce extraordinary *luftmenschen*-like photographs of jumping subjects, from models and naked muses to fruit, objects and numerous celebrities, including Robert Oppenheimer and Marilyn Monroe. Halsman had no less exhaustive energies animating his life, which was shaped more by heaviness and trauma than the lightness his images convey.

Like so many other levitators and manufacturers of levitative imagery and artworks, Halsman's life as a Jew was racked with persecution. Before he entered America as a migrant during the Second World War, his life was already marked by violence, stasis and escape. Austin Ratner's novel *The Jump Artist* (2009) is loosely based on Halsman's childhood and young adulthood, when he was tried and convicted of murdering his father when hiking on the Zamser, a mountain path in the Austrian Tyrol. Halsman was imprisoned by an Austrian Nazi court, and Ratner quotes from a letter the former sent to Ruth, his girlfriend, from Innsbruck prison in 1929: 'Tell me, have you ever dreamt of flying?' Halsman frequently dreamed of flying, perhaps a response to his incarceration. He was eventually released, and escaped to Marseilles, where he would be trapped and unable to obtain a visa to the United States, until Albert Einstein stepped in on his behalf, petitioning the government to accept him.

With camera in hand, Halsman soon attained his own status as one of the world's top photographers. One of the techniques he became most famous for was to encourage his subjects to jump, and thus would suspend them in photographic time and space, for ever. Halsman evolved the process as a way to obtain a particular truth from his subjects, something he believed missing in ordinary

photography. It was difficult to get behind the figurative masks worn by his many famous faces.

In Dalí and Halsman's collaborations on jump photography, there was also something visceral and ecstatic about the means by which their photographs were achieved. Dalí's enthusiasm for and interest in levitation – and jumping – may come from his youth. At some length Dalí describes leaving the Ritz Hotel in Madrid and running through the streets. But the sprint which he expects to be noticed by passers-by is ignored, the pedestrians indifferent to his business. Dalí's response is to leap. He is apparently good at it, 'adept at high jumping', and so he makes each leap larger and more powerful than the previous. This does the trick. Passers-by gawp and stare, which delights Dalí further. His audience helps hold his very temporary levity together.[28]

The origins of Dalí's interest may have come even earlier. Dalí describes how, at the Marist school in Figueras, when he was sixteen years old, he had the idea to throw himself from the top of a stone staircase in the playground. What he remembers of the event is telling. At first he backed away. The next day, with his classmates in tow, he made the 'leap into the void', falling with a thump and a bump onto the concrete surface, before his friends came to his aid. Both the leap and fall are exhilarating to him. Dalí describes an 'intense and inexplicable joy' that came upon him. And, even though he was embarrassed at the attention his friends gave him, as for stunt artists there is perhaps something addictive about it. Four days later he did the same thing again, uttering a scream at the start of his leap so that everyone in the playground, including the Brother Superior, would see him. His delight was 'indescribable' and the pain 'insignificant'.[29]

As the young Dalí's fame reached its climax, and he performed the stunt a few times, he describes an atmosphere of miraculous proportions before he embarked upon yet another leap. His memory paints a Renaissance portrait as familiar as a Christian Assumption:

Philippe Halsman, *Robert Oppenheimer*, 1958.

the sky, on fire from the setting sun, was massed with sublime
clouds in the form of rampant leopards, Napoleons and caravels,
all dishevelled; my upturned face was illuminated by the thousand
lights of apotheosis. I descended the stairway step by step, with a
slow deliberation of blind ecstasy so moving that suddenly a great
silence fell among the shouting whirlwind in the play-yard. I
would not at that moment have changed places with a god.[30]

As with the Surrealist tendency to float female muses, which Dalí
would continue into his painting, his collaborations with Halsman
were no less subject to this floatation of female autonomy.

Antipode

The *luftmensch*'s groundlessness has found form in other
marginalized and excluded communities. Antipodean versions
of these characters might be found in the forced groundlessness
of indigenous populations. These energies can be found in the
writings of Australian writer Arnold Zable.[31] Like others, the exilic
movements of the Jewish *luftmensch* in Australia sit strangely at odds
with the similar exilic movements of the population of Indigenous
Aborigines, vanished in the history of Australia's racist policies and
the rising walls, fences and expansion of its contemporary borders.
As Gay Breyley writes, 'all it takes is a generation of dispossession
or constriction of conversation space to render even the Indigenous
person a Luftmensch.'[32]

The most explicit examination of these themes can be found
in Kim Scott's novel *Benang* (1999). The story is of Harley, one of
Australia's lost generation of stolen Aboriginal children, who is
adopted into a white family. Harley's new grandfather is a violent
eugenicist, inspired by the English Australian A. O. Neville, who
from 1915 held the office of Chief Protector of Western Australia's
Department of Aboriginal Affairs, and was a chief architect of their

policy of child removal. Neville expressed his association of ascent and civilization through the department's policy of seeking to 'breed out colour': 'As I see it, what we have to do is uplift and elevate these people to our plane.'[33] In *Benang*, Harley begins to levitate.

Harley's levitations are the figural equivalent to Neville's ideas of racial ascent. Harley has levitated because he is groundless, his Aboriginal heritage taken out from under him.[34] Elevated to Neville's plane, Harley learns how to float. As with our other levitators, however, the experience is highly confusing. He wakes up finding his vision is obscured; his eyes are blinded by the proximity of his face to the ceiling up to which he has hovered. Harley's reaction is, quite rightly, shock. He pushes out his hands and shoots rapidly from the top of the room. Levitation is short-lived:

> I fell. Still groggy from the collision with the floor, and once more floating towards the ceiling, I kicked out and managed to hook my feet in the wrought-iron bedstead. It was an awkward and clumsy process but I succeeded in securing the bed-sheet (which must have fallen from the ceiling) and inserting myself beneath it. And there I lay, secure but trembling, staring at my hands which gripped the sheet so tightly.[35]

Harley soon learns that his levitations can be learned and perfected, and finally begins to get the hang of it by 'tentatively experimenting'. He begins to realize his propensity for elevation is just that: it requires relaxation, that he let his mind go. Although he feels weak, he recognizes that it is obviously 'not from supporting my body's weight'.[36]

Harley's levitation is not a simple objectification, but a self-conscious deprecation familiar to the *luftmensch*. He compares himself to a lampshade, and wonders if it is what his grandfather meant when he 'said I was most brightest and most useful in an uplifted state'.[37] Harley begins to reflect on his elevated state, finding himself easing into the air and hovering 'like a balloon anchored by a fine line. I was more comfortable that way.' But he fears his state of being 'let adrift, and that it came so naturally to me'.[38] Harley feels his levity as uncontrollable, a state he struggles to retain autonomy over, as he is subjected to the whims and wishes of the wind. In one scene he almost becomes a windsock, as his trousers are caught on some guttering:

> and there I was; uplifted and spread out to the wind, which whistled through me, and in and out of orifices, singing some spiteful tune. I could not concentrate on any sort of story, no narrative. My trousers ripped a bit more.[39]

Neither can Harley control the recognition of difference his levity and racial descent installs in those who encounter him, despite his clothes and general acculturation – or apparent ascent – to whiteness. He experiences a feeling of embarrassment and even awkwardness: 'the sudden silence – the temporary laughter and disbelief – of distant nephews nieces cousins grannies when they see me come gliding in above the fire. I hover in the campfire smoke, and hum with the resonance of that place.'

Harley's elevation, his raising timed to the march of the colonial regime, is similar to a variety of projects that have tried to make Australia's landscapes of colonialism and colour unfamiliar and unsettled. Lisa Slater understands Harley's propensity to elevate in the context of Ken Gelder and Jane Jacobs's notion that the Indigenous population is able to produce a range of special effects that disturb colonial narratives, 'unsettling to the rational colonial project as it exposes its lack of power to maintain order and limit life to that which abides by its logic'.[40]

In a similar vein, Kei Miller's evocative tale set around a Jamaican levitating preacher, Alexander Bedward, runs a magical narrative of colonial and class divisions, racial tensions and escalating gang violence in his fictional town of Augustown, based on the real August Town of Jamaica.[41] Bedward was a real Christian preacher who garnered 30,000 followers. Proclaiming that they would ascend to Heaven, Bedward led a mass rally from August Town to Kingston in 1921. He was arrested and put on trial, before being remanded in a psychiatric asylum.[42]

iLevitate

With its humour, the figure of the *luftmensch* reveals something entirely domestic about the levitator. 1980s New York situates the fortresses of light in Cynthia Ozick's short story 'Levitation' (1982). At a dinner party of a Brooklyn couple, everything goes topsy-turvy. In many respects, the home is not the enemy of levitation, despite the latter's capacity to detach, and especially given the tendency of many nineteenth- and early twentieth-century mediums to work under the (potentially augmented) control of a darkened house or apartment. Or we might recall Kabakov's apartment installation.

In Ozick's story, the rooms of the two writers' apartment shine, glinting with the glare of glasses and candles. Materials and conversations seem to shimmer in the air, all afloat in eddies and vortices. In the empty fireplace a newspaper log is lit, which dies quickly. A Holocaust survivor begins talking, describing a death camp. At this moment everything changes. The room begins to lift. 'It ascended. It rose like an ark on waters':

> It seemed [to Lucy] that the room was levitating on the little grains of the refugee's whisper . . . they were being kidnapped, these Jews by a messenger from the land of the dead . . . The room was ascending . . . it grew smaller and smaller, more and more remote . . . she craned after it. A glory of their martyrdom.[43]

In the same year as Ozick's short story, the American Larry Walters became known as the Lawn Chair Pilot, floating himself up to 16,000 ft (4,900 m) on 2 July 1982. Not only did Walters's ascent happen in a quotidian, suburban setting and through the most ordinary of equipment – balloons and a lawn chair – it also reveals just how ordinary or DIY levitation can be. Walters was noticed by a nearby Trans World Airlines flight before descending back to relative safety.

The *New York Times* would identify Walters as perfectly qualified for the designation *luftmensch* in a review of the Broadway play based on his ascent, *The Ballad of Larry the Flyer*.[44] But this is not a simple levitational act; in fact the story is a sad one, as Walters committed suicide almost a decade after his flight. And yet, Walters shares something of the myth-making we see common to levitators and which Kabakov's work built on. Walters had dreamed of flying from an early age, and like Kabakov's piece, his house and his bedroom could be found adorned with imagery of early aviators and astronauts. Somehow, Walters's rise into the lower atmosphere appears just that bit more buffoonish, perhaps because it was so low-tech and foolhardy. He used an air pistol to deflate the balloons.

Contemporary levitative photography has built on these quotidian senses of levitational imagery. Now anyone can levitate through Photoshop or simple apps available on their smartphones. This has created some beautiful and ambiguous imagery, but the tendency is also to repeat some of the more sexualized tropes of levity seen throughout the book. Serbian artist Mina Sarenac exposes female models to levitated suspension against backdrops of urban ruination. The models appear almost prostrate in beautiful yet vulnerable poses, attired in frippery and drapery of the Russian Ballet amid surroundings of dilapidated industrial buildings, adorned with peeling paint and graffiti.

This is not the only form of female levity that we can find in the more contemporary trends for levitation in photography. Some artists have found ways of harnessing such a manner of photographic and gendered exposure to explore issues of womanhood and even disease. Harnessing is the right word when we consider a series of photographs produced by Sam Taylor-Johnson (formerly Taylor-Wood). Taylor-Johnson's *Suspended* series sees her levitating in numerous poses, attired in a vest and underwear. The photographs were enabled by a collaboration with an apparatus usually associated with bondage, requiring a restrictive harness, cables and strings to suspend her from the ceiling. In the final imagery her bonds have been doctored out so that her levity appears effortless rather than mechanically derived.

The series begins with *Escape Artist* (2008), where Taylor-Johnson experimented with the magician's and escapologist's tricks, culminating in an image in which she appears to be suspended by balloons. Themes of confinement and levitational escape are entwined through Taylor-Johnson's self-portraits. Her body looks highly vulnerable. In some poses she appears depleted, perhaps in ecstasy. In others she looks slumped, perhaps thrown or used up. Her face is never seen, and sometimes obscured by her arms; in others her hair provides a veil. Her legs are pulled up against her behind; in another she looks lifeless, possibly dead or in uncomfortable slumber.

For some commentators the photographs are a liberation, removing Taylor-Johnson from the desiring male gaze, and the restrictive adornments of exploitative sex. In the images in her *Bram Stoker's Chair* series (2005), not only are the supports removed, but so is the shadow of the chair. Just as Stoker's Dracula achieves no shadow, Taylor-Johnson's levitation becomes an abstraction of support.

In these series we begin to achieve a more sustained relationship with levitation and through these supports and others seen in this book, such as the cross of crucifixion, the possibility of an association between levitation and death, or the act of death. Of course, the play with shadow in Taylor-Johnson's *Bram Stoker* series is a reminder that Dracula was the living dead, but levitation shares more than a passing resemblance or a confusion with hangings and capital punishment, even if the wires have been cut or Photoshopped out. These are the most extreme forms of passivity we could conceive of and their meaning is only occasionally made clear.

Amy Spanos perhaps brings this into focus in her stylized and sexualized images of young women. Some are levitating, some dangled by puppet strings; others are suspended in images that gesture towards explicit sexual violence, but they are not quite the swaying bodies hanging from a hangman's scaffold.[45]

We can conclude this book with the continuing ambiguity of lightness that levitation appears to perform. Somehow, levitation can speak to both light and weighty matters. It moves between visceral bodily experiences, dreamlike states of rapture that leave the body behind, and imaginative and phantasmic utopian literature, to heavy textual histories or painstaking forms of measurement. Levitation supplies us with a record of some of the most complete and obvious forms of exploitation, inequality and even violence. The levitator somehow subsists and coexists with expressions of freedom, emancipation and empowerment. The levitator is anything but the Apollonian eye usually reserved for gods, kings and the powerful, but a far more ambiguous and vulnerable figure.

References

1 Balance

1 Javier Caletrio and Thomas Birtchnell, eds, *Elite Mobilities* (London, 2014).

2 See for example Mark Dorrian, *Seeing from Above* (London, 2014); Peter Adey, Mark Whitehead and Alison Williams, *From Above: War, Verticality and Violence* (London, 2014).

3 Jason King, 'Which Way is Down? Improvisations on Black Mobility', *Women and Performance: A Journal of Feminist Theory*, XIV/1 (2004), pp. 25–45.

4 U. Boccioni, C. Carrà, L. Russolo, G. Balla and G. Severini, 'Manifesto of the Futurist Painters', in *Futurist Manifestos*, ed. Umbro Apollonio (London, 2009), p. 25; see also Constance Classen, *The Colour of Angels: Cosmology, Gender and the Aesthetic Imagination* (London, 1998).

5 Mircea Eliade, *Shamanism: Archaic Techniques of Ecstasy* (New York, 1989).

6 Eliade cited in Douglas Allen, 'Eliade and History', *Journal of Religion*, LXVIII/4 (1988), p. 554.

7 Mark Edwards, *Neoplatonic Saints: The Lives of Plotinus and Proclus by their Students* (Liverpool, 2000).

8 John F. Hutchinson, 'Disasters and the International Order: Earthquakes, Humanitarians, and the Ciraolo Project', *International History Review*, XXII/1 (2000), pp. 1–36.

9 Cited in Tomas Hägg and Philip Rousseau, *Greek Biography and Panegyric in Late Antiquity* (San Diego, CA, 2000), p. 242.

10 Ibid., p. 241.

11 Joel Marcus, *Mark: 8–16* (Anchor Yale Bible Commentaries) (New Haven, CT, 2000), p. 1110.

12 Gregory Shaw, 'The Role of *Aesthesis* in Theurgy', in *Iamblichus and the Foundations of Late Platonisim*, ed. Eugene Afonasin, John M. Dillon and John Finamore (Leiden, 2012), p. 109.

13 *The Canon of Medicine of Avicenna* [980–1037] (New York, 1973).

14 Ibid., p. 37.
15 Jason König, *Athletics and Literature in the Roman Empire* (Cambridge, 2005), p. 320.
16 From Anonymous, 'Ropewalkers, Acrobats and Jugglers', *Duffy's Hibernian Magazine* (1861), p. 27.
17 Friedrich Herr, *The Medieval World* (London, 1962), p. 333.
18 Eugene Jolas, *Eugene Jolas: Critical Writings, 1924–1951* (Boston, MA, 2009), p. 291.
19 Cited in Arthur Watson, 'On the Funambulist', *The Reliquary and Illustrated Archaeologist*, X (1904), pp. 217–31.
20 Ibid.
21 Froissart quoted ibid., p. 227.
22 Denys Turner, *The Darkness of God: Negativity in Christian Mysticism* (Cambridge, 1995), p. 3.
23 John Tolan, 'Anti-hagiography: Embrico of Mainz's *Vita Mahumeti*', *Journal of Medieval History*, XXII/2 (1996), p. 39.
24 Veronica Della Dora, *Landscape, Nature, and the Sacred in Byzantium* (Cambridge, 2016), p. 149.
25 Alan Gomes, 'The Rapture of the Christ: The "Pre-ascension Ascension" of Jesus in the Theology of Faustus Socinus (1539–1604)', *Harvard Theological Review*, CII/1 (2009), pp. 102, 1, 75–99.
26 Hilary Powell, 'Following in the Footsteps of Christ: Text and Context in the Vita Mildrethae', *Medium aevum*, LXXXI/1 (2013), pp. 23–43.
27 Indeed, Michel Serres finds a 'displacing of the king's body', as an emperor descends in his death to his grave and takes form in a tomb or pyramid which blocks out the sun once more, and 'on the sunbathed earth geometry is born'. Michel Serres, *Detachment* (Ann Arbor, MI, 1989), p. 74.
28 Kathleen Giles Arthur, 'Descent, Elevation and Ascent: Oppositional Forces in the Strozzi di Mantova Chapel', in *Gravity in Art: Essays on Weightlessness in Painting, Sculpture and Photography*, ed. Mary Edwards and Elizabeth Bailey (Jefferson, NC, 2012), p. 60.
29 Lisa Rafanelli and Erin Benay, *Faith, Gender and the Senses in Italian Renaissance and Baroque Art: Interpreting the 'Noli me tangere' and Doubting Thomas* (Aldershot, 2015), p. 74.
30 Azhar Abidi, 'The Secret History of the Flying Carpet', *Southwest Review*, XCI/3 (2006), p. 134.
31 Carl Schmitt, *Political Theology* [1922] (Chicago, IL, 2005), p. 56.
32 Ibid., pp. 48–9.
33 See Sanja Dejanovic, *Nancy and the Political* (Edinburgh, 2015), p. 4.
34 A. P. Martinich, *The Two Gods of Leviathan: Thomas Hobbes on Religion and Politics* (Cambridge, 1992), p. 363.

35 Peter Goodrich, *Legal Emblems and the Art of Law: Obiter Depicta as the Vision of Governance* (Cambridge, 2013), p. 123.
36 Denis Cosgrove, *Apollo's Eye* (Baltimore, MD, 2001), p. 2.
37 Goodrich, *Legal Emblems*, p. 89.
38 Cornelia D. J. Pearsall, *Tennyson's Rapture: Transformation in the Victorian Dramatic Monologue* (Oxford, 2008), p. 93.
39 Theodoret cited in Charles M. Strang, 'Digging Holes and Building Pillars: Simeon Stylites and the "Geometry" of Ascetic Practice', *Harvard Theological Review*, CIII/4 (2010), p. 467.
40 Edward Gibbon, *The History of the Decline and Fall of the Roman Empire* (Oxford, 1837), pp. 578–9.
41 Peter Goodrich, 'Lex Laetans: Three Theses on the Unbearable Lightness of Legal Critique', *Law and Literature*, XVII/3 (2005), p. 305.
42 Jean-Luc Nancy, *The Creation of the World; or, Globalization* (New York, 2007), p. 97.
43 Peter Gratton, *The State of Sovereignty: Lessons from the Political Fictions of Modernity* (New York, 2012), p. 205.
44 Jean Paul, *Levana; or, The Doctrine of Education* (London, 1848), p. 309.
45 Thomas De Quincey, *Confessions of an English Opium-Eater and Other Writings* [1821] (Oxford, 2013) p. 138.
46 Jean Paul, *Levana*, p. 323.
47 Indeed, for Nancy, sovereignty is more akin to being above the mountain than being the mountain itself. Sovereignty in this system of ideas appears to rise above the body and separate itself, to an absolute elevation detached from, but part of, something like a legal system; Nancy, *The Creation of the World*, p. 97.
48 Jacqueline Rose, *Godly Kingship in Restoration England: The Politics of the Royal Supremacy, 1660–1688* (Cambridge, 2011), p. 142.
49 Goodrich, 'Lex Laetans', p. 303.
50 Blaise Cendrars, *Sky: Memoirs*, trans. Nina Rootes (London, 1996), p. 61.
51 'Then I started wondering how there could be such a bright fire in that room, for the rays of light could only have come from a very large and intense fire.' Ibid., p. 96.
52 G. K. Chesterton, *St Thomas Aquinas* (New York, 1933).
53 Jung explores the groaning of holy men and women 'as creative powers and potentialities', evidence of a yearning to be flung upwards. Carl Jung, *Flying Saucers: A Modern Myth of Things Seen in the Sky* [1958] (New York, 2014), p. 56.
54 Elizabeth Bailey, 'The Floating Book: A Reading of Saint Dominic's Miraculous Book in Italian Art in the Late Thirteenth through the Early Fifteenth Centuries', in *Gravity in Art*, ed. Edwards and Bailey, p. 88.
55 Teresa of Ávila, *The Way of Perfection* [1919] (New York, 2007), p. 64.

56 Ibid., p. 179.

57 Ibid.

58 *The Life of Saint Teresa, Written by Herself*, trans. John Dalton (Oxford, 1851), p. 188.

59 Gavin Pretor-Pinney, *The Cloudspotters Guide: The Science, History and Culture of Clouds* (New York, 2006).

60 Susanne Warma, 'Ecstasy and Vision: Two Concepts Connected with Bernini's Teresa', *The Art Bulletin*, LXVI/3 (1984), pp. 508–11.

61 Teresa's is also a non-secular affective management of emotions, drives and tears as outlets, like a pot boiling uncontrollably.

62 Cited in Constance Classen, *The Colour of Angels: Cosmology, Gender and the Aesthetic Imagination* (London, 1998), p. 43.

63 Laura Marchetti, 'Light as an Original Metaphor', *Semiotica*, CXXXVI/1/4 (2001), p. 260.

64 Cristina Mazzoni, *Saint Hysteria: Neurosis, Mysticism and Gender in European Culture* (New York, 1996), pp. 38–9.

65 Krafft-Ebing quoted ibid., p. 41.

66 Italo Calvino, *Six Memos for the Next Millennium* (Cambridge, MA, 1988), p. 27.

67 Jan Machielsen, *Martin Delrio: Demonology and Scholarship in the Counter-Reformation* (Oxford, 2015).

68 Calvino, *Six Memos*, p. 27.

69 Lyndal Roper, 'Witchcraft and the Western Imagination', *Transactions of the Royal Historical Society* (Sixth Series), 16 (2006), pp. 117–41.

70 Martin Antoine Del Rio and P. G. Maxwell-Stuart, eds, *Investigations into Magic* (Manchester, 2000), p. 197.

71 Ibid.

72 Robert Paltock, *The Life and Adventures of Peter Wilkins Among the Flying Nations of the Seas* (London, 1833), p. iii.

73 Chesterton, *St Thomas Aquinas*, p. 3.

74 Wolfgang Grayson, *Witchcraft Persecutions in Bavaria: Popular Magic, Religious Zealotry and Reason of State in Early Modern Europe* (Cambridge, 2003), p. 360.

75 Milan Kundera, *The Unbearable Lightness of Being* (London, 1984), p. 4.

76 Emine Sevgi Özdamar, *Life is a Caravanserai*, trans. Luize Von Flotow (Middlesex, 2009).

77 'Lambertini Criteria', *New York Times* (5 December 2008), Opinion Pages, www.nytimes.com.

78 Fernando Vidal, 'Miracles, Science, and Testimony in Post-Tridentine Saint-making', *Science in Context*, XX/3 (2007), pp. 481–508.

79 Cited in Michael Grosso, *The Man Who Could Fly: St Joseph of Copertino and the Mystery of Levitation* (Lanham, MD, 2016), p. 86.

80 My reading of Clubbe owes much to Steven Connor's wonderful essay 'Absolute Levity', *Comparative Critical Studies*, vi/3 (2009), pp. 411–27.

81 John Clubbe, *Physiognomy: A Sketch Only of a Larger Work Upon the Same Plan* (London, 1763), p. 12.

82 Ibid., p. 13.

83 Ibid., p. 16.

84 Ibid., p. 17.

85 Ibid., p. 22.

86 Lucia Dacome, 'Living with the Chair: Private Excreta, Collective Health and Medical Authority in the Eighteenth Century', *History of Science*, xxxix (2001), p. 489.

87 Clubbe, *Physiognomy*, p. 27.

88 Frank E. Manuel, *The Religion of Isaac Newton: The Fremantle Lectures* [1973] (Oxford, 1974), p. 100.

89 Newton quoted ibid., p. 101.

90 Ibid., p. 102.

91 Oettermann quoted ibid., p. 15.

92 Monck Mason, *Aeronautica; or, Sketches Illustrative of the Theory and Practice of Aerostation* (London, 1838), p. 117.

93 Goodrich, 'Lex Laetans', pp. 297–8.

94 Ibid.

95 Ibid., p. 313.

96 Ibid.

97 Bayla Singer, *Like Sex with Gods: An Unorthodox History of Flying* (College Station, tx, 2003), p. 161.

98 Nicola Masciandaro, 'Grave Levitation', *Loveeee Journal*, ed. C. Rizzo and L. Amara (2013), pp. 108–9.

2 Faking on Air

1 Sarah Dadswell, 'Fakirs, Fakers and Magic: Yoga in the Transnational Imagination, 18th–20th Century', ntq (February 2007), pp. 258–63.

2 Marina Warner, *Stranger Magic: Charmed States and the Arabian Nights* (Cambridge, ma, 2011), p. 77.

3 Dadswell, 'Fakirs, Fakers and Magic', pp. 258–63.

4 Catherine Peters, *The King of the Inventors: A Life of Wilkie Collins* (Hamburg, 1991).

5 Henry Mayhew, *London Labour and the London Poor*, vol. iii (London, 1861), p. 54.

6 Louis Jacolliot, *Occult Science in India and Among the Ancients: With an Account of their Mystic Initiations and the History of Spiritism* (New York, 1861), pp. 237–8.

7   *Memoirs of the Emperor Jahangueir, Written by Himself; and Translated from a Persian Manuscript by Major David Price* (London, 1829), p. 102; emphasis mine.

8   Laura Marchetti, 'Light as an Original Metaphor', *Semiotica*, cxxxvi/1/4 (2001), pp. 245–68.

9   In Peter Lamont, *The Rise of the Indian Rope Trick* (New York 2005), p. 36; emphasis mine.

10 Ibid.

11 'The Luminous Fountain at the Pantopicon', *Illustrated London News* (11 November 1854), p. 456.

12 'The Royal Panopticon of Science and Art, Leicester Square', *Illustrated London News* (31 January 1852), p. 96.

13 Caren Kaplan, *Aerial Aftermaths* (Durham, NC, 2016), p. 164.

14 Stephan Oettermann, *The Panorama: History of a Mass Medium* (Cambridge, MA, 1997), p. 127; emphasis mine.

15 Gabriel Williams, 'Italian Tricks for London Shows: Raffaele Monti at the Royal Panopticon', *Sculpture Journal*, xxiii/2 (2014), pp. 131–43.

16 Richard Tonson Evanson, *Nature and Art; or, Reminiscences of the International Exhibition, Opened in London on May the First, 1862: A Poem, with Occasional Verses, and Elegiac Stanzas* (London, 1868), p. 63.

17 Ibid., p. 64.

18 Williams, 'Italian Tricks for London Show', pp. 131–43.

19 Robert D. Aguirre, 'William Bullock (1790–1844): British Museum Curator and Showman in Mexico', in *The Human Tradition in the Atlantic World, 1500–1850*, ed. Karen Racine and Beatriz G. Marrigonian (Lanham, MD, 2010), p. 225.

20 Harry Houdini, *The Unmasking of Robert-Houdin* (London, 1908), p. 102.

21 Robert-Houdin, *Memoirs of Robert-Houdin* (Philadelphia, PA, 1859), p. 90.

22 Elizabeth Ezra, *Georges Méliès* (Manchester, 2000), p. 9.

23 'Black Art Secrets', *Chicago Tribune* (3 October 1897), p. 46.

24 Alfred Giebler, 'Rubbernecking in Filmland', *Motion Picture World* (1919), pp. 1623–4.

25 Ibid., p. 1624.

26 Laurence Talairach-Vielmas, *Moulding the Female Body in Victorian Fairy Tales and Sensation Novels* (Aldershot, 2013).

27 Ezra, *Georges Méliès*, p. 90.

28 Elizabeth Chesney, *The Rabelais Encyclopedia* (New York, 2004), p. 2.

29 Mikhail Bakhtin, *Rabelais and His World* (Bloomington, IN, 1965).

30 Frances Larsen, *Severed: A History of Heads Lost and Heads Found* (London, 2014).

31 Yelena Primorac, 'Illustrating Wilde: An Examination of Aubrey Beardsley's Interpretation of *Salome*', *The Victorian Web* (2009), www.victorianweb.org.

32 It is not incidental that Disney's fairly dull reimagination of the tale of *Sleeping Beauty* in the recent *Maleficent* (2014) sees Angelina Jolie's character shorn of her wings by her lover. The scene has been compared to rape.

33 Laura Hillenbrand, *Seabiscuit: An American Legend* (New York, 2001), p. 149.

34 Hana Worthen, 'Dramaturgy of Desire, Ethics of Illusion in Kristian Smeds's *Mr Vertigo*', *Contemporary Theatre Review*, xxii/3 (2012), pp. 400–411.

35 John S. Doskey, 'The European Journals of William Maclure', *American Philosophical Society* (1988), p. 365.

36 Polly/Arianna is actually based on a real balloonist, Lily Cove, who died in a balloon/parachute jump in Haworth at a gala in 1906. It was thought that her parachute lines may have been interfered with by a jealous lover. While the inquest considered suicide, it appeared to onlookers that she deliberately released herself from the parachute so as to avoid drowning in the lake she appeared to be falling towards. Curiously, Cove was managed, like Polly, by an experienced balloonist and parachutist, Captain Frederick Bidmead. During the stunt, Lily would sit on a trapeze suspended beneath the balloon. Once Lily jumped from the balloon, a line attached to the balloon would release a parachute, opening it, and allowing her to descend safely.

37 Jane Urquhart, *Changing Heaven: A Novel* (Toronto, 1990), p. 7.

38 We could think about other moving stories some 'found' balloons can render. Derek P. McCormack, 'Atmospheric Things and Circumstantial Excursions', *Cultural Geographies,* xxi/4 (2014), pp. 605–25.

39 Urquhart, *Changing Heaven*, p. 36.

3 Science, Spiritualism and Scepticism

1 H. P. Blavatsky, letter to her sister, 1875, *Path Magazine*, ix (1895), pp. 379–80.

2 H. P. Blavatsky, *Isis Unveiled: A Master Key to the Mysteries of Ancient and Modern Science and Theology* [1877] (London, 2006), p. 446.

3 Footnote to 'An Indian Aethrobat', *The Theosophist*, i/5, (1880), p. 120.

4 *The Theosophist*, iii/6 (1882), pp. 163–4.

5 Hazrat Inayat Khan, *The Sufi Message of Hazrat Inayat Khan: The Sufi Teachings*, vol. ix (Cairo, 1963).

6 'Modern Spiritualism', *English Mechanic and the World of Science* (9 October 1874), p. 96. See James Joyce's allusions to this phrase in James Joyce Online Notes, www.jjon.org/joyce-s-allusions/forty; the phrase also coined the popular satirical caricature of Mrs Fitzherbert, who would marry George iv when he was Prince Regent in 1785.

7 'Levitation', *The Spectator* (16 January 1875), p. 12.

8 Molly Whittington-Egan, *Mrs Guppy Takes a Flight* (Castle Douglas, 2014), p. 110.

9 See Steven Connor, *Dumbstruck: A Cultural History of Ventriloquism* (Oxford, 2000).

10 Hereward Carrington, *The Problems of Psychical Research Experiments and Theories in the Realm of the Supernormal* (New York, 1921).

11 Harry Price, 'The Mechanics of Spiritualism', in Price, *Fifty Years of Psychical Research* (London, 1939).

12 In James Glaisher, ed., *Travels in the Air*, 2nd edn (London, 1871), p. 147.

13 Camille Flammarion, *Mysterious Psychic Forces: An Account of the Author's Investigations in Psychical Research, Together with Those of Other European Savants* (Boston, MA, 1909), p. 83.

14 Ibid., p. 123.

15 See Steven Connor, 'Pregnable of Eye: X-rays, Vision and Magic' (2008), www.stevenconnor.com/xray.

16 Olivier Leroy, *La lévitation: Contribution historique et critique à l'étude du merveilleux* (Paris, 1928).

17 'Image, Technology, Enchantment: Marina Warner in Conversation with Dan Smith', in *The Machine and the Ghost*, ed. Sas Mays and Neil Matheson (Manchester, 2012), p. 125.

18 Flammarion, *Mysterious Psychic Forces*, p. 10.

19 Carlos S. Alvarado, 'Eusapia Palladino: An Autobiographical Essay', *Journal of Scientific Exploration*, IIV/1 (2011), pp. 88–9.

20 Brian Inglis, 'Parapsychologist', *Encounter* (1983), pp. 53–4.

21 Ibid., p. 53.

22 Arthur Koestler, *Darkness at Noon* (New York, 1940), p. 262.

23 Ernesto Spinelli, *The Mirror and the Hammer* (London, 2002), p. 156.

24 Arthur Koestler, 'Yoga Unexpurgated: (I)', *Encounter* (1959), pp. 7–26.

25 Ibid., p. 23.

26 Ibid., p. 19.

27 Ibid.

28 Peter Kurth, 'Koestler's Legacy: Pushing my Luck', unpublished article for *Vanity Fair*, available at https://peterkurth.wordpress.com.

29 Inglis, 'Parapsychologist', p. 56.

30 J. B. Hasted, D. J. Bohm, E. W. Bastin and D. O'Regan, untitled news item, *Nature*, CCLIV (1975), pp. 470–72.

31 Rosalind Heywood, *ESP: A Personal Memoir* (London, 1964), p. 185.

32 I. Starr, A. J. Rawson and H. A. Schroeder, 'Apparatus for Recording the Heart's Recoil and the Blood's Impacts in Man (Ballistocardiograph), Experiments on the Principles Involved, Records in Normal and Abnormal Conditions', *Proceedings of the American Physiological Society. 50th Annual Meeting of the American Journal of Physiology* (1938), pp. 123–95.

33 J. B. Hasted, D. Robertson and E. Spinelli, 'Recording of Sudden Paranormal Changes of Body Weight', *Research in Parapsychology* (1982), pp. 105–6.

34 J. B. Hasted, 'Speculations about the Relation between Psychic Phenomena and Physics', *Psychoenergetic Systems*, III (1978), pp. 243–57.

35 Guy Lyon Playfair, *This House is Haunted: The True Story of the Enfield Poltergeist* (Stroud, 2007).

36 See Peter Lamont's terrific biography of Home, *The First Psychic: The Peculiar Mystery of a Notorious Victorian Wizard* (London, 2005), pp. 184–94.

37 Guy Lyon Playfair and Maurice Grosse, 'Enfield Revisited: The Evaporation of Positive Evidence', *Journal of the Society of Psychical Research* (1988), pp. 208–19.

38 Bart Shultz, *Eye of the University: Henry Sidwick, an Intellectual Biography* (Cambridge, 2004), p. 693.

39 Ibid., pp. 217–18.

40 Henry Sidwick, letter to the editor, *British Medical Journal*, II (1895), p. 1263.

41 Ibid.

4 Reverie, Dreams and the Surreal

1 'Meditation: Storming a British Citadel', *India Today* (31 August 1980), p. 179.

2 Horatia Harrod, 'Terry Gilliam Interview', *The Telegraph* (14 March 2014).

3 N. Pevsner, *Buckinghamshire* (Cambridge, MA, 1984), p. 475.

4 'Consciousness-based Education', Maharishi University of Management, www.mum.edu, accessed 21 October 2016.

5 Susan E. Harding and Michael A. Thalbourne, 'Transcendental Meditation, Clairvoyant Ability and Psychological Adjustment', in *Research in Parapsychology*, ed. W. G. Roll and J. Beloff (Metuchen, NJ, 1980), pp. 71–3.

6 'Maharishi Effect', Maharishi University of Management, www.mum.edu, accessed 21 October 2016.

7 'Counter-terrorism and Peace through Meditation', Golden Dome, www.goldendome.org/_defense.htm, accessed 21 October 2016.

8 Adam Gollner, *The Book of Immortality: The Science, Belief, and Magic behind Living Forever* (New York, 2014), p. 183.

9 'Evolution of Man', Golden Dome, http://goldendome.org/EvolutionOfMan/index.htm, accessed 21 October 2016.

10 Daniel Ogilvie, *Fantasies of Flight* (Oxford, 2004), pp. 31–44.

11 Cited in Arthur Scherr, 'Leonardo da Vinci, Sigmund Freud, and Fear of Flying', *Midwest Quarterly*, XLII/2 (2001), p. 119.

12 Ibid.; emphasis mine.

13 Marina Warner, 'Freud's Couch: A Case-history', *Raritan*, XXXI/2 (2011), p. 161.

14 Ibid., p. 147.

15 June O. Leavitt, *The Mystical Life of Franz Kafka* (Oxford, 2012), p. 90.

16 Cited ibid., p. 22.

17 Franz Kafka, 'Description of a Struggle', in *The Collected Works*, vol. I
    (New York, 1971), p. 284.

18 Scherr, 'Leonardo da Vinci, Sigmund Freud, and Fear of Flying', p. 120.

19 Carl Jung, *The Collected Works of C. G. Jung*, Complete Digital Edition,
    ed. Gerhard Adler, Michael Fordham and Herbert Read (e-book, 2013).

20 Jung cited in Ogilvie, *Fantasies of Flight*, p. 111.

21 Jung, *The Collected Works*, vol. I.

22 Wade Davis, *Into the Silence: The Great War, Mallory and the Conquest of
    Everest* (London, 2012), p. 107.

23 Ibid., p. 219.

24 Salman Rushdie, *The Satanic Verses* [1988] (New York, 2011), p. 196.

25 Ibid., p. 198.

26 T. S. Blakeney, 'Maurice Wilson and Everest, 1934', *Alpine Club Journal* (1934),
    p. 270.

27 Constantin A. Marinescu, 'Levitating Gods and Dream Imagery on Roman
    Coinage', in *Gravity in Art: Essays on Weightlessness in Painting, Sculpture and
    Photography*, ed. Mary Edwards and Elizabeth Bailey (Jefferson, NC, 2012), p. 22.

28 C. Golden, S. R. Bissette and T. E. Sniegoski, *The Monster Book* (New York
    2000).

29 Cited in Constance Classen, *The Colour of Angels: Cosmology, Gender and the
    Aesthetic Imagination* (London, 1998), pp. 136–7.

30 Peter Gabriel Bergmann, *The Riddle of Gravitation* (London, 1968), frontispiece.

31 Juliana Gonzalez, 'Remedios Varo's World and Fantasy World', in Ricardo Ovalle,
    Remedios Varo: catálogo razonado (Mexico City, 2008), p. 90.

32 Ibid.

33 I am of course making allusions to Hannah Arendt's term based on her analysis
    of the trial of Adolf Eichmann and the Nazi regime; Hannah Arendt, *Eichmann in
    Jerusalem* (New York, 1963).

34 Remedios Varo, cited in Ovalle, *Remedios Varo*, p. 107.

35 Tatiana Flores, 'Strategic Modernists: Women Artists in Post-revolutionary
    Mexico', *Woman's Art Journal*, XXIX/2 (2008), pp. 12–22.

36 The Mexican Museum, San Francisco, *Leonora Carrington: The Mexican Years,
    1943–1985* (Mexico City, 1991), p. 33.

37 Sylvère Lotringer, 'Evil Influences', *Semiotext(e)*, at www.semiotexte.com,
    accessed 21 October 2016.

38 Tsu-Chung Su, 'Artaud's Journey to Mexico and His Portrayals of the Land',
    CLCWeb: Comparative Literature and Culture, XIV/5 (2012), available at
    http://docs.lib.purdue.edu/clcweb.

39 Antonin Artaud, *Artaud Anthology*, ed. Jack Hirschman (San Francisco, CA, 1963), p. 68.
40 Ibid., p. 64.
41 Ibid., p. 65.
42 Terri Geis, 'The Voyaging Reality: María Izquierdo and Antonin Artaud, Mexico and Paris', *Papers of Surrealism* (Winter 2005), pp. 1–12.
43 Antonin Artaud and Jack Hirschman, *Artaud Anthology* (San Francisco, CA, 1963), p. 202.
44 Salvador Dalí, *The Secret Life of Salvador Dalí* (New York, 1942), p. 88.
45 Robert Descharnes and Gilles Neret, *Salvador Dalí, 1904–1989: The Paintings* (Cologne, 2007), p. 423.
46 Ibid., p. 407.
47 'Suspensors', *Dune Wiki*, http://dune.wikia.com/wiki/Suspensors, accessed 21 October 2016.
48 Frank Herbert, *Dune: Terminology of the Imperium* (Berkeley, CA, 1977), p. 513.
49 So successful was he in removing the cable that in a recent interview Sokolsky joked that incredulous questioners have found it more convincing that he invented Photoshop, in 1963. David Warner, 'Interview with Melvin Sokolsky', *Lens Flare* (2010), https://vimeo.com/6680829.
50 Wilhelm Fraenger, *Hieronymus Bosch* (Basel, 1994), p. 44.

5 Super

1 Jennifer Homans, *Apollo's Angels: A History of Ballet* (London, 2010), p. 172.
2 Cited in Sally Banes, *Dancing Women: Female Bodies Onstage* (New York, 2013), p. 14.
3 Carol Lee, *Ballet in Western Culture: A History of its Origins and Evolution* (New York, 2002), p. 191.
4 Anna Furse, 'Being Touched', in *A Life of Ethics and Performance*, ed. J. Matthews and D. Torevell (Cambridge, 2011), p. 54.
5 Ibid., p. 55.
6 Daniel Pick suggests there is a genealogical line between Nordier and Du Maurier, but numerous attempts at plagiarism were unsuccessful, a court deciding that while the names used in the book were lifted from Nordier and elsewhere, the work itself was original. George Du Maurier, *Trilby*, ed. Daniel Pick (Cambridge, 2006).
7 Judith Chazin-Bennahum, *The Lure of Perfection: Fashion and Ballet, 1780–1830* (New York, 2004), p. 215.
8 Peter Conrad, 'A Tale of Two Cities', *The Guardian* (9 October 2005), www.theguardian.com.

9 Peter Milton, 'Notes on: *Points of Departure I: Mary's Turn*',
   www.petermilton.com/documents/cat116.htm, accessed 15 November 2016.

10 Homans, *Apollo's Angels*, p. 156.

11 Cyril Beaumont, *Vaslav Nijinsky* (London, 1932).

12 Nijinsky cited in Michael White and Rhea Murphy, *In the Zone: Transcendent
   Experience in Sports* (New York, 1995).

13 Nandor Fodor, 'Could Nijinsky Defy Gravitation?', *The Winnipeg Tribune*
   (2 March 1940), p. 30.

14 Suzanne Farrell, *Holding On to the Air: An Autobiography* (New York, 1990),
   p. 13.

15 Otto Rank, *The Trauma of Birth* [1929] (London, 1993), p. 77.

16 Joel D. Black, 'Levana: Levitation in Jean Paul and Thomas De Quincey',
   Comparative Literature, XXXII/1 (1980); emphasis mine.

17 P. L. Travers, *Mary Poppins* (Boston, MA, 1964), p. 47.

18 Black, 'Levana', p. 42.

19 Ibid., p. 117.

20 Ibid., p. 271

21 Ibid., p. 32; emphasis mine.

22 Ibid., p. 33.

23 Ibid., p. 35.

24 Georgia Grilli, *Myth, Meaning and Symbol in 'Mary Poppins'* (London, 2013), p. 46.

25 White and Murphy, *In the Zone*.

26 Ira Berkow, 'Jordan Hovers on Air', *New York Times* (8 May 1988),
   www.nytimes.com.

27 'Back to Earth: No One's Accusing Michael Jordan of . . .', *Chicago Tribune*
   (22 February 1990), http://articles.chicagotribune.com.

28 Jason King, 'Which Way is Down? Improvisations on Black Mobility', *Women and
   Performance: A Journal of Feminist Theory*, XIV/1 (2004), pp. 40–41.

29 Graham M. Jones, 'The Family Romance of Modern Magic: Contesting Robert-
   Houdin's Cultural Legacy in Contemporary France', in *Performing Magic on the
   Western Stage*, ed. F. Coppa, L. Hass and J. Peck (Basingstoke, 2008), pp. 33–60.

30 Adnan Morshed, *Impossible Heights: Skyscrapers, Flight, and the Master Builder*
   (Minneapolis, MN, 2015).

31 Ibid., p. 167.

32 Richmond Barbour, *Before Orientalism: London's Theatre of the East, 1576–1626*
   (Cambridge, 2003), p. 48.

33 William Gilbert, *On the Lodestone and Magnetic Bodies: And On the Great
   Magnet of the Earth*, trans. P. Fleury Mottelay (London, 1893), p. 144.

34 Ibid., p. 181.

35 Roger Stites, *Revolutionary Dreams: Utopian Vision and Experimental Life in the
   Russian Revolution* (Oxford, 1989), p. 175.

36 Alexander Bogdanov, *Red Star* (Bloomington, IN, 1908), p. 29.

37 Ibid., p. 38.

38 H. G. Wells, *The First Men in the Moon* (London, 1901).

39 Robert M. Philmus and David Y. Hughes, eds, *H. G. Wells: Early Writings in Science and Science Fiction* (Los Angeles, CA, 1975), p. 230.

40 Eric Bunge, 'Jealousy: Modern Architecture and Flight', *Cabinet*, XI (Summer 2003), available at www.cabinetmagazine.org.

41 Peter Conrad, *Modern Times, Modern Places* (New York, 1999), p. 104.

42 El Lissitzky, 'The Reconstruction of Architecture in the Soviet Union (1929)', trans. Eric Dluhosch, in El Lissitzky, *Russia: An Architecture for World Revolution* (Cambridge, MA, 1970), p. 63.

43 Krutikov in Selim Omarovich Khan-Magomedov, *Georgii Krutikov: The Flying City and Beyond* [2005] (Barcelona, 2015), p. 85.

44 John Bowlt, 'Body Beautiful: The Artistic Search for the Perfect Physique', in *Laboratory of Dreams: The Russian Avant-garde and Cultural Experiment*, ed. John Bowlt and Olga Matich (Stanford, CA, 1996), p. 58.

45 Cited in Alla Vronskaya, 'Two Utopias of Georgii Krutikov's "The City of the Future"', in *Distance and Cities: Where Do We Stand?*, ed. Gunter Gassner, Adam Kaasa and Katherine Robinson (London, 2012), p. 48.

46 Selim Omarovich Khan-Magomedov, *Georgii Krutikov*, p. 47.

47 Ibid., p. 85.

48 Ibid., p. 66.

49 Ibid.

50 Michel de Certeau, *The Practice of Everyday Life*, trans. Steven Rendall (Berkeley, CA, 1984).

51 Ibid., p. 92.

52 Ibid.

53 Scott Bukatman, *Matters of Gravity* (Durham, NC, 2004), p. 49.

54 I am grateful to Martin Dodge, whose writings on helicopter urbanism in Manchester and Liverpool alerted me to René Ravo's illustrations. Martin Dodge and Martin Brook, 'Helicopter Dreaming: The Unrealised Plans for City Centre Heliports in the Post-war Period', http://personalpages.manchester.ac.uk/staff/m.dodge/Heliport_dreaming-wp.pdf, accessed 15 November 2016.

55 We might be inspired by early Danish cartoons showing British aerial progress, depicting the consequences of Blériot's crossing of the Channel in an aeroplane, and air show goers at Hendon, the north London suburb. In an edition of the magazine *Blæksprutten* in 1909, a cartoon captioned 'Crossing the Channel' showed human bodies in suspension in the air, presumably mid-leap, crossing the Channel, which has become a canal.

56 Ian Ellis, 'History of the Propeller Beanie and the Ultimate Propeller-head Geek', http://todayinsci.com, accessed 21 October 2016.

57 Neal Curtis, *Sovereignty and Superheroes* (Oxford, 2015), p. 155.

58 Derek Gregory, 'The Angel of Iraq', *Environment and Planning D: Society and Space*, XXII (2004), pp. 317–24.

59 Alan Moore and Dave Gibbons, *Watchmen*, 4 (Burbank, CA, 1986).

60 Jeffrey Kripal, *Mutants and Mystics: Science Fiction, Superhero Comics, and the Paranormal* (Chicago, IL, 2011).

61 Connor, 'Absolute Levity', p. 426.

62 Kathryn Hixson, 'Nauman: Good and Bad (1994)', in *Bruce Nauman*, ed. R. C. Morgan (Baltimore, MD, 2002), pp. 108–15.

6 Anti-gravity

1 Aaron Schuster, 'The Cosmonaut of the Erotic Future', *Cabinet*, XXXII (Winter 2008/9), www.cabinetmagazine.org.

2 Hito Steyerl, 'In Free-fall: A Thought Experiment on Vertical Perspective', *E-flux*, XXIV (April 2011) www.e-flux.com.

3 On Wolfe's other examination of a metaphorical vertical fall, see my exploration of his writing in relation to other literary excursuses on Manhattan excesses during the 1980s in Peter Adey, *Air* (London, 2014).

4 See important feminist explorations of early test flight, especially Didier DeLyser's produced film *Pancho Barnes and the Happy Bottom Riding Club*, dir. Nick Spark (2009), ASIN: B002NHX1YK.

5 Fritz Haber and Heinz Haber, 'Possible Methods for Producing Gravity-free State for Medical Research', *Journal of Aviation Medicine*, XXI/5 (1950), pp. 395–400.

6 Ibid.

7 Joe Kittinger and Craig Ryan, *Come Up and Get Me: An Autobiography of Colonel Joe Kittinger* (Albuquerque, NM, 2011).

8 Craig Ryan, *Sonic Wind: The Story of John Paul Stapp and How a Renegade Doctor Became the Fastest Man on Earth* (New York, 2015).

9 Department of the Air Force, *Animals in Rocket Flight* (1953), available at www.archive.org.

10 Tom Wolfe, *The Right Stuff* [1979] (New York, 2005), p. 259

11 Emmanuel Levinas, *Difficult Freedom: Essays on Judaisim* (Baltimore, MD, 1997).

12 Jacques Derrida and Geoffrey Bennington, *Jacques Derrida* (Chicago, IL, 1999), pp. 134–5.

13 Hannah Arendt, *The Human Condition*, 2nd edn (Chicago, IL, 2013), p. 1.

14 Howard Caygill, *Levinas and the Political* (London, 2013), p. 91.

15 Emmanuel Levinas, *Discovering Existence with Husserl*, trans. Richard A. Cohen and Michael B. Smith (Evanston, IL, 1998), p. 165.

16 Emmanuel Levinas, *Of God Who Comes to Mind*, trans. Bettina Bergo (Stanford, CA, 1998), p. 7.

17 Ibid., p. 8.
18 Scott Palmer, *Dictatorship of the Air* (Cambridge, 2006).
19 Paul Froese, 'Forced Secularization in Soviet Russia: Why an Atheistic Monopoly Failed', *Journal for the Scientific Study of Religion* (2004), pp. 35–50.
20 Walter Kolarz, *Religion in the Soviet Union* (New York, 1961), p. 20.
21 Hermann Potočnik, *The Problem of Space Travel: The Rocket Motor* [1928] (Washington, DC, 1995), p. 83.
22 Tom Jones, 'Lost in Space: Microgravity's Mysterious Side Effect: Stuff Disappears', *Air and Space Magazine* (September 2010), www.airspacemag.com.
23 C. M. Oman, I. P. Howard, T. Smith et al., 'The Role of Visual Cues in Microgravity Spatial Orientation', in *The Neurolab Spacelab Mission: Neuroscience Research in Space*, ed. Jay Buckey and Jerry Homick (Houston, TX, 2003), pp. 69–82.
24 Donald J. Kessler and Burton G. Cour Palais, 'Collision Frequency of Artificial Satellites: The Creation of a Debris Belt', *Journal of Geophysical Research*, LXXXIII/A6, (1978), pp. 2637–46.
25 'Religion and Space: A High Vantage Point', *The Economist: Erasmus Blog*, www.economist.com/blogs/erasmus, 22 July 2014.
26 Jed Mercurio, *Ascent* (London, 2007).
27 Ibid., p. 27.
28 For the detail on this rivalry, I am indebted to Stephen Petersen's excellent article on the topic, 'Innovation and the Rhetoric of Plagiarism: The Klein/Takis Rivalry', *Visual Resources: An International Journal of Documentation,* XVI/2 (2011), p. 156.
29 Cited in Thomas McEvilley, 'Yves Klein: Messenger of the Age of Space', in Thomas McEvilley, *The Triumph of Anti-art: Conceptual and Performance Art in the Formation of Post-modernism* (Kingston, NY, 2005), p. 55.
30 Sidra Stich, *Yves Klein* (New York 1994), p. 159.
31 Sarah Wilson, 'Voids, Palimpsests, Kitsch: Paris Before Klein', in *Voids/Vides* (Paris, 2009), pp. 192–7.
32 Cited in Stich, *Yves Klein*, p. 159.
33 Ibid., p. 160.
34 Cited in Nuit Banai, *Yves Klein* (London, 2014), p. 126.
35 Cited in McEvilley: 'Yves Klein: Messenger of the Age of Space', p. 69.
36 Ibid.
37 Christine Buci-Glucksmann, François Boissonnet, Jean-François Lyotard and Gilles Chatelet, 'L'atelier de Takis: Tous deux, l'artiste et le savant sont tellement proches', *Rue Descartes*, X (1994), pp. 155–67.
38 Eduardo Kac, 'Against Gravitropism: Art and the Joys of Levitation', in *I Levitate, What's Next*, ed. Aleksandra Kostić (Maribor, Slovenia, 2000), pp. 88–97.
39 Ibid.

40 Frank Pietronigro, 'Drift Painting in a Microgravity Environment and the Zero Gravity Arts Consortium', paper presented at the 7th Space and the Arts Workshop, 18–21 May 2004, co-organized by Leonardo/Olats, the IAA, the Ours Foundation and the European Space Research and Technology Centre (ESTEC), available at www.pietronigro.com, accessed March 2015.
41 Frank Pietronigro, 'How it Felt to Float Like an Angel: Expansion', at www.pietronigro.com, accessed March 2015.
42 Frank Pietronigro, 'Expanding the Heart: A 21st-century Artonaut Contemplates Spaceflight', *Journal of Space Philosophy*, II/1 (2013), pp. 1–12.
43 Ibid., p. 8.
44 Chris Hadfield, *An Astronaut's Guide to Life on Earth* (London, 2013), p. 260.
45 Joseph Gelmis, 'An Interview with Stanley Kubrick', in *The Film Director as Superstar* (New York, 1970), available at www.visual-memory.co.uk, accessed 21 October 2016.
46 G. F., 'How Does Copyright Work in Space?', *The Economist* (22 May 2013), www.economist.com/blogs/economist-explains.
47 Hadfield, *An Astronaut's Guide to Life on Earth*, p. 270.
48 Ibid., p. 272.
49 Boris Groys, *Ilya Kabakov: The Man Who Flew into Space from his Apartment* (London, 2006), p. 2.
50 Ibid., pp. 6–7.

7 Exorcize the Pentagon

1 It is actually a Marriott hotel in Los Angeles.
2 Scott Bukatman, *Matters of Gravity: Special Effects and Supermen in the 20th Century* (Durham, NC, 2003), p. 2.
3 Ibid.
4 Ibid.
5 Kathryn Hixson, 'Nauman: Good and Bad', in *Bruce Nauman*, ed. Robert C. Morgan (Baltimore, MD, 2002), p. 114.
6 Ibid.
7 'Invasions and Fakes: Susan Hiller in Conversation with Alexandra Kokoli', in *The Machine*, ed. Sas Mays and Neil Matheson (Manchester, 2013), p. 106.
8 Lewis Mumford, *The City in History: Its Origins, its Transformations, and its Prospects* (New York, 1997), p. 432.
9 Ibid.
10 Richard J. Honigman, 'Pentagon Rising', *Oracle*, I/10 (October 1967), p. 31.
11 Gerard DeGroot, *The Sixties Unplugged: A Kaleidoscopic History of a Disorderly Decade* (London, 2009), p. 380.

12 Paul Krassner, *Confessions of a Raving, Unconfined Nut: Misadventures in the Counterculture* (New York, 1993).

13 'The Quest for Spiritual Survival', *Life* (9 January 1970), p. 26.

14 Allen Cohen, 'The San Francisco Oracle: A Brief History', in *Insider Histories of the Vietnam Era Underground Press*, ed. Ken Wachsburger (East Lansing, MI, 2012), p. 167.

15 Ibid.

16 Steven Levine, 'Notes from the Genetic Journal', *Oracle*, I/10, n.p.

17 Allen Cohen, 'Returning from Mexico', *Oracle*, I/12 (1969).

18 Joseph P. Laycock, 'Levitating the Pentagon: Exorcism as Politics, Politics as Exorcism', *Implicit Religion*, XIV/3 (2011), p. 300.

19 Honigman, 'Pentagon Rising'.

20 Laycock, 'Levitating the Pentagon', pp. 300–301.

21 Harriet Hawkins, 'Levitated Mass', in *Global Undergrounds: Exploring Cities Within*, ed. Paul Dobraszczyk, Carlos López Galviz and Bradley L. Garrett (London, 2015).

22 David L. Ulin, 'Sidewalking Along the Miracle Mile', *Places Journal* (2015), https://placesjournal.org.

23 Ibid.

24 Miller quoted ibid.

25 Regis Perray, 'Ground', *Les mots propres* (2012), at www.regisperray.eu.

26 Jean-Marc Huitorel, 'On Earth as it Is in Heaven', trans. Tony Coates (2013), at www.regisperray.eu.

27 Allen Ginsberg, 'Renaissance or Die', *Oracle*, I/5, (1967), p. 21.

28 Alex Houen, '"Back! Back! Back! Central Mind-machine Pentagon . . .": Allen Ginsberg and the Vietnam War', *Cultural Politics*, IV/3 (2008), pp. 351–74.

29 The Allen Ginsberg Project, 'Spontaneous Poetics 96 – (Artaud 2)' (2013), http://ginsbergblog.blogspot.co.uk.

30 Cited in Houen, '"Back! Back! Back!"', p. 360.

31 Ibid., p. 363.

32 Keith Richards, *Life: Keith Richards* (London, 2010), p. 241.

33 Ronald E. Kisner, 'Earth, Wind and Fire', *Jet* (1978), p. 15.

34 Rickey Vincent, 'It's Elemental', *Vibe* (1999), p. 128.

35 Philip Bailey, Keith Zimmerman and Kent Zimmerman, *Shining Star: Braving the Elements of Earth, Wind and Fire* (Cambridge, 2014).

36 Norman Mailer, *The Armies of the Night: History as a Novel, the Novel as History* (New York, 1968), p. 133.

37 Ibid., p. 129.

38 Ibid., p. 121.

39 Ibid., p. 127.

40 Santanu Das, 'Reframing First World War Poetry: An Introduction',
    in *The Cambridge Companion to the Poetry of the First World War*,
    ed. Santanu Das (Cambridge, 2013), p. 16.
41 Vincent Sherry, 'First World War Poetry: A Cultural Landscape', ibid., p. 45.
42 Cited in Joseph P. Laycock, 'Levitating the Pentagon: Exorcism as Politics,
    Politics as Exorcism', *Implicit Religion,* XIV/3 (2011), pp. 295–318.
43 DeGroot, *The Sixties Unplugged*, p. 380.

8 Luftmenschen

1 Steven Levine, 'Lovebeast', *Oracle*, I/5 (1967).
2 Arie M. Dubnov, '"True Art Makes for the Integration of the Race": Israel Zangwill
   and the Varieties of the Jewish Normalization Discourse in Fin-de-siècle Britain',
   in *New Directions in Anglo-Jewish History*, ed. G. Alderman (Brighton, MA, 2010).
3 Sandor Gilman, *Jewish Self-hatred: Anti-Semitism and the Hidden Language of
   the Jews* (Baltimore, MD, 1992).
4 Sander L. Gilam, 'Anti-Semitism and the Body in Psychoanalysis', *Social
   Research*, LVII/4 (1990), p. 9.
5 Dubnov, '"True Art Makes for the Integration of the Race"', p. 101.
6 Ibid.
7 Przemysław Strożek, 'Footballers in Avant-garde Art and Socialist Realism',
   in *Handbuch der Sportgeschichte Osteuropas*, ed. Anke Hilbrenner, Ekaterina
   Emeliantseva, Christian Koller, Manfred Zeller and Stefan Zwicker (Bonn, 2015),
   available at www.ios-regensburg.de.
8 Ibid.
9 Maria Tsantsanoglou, 'The Soviet Icarus: From the Dream of Free Flight to the
   Nightmare of Free Fall', in *Utopian Reality*, ed. Christina Lodder, Maria Kokkori
   and Maria Mileeva (Leiden, 2013), pp. 43–56.
10 Benjamin Harshav, *The Polyphony of Jewish Culture* (Stanford, CA, 2007),
    pp. 218–20.
11 Iakov Tugendhol'd, 'The Artist Marc Chagall', in *Marc Chagall and the Jewish
    Theater*, ed. Benjamin Harshav (New York, 1992), p. 141.
12 Ibid., p. 142.
13 Iris Bruce, 'Kafka and Jewish Folklore', in *The Cambridge Companion to Kafka*,
    ed. Julian Preece (Cambridge, 2002), pp. 150–69.
14 Ibid., p. 325.
15 Ibid., p. 327.
16 Ibid
17 Franz Kafka, *The Complete Stories* (New York, 1971), p. 335.
18 Weizmann cited in in Morris Rothenberg, *Trial and Error: The Autobiography of
    Chaim Weizmann* (New York, 1949), p. 493.

19 Max Nordau, *Degeneration*, trans. from 2nd German edn (London, 1895), p. 118.

20 Ibid., p. 111.

21 Dan Miron, 'The Literary Image of the Shtetl', *Danish Jewish Studies*, I/3 (1995), p. 21.

22 Brian Swann, 'The Luftmensch', *Minnesota Review*, VIII/2 (1977), p. 16.

23 Ber Borochov, *Class Struggle and the Jewish Nation: Selected Essays in Marxist Zionism* (London, 1984), p. 170.

24 Arial Bubinstein, *Economic Fables* (New York, 2012), p. 177.

25 Boaz Neumann, *Land and Desire in Early Zionism* (Lebanon, NH, 2011) p. 116.

26 Ibid., p. 16.

27 Ibid., p. 75.

28 Salvador Dalí, *The Secret Life of Salvador Dalí* (New York, 1942), pp. 183–4.

29 Ibid., p. 15.

30 Ibid.

31 Gay Breyley, '"Kissing the Noose of Australian Democracy": Misplaced Faiths and Displaced Lives Converse over Australia's Rising Fences', *borderlands e-journal*, II/3 (2003), www.borderlands.net.au.

32 Ibid.

33 Auber O. Neville, *Australia's Coloured Minority: Its Place in the Community* (Sydney, 1947), p. 57.

34 See Alison Ravenscroft, *The Postcolonial Eye: White Australian Desire and the Visual Field of Race* (Aldershot, 2013), p. 149.

35 Lisa Scott, *Benang* (Fremantle, 1999), p. 11.

36 Ibid., p. 12.

37 Ibid., p. 13.

38 Ibid.

39 Cited in Lisa Slater, 'Kim Scott's *Benang*: An Ethics of Uncertainty', *Journal of the Association for the Study of Australian Literature*, IV (2005), p. 146.

40 Ibid., p. 150.

41 Kei Miller, *Augustown* (London, 2016).

42 Roxanne Watson, 'The Native Baptist Church's Political Role in Jamaica: Alexander Bedward's Trial for Sedition', *Journal of Caribbean History*, XLII/2 (2008), p. 231.

43 Cynthia Ozick, *Levitation: Five Fictions* (New York, 1982), p. 16.

44 Lawrence van Gelder, 'What has 4 Legs, 42 Balloons and Flies?', *New York Times* (15 August 2001), p. E1.

45 V.A.C. Gattrell, *The Hanging Tree: Execution and the English People, 1770–1868* (Oxford, 1996), p. 605.

Acknowledgements

I'm especially grateful to a period of leave spent at the Institute for Advanced Studies at Durham University, where I stayed as a fellow for their 'light' theme in the spring of 2014, and to Trevelyan College for putting me up. The fellowship, combined with the time and financial support of a Philip Leverhulme Prize, proved invaluable. To Veronica Strang, as director of the Institute, Martyn Evans, Principal of Trevelyan College, and to the administrators Linda and Audrey: a huge thank you. The dynamic of the group of fellows there was particularly inspiring and special thanks must go to Julie Westerman, with whom I collaborated on a levitation photographic project, Ulisses Barres de Almeida, Lesley Chamberlain, Jill Clarke, Tim Edensor, Peter Gratton, Norman Kleiman and Brad Tebo. I doubt there are many other places in the world where this kind of community can be supported, and I gained so much from having the time to read, think and discuss ideas there. I talked with the always inspiring Durham and Newcastle academics, including Ben Anderson, Rachel Colls, Martin Coward, Steve Graham, Angharad Closs Stephens, Noam Leshem and Phil Steinberg, and was elevated by the place and surroundings of Durham Cathedral, Lindisfarne and the Northumberland landscape.

As always, Royal Holloway has been a brilliant home for developing this project, although at times I've kept it quiet! Klaus Dodds, Harriet Hawkins, Rachael Squire and Pip Thornton provided comments on various parts of the manuscript. Barry Langford made very helpful film recommendations, as did Jeremy Crampton, and I learned a lot when I presented some of these ideas at the conference 'Power and Space in the Drone Age' at Université de Neuchâtel organized by Francisco Klauser in 2015.

Photo Acknowledgements

The author and publishers wish to express their thanks to the below sources of illustrative material and/or permission to reproduce it:

Anonymous, *The Unmasking of Robert-Houdin* (New York, 1908): p. 58; photos author: p. 216; photos Leo Bourdreau: pp. 168, 169; photos British Library: pp. 64, 68; © Remedios Varo, DACS/VEGAP 2016: pp. 132, 133; Luis Figuier, *Les Mystères de la science* (Paris, 1880): p. 109; © FOTO: FORTEPAN: p. 163; *Psychical Review*, vol. II (London, 1893–4): p. 99; © Philippe Halsman/Magnum Photos: p. 256; © Nelly Ben Hayoun: p. 211; Thomas Hobbes, *Leviathan* (London, 1651): p. 26; photos Elissa Malcohn: p. 161; photos Metropolitan Museum of Art: pp. 34, 37, 47; © Peter Milton: p. 148; photos MIT Museum Collection, Cambridge, MA: p. 203; Thomas Nachlik and Rich Johnston, *The Flying Friar* (London, 2006): p. 173; photos NASA: pp. 190, 196, 197, 199; photos National Library of Congress, Washington, DC: pp. 51, 73 (left and right), 80, 82, 229; © Roberto Nieto: p. 163; photos Musée d'Orsay, Paris: p. 79; Frank R. Paul, *Amazing Stories* (New York, 1928): p. 174; © Régis Perray: p. 233; Herman Potočnik, *Das Problem der Befahrung des Weltraums – der Raketen-motor* (Berlin, 1929): p. 198; photos Prado Museum, Madrid: p. 36; John Quincy, *Medica Static* (London, 1718): p. 48; Reale Accademia Ercolanese di Archeologia, *Le Antichità di Ercolano* (Naples, 1757–92): p. 14; © The Royal National Theatre, London: p. 85; photos Saatchi Gallery, London: p. 88; Chagall ®/© ADAGP, Paris and DACS, London 2016: p. 247; © The Science Museum, London: p. 105; © Melvin Sokolsky: p. 144; © Mungo Thompson: p. 234 (top and bottom); © Trustees of the British Museum, London: p. 121; © Victoria and Albert Museum, London: pp. 27, 66, 78, 146, 150; photos The Walters Art Gallery, Baltimore, MD: p. 23; photos Wellcome Library, London: p. 41; George Wither, *A Collection of Emblems* (London, 1635): p. 53; photos The Wolfsonian–Florida International University, Miami Beach, FL: p. 161.

Index

2001: A Space Odyssey (film) 119,
198–200, 209–10

Aborigines 258–60
aerial cities 50, 159–73
Akindinov, Alexey, *Gagarin's Breakfast
193*
Aladdin (film) 153
Alexander the Great 22, 163
Amrany, Omri, and Julie Rotblatt-
Amrany, *The Spirit 157*
animal levitation 46, 60, 188–9, 248–50
Aquinas, Thomas 34, 42
Arendt, Hannah 191
Aristotle 12
Artaud, Antonin 137–40, 143, 235
Atherton, John, *New York World's Fair
1939 161*
Aurelius, Marcus 17
Auster, Paul, *Mr Vertigo* (book) 81

ballet 147–52
ballooning 51–4, 63–4, 81–6, 94, 193,
262–3
Barrie, J. M., *Peter Pan* (book) 152
Beardsley, Aubrey 77–8
The Climax 78

Bedknobs and Broomsticks (film) 43
Berruguete, Pedro, *St Dominic and the
Albigensians 36*
birth 150–51
and levitation 16–17, 28–9, 151–2,
209
Blanchard, Sophie (balloonist) 81–2
Blavatsky, Helena 88–90, 122, 131
Bohm, David J. 104
Bosse, Abraham, *Frontspiece for
Leviathan 26*
Bowie, David 209–10
Brailes, William de, *The Ascension 23*
Brazil (film) 112–15, 140
broomsticks 41, 43
bubbles 77, 142–5
Buffy the Vampire Slayer (TV series)
129–31
Burges, William, *St Simeon Stylites 27*

Carrington, Hereward 92–3, 98
Carrington, Leonora 131, 135–7, 142
Certeau, Michel de 172–3
Chagall, Marc 170, 244–8
The Stroll 248–9
Christianity 16, 18–21, 35, 84, 138–40, 226,
252, 261

God 17–19, 22, 25, 38–9, 46, 51, 81, 139, 192–3
heavens, the 11–13, 19–23, 28, 31, 50–53, 64, 139–40, 193
Jesus 13, 21–3
Chronicle (film) 182–4
cinema 75–80, 81, 142
Cirque du Soleil 86
clouds 38, 41–2, 114, 147, 156, 217–19
Cohen, Allen 222, 225–7
Cold War, the 186–215, 235
Collins, Wilkie, *The Moonstone* (book) 57
Copperfield, David (magician) 75, 236
Crystal Palace 65, 111

Dalí, Salvador 140–43, 255–8
Darget, Louis 96
death 263–4
Delrio, Martin (theologian) 40–43
Derrida, Jacques 191
Devéria, Achille, *Marie Taglioni / (Sylphide) 146*
Deyneka, Aleksandr, *The Football Player* 245–6
Diogenes 22, 163
Du Maurier, George, *Trilby* (book) 72, 75
Dune (film) 142, 220
Dynamo (magician) 75

Ebbsfleet stone 21
Enfield poltergeist 106–9
Enlightenment, the 12, 50, 54, 152, 159
exceptional powers 28–9
Eyes Wide Shut (film) 44

fairy tales 82–6, 130, 131
fakir, the 56–62, 67–9, 72
Fatboy Slim 219–20
Figuier, Louis, *Les Mystères de la science 109*

Flammarion, Camille 94
flying carpet 24–5, 56–7, 118–20, 152–4, 213
footballers 245–6
Freud, Sigmund 119–20, 126, 131, 151
funambulism (tightrope walking) 14–17, 101, 217–20
Futurism 9, 140, 171
    see also Italian Futurists

Gagarin, Yuri 191–2, 200–201, 204, 205, 208, 214, 239, 245
Geller, Uri 104
gender politics 40–45, 49–50, 85–6, 91–7, 123–4, 129–31, 141–5, 148–9, 185, 227
in photography 262–4
in Surrealism 131–42
Ghostbusters (film) 123–4
Gothic architecture 15, 111
Gravity (film) 194–5, 197–8
Great Exhibition (1854) 62, 64, 65, 115
Green, Valentine, *A Representation of Mr Lunardi's Balloon as Exhibited in the Pantheon, 1784 64*
Guppy, Agnes 65, 91–4

Halsman, Philippe, *Robert Oppenheimer 256–7*
Hasted, J. B. 104–9
health 13, 11
Heizer, Michael 228, 230–33
    Levitated Mass 229
helicopters 175–7, 237–8
Herrmann, Alexander 72–3, 76
Hobbes, Thomas, *Leviathan* (book) 25–6, 139
Holocaust, the 101, 244, 253, 261
home improvement 125–6
Houdini, Harry 58, 60, 69–75, 76
hoverboard 217, 218

Hugo (film) 70–71
hypnosis 55, 61, 69–76

India 89, 102, 111, 128–9
Institut Général Psychologique 92
Inuit communities 10
Islam 57
    folklore 45
    Muhammad 18, 19, 164
    Quran, the 23–4
Israel 250, 253
    magicians 55–62, 80
Italian Futurists 9

jaduwallah 57–8, 60–61
Jamaica 260–61
Jordan, Michael 157–9
Judaism 203, 243–65
Jung, Carl 35, 109, 126–7, 131, 154, 240

Kabakov 213–15, 261–2
Kafka, Franz 121–3
Kármán Line, The (film) 44
Kellar, Harry 81, 90
Koestler, Authur 100–105, 118
Krutikov, Georgii 170–72
Kundera, Milan, *The Unbearable Lightness of Being* (book) 44, 123

laboratories 98–100, 187
language and levitation 246–8, 253–4
Laputa: Castles in the Sky (film) 165
Likhanov, Albert, *Syn Rossii* (book) 200
Lock, Melchior 120
    Tortoise and Separate View of a Walled, Coastal Town in the Veneto 121

Macdonald, George, 'The Light Princess' 83, 86, 152
Macuga, Goshka, *Madame Blavatsky 88*

magic 12, 24, 40, 43–4, 55–7, 60–61, 68, 70–81, 104, 118, 120, 131, 137, 153–7, 263
magnetism 8, 24–5, 54, 89, 93, 163–5, 171, 182, 185, 202–5
    maglev technology 8
Malevich, Kazimir 169–70, 245, 215
Man on Wire (film) 217–19
many universe theory 106
Mary Poppins (books and film) 154–6
Méliès, George 71, 75–8, 80, 143
Mercury Project 189–91
Mexico 131, 134–40, 226–7
Milan Commission, the 98–100
Milton, Peter, *Points of Departure ı: Mary's Turn 148*
Monti, Raffaele 64–7, 115
Moreau, Gustave, *The Apparition 79*
mountains 18, 19, 25, 29, 45, 104, 122, 127–9, 138, 141, 163
    Mount Everest 127–9
Muybridge, Eadweard 80

Nancy, Jean-Luc 25, 28–9
National Geographic 7
Natural Law Party 117–18
Nauman, Bruce 220–21
    Failing to Levitate in the Studio 184
Neoplatonism 12, 13, 18, 35, 67, 81, 84, 138, 203–5
Nesbit, Edith, *The Phoenix and the Carpet* (book) 152–4
New York World's Fair (1939) 159–61, 175
Newton, Isaac 11, 50–51
Nietzsche, Friedrich 243
Nijinsky, Vaslav 150–51
nuclear mysticism 140–42

ontology 11
oppositional forces 11–13, 39, 50, 187

Oracle (magazine) 222–3, 225–7, 235, 243
Orwell, George 100–102
Owen, Wilfred 239–40
Özdamar, Emine Sevgi, *Life is a Caravanserai* (book) *45–6*
Ozick, Cynthia, 'Levitation' 11

Palladino, Eusapia 91–100, 109, 251
Paolo, Giovanni di, *St Catherine of Siena 37*
Paul, Jean 29–31, 152
Pentagon, the 221–4, 227–8, 223–41
Perray, Régis, *6th Day of Displacement* 233
Petit, Philippe 217–20
    see also *Man on Wire* (film)
photography 62, 63, 80, 92, 94, 95–100, 107, 142, 145, 149, 177, 185, 204–6, 221, 241, 245, 255–7, 262–4
    Boston, Bernie 241
    Halsman, Philippe 255–7
    Hiller, Susan 221
    jump photography 255–8
    Käsebier, Gertrude 149
    Klein, Yves 202–6
    Lissitzky, El 245
    Photoshop 262–4
    Sarenac, Mina 262
    Sokolsky, Melvin 142–35
    Taylor-Johnson, Sam 263–4
Plato 11
Potočnik Herman 194–5, 198–200, 207, 213, 215
Prague 121–2
Pretor-Pinney, Gavin, *Cloudspotters' Guide* (book) *38*
Price, Harry 61, 94
quantum physics 106

Rados, Luigi, *Sophie Blanchard in Milan 82*

raising 221–4, 228–42
rhythm 236–7
Robert-Houdin, Jean-Eugène 58, 69–72, 76, 159
Roman religion 16, 129
Róna, Jaroslav, *Franz Kafka 123*
rope tricks 60–62, 69
Rowling, J. K., *Harry Potter 43*
Royal Panopticon of Science and Art 62–7
Rushdie, Salman, *The Satanic Verses* (book) 128–9

saints
    St Augustine 15–17, 29, 35
    St Catherine of Siena 35, 36–8
    St Dominic of Osma 35–6
    St Joseph of Cupertino 32, 33, 39, 45–6, 173
    St Teresa of Âvila 35, 38, 40, 141, 218
    see also Christianity
Santa Clause: The Movie (film) 156–7, 159
Sassetta, Il, *The Blessed Ranieri Rasini Freeing Poor People from Prison in Florence 136*
Schmitt, Carl 25, 28
Schongauer, Martin, *The Temptation of St Anthony 34*
science fiction 99, 161, 165, 171, 175–8, 225
Science Museum, London 105
Scott, Kim, *Benang* (book) 258–60
séance 88, 90, 92, 94–6
shamanic practices 10, 40, 156, 222, 227
sleep
    dreams 114–15, 119–25, 142–5, 151, 225
    nightmares 126–35
Society for Psychical Research 92, 104, 110

soil 250–54
Sokolsky, Melvin 142–4
    'Over New York' *144*
sovereignty 18–31, 52–4
space travel 186–215
    International Space Orchestra 211
    International Space Station 195, 196,
    209–12
    space copyright 211–12
    space debris 198
    Sputnik 189, 191
Sparked (film) 86
*Star Wars: Episode v – The Empire
    Strikes Back* (film) 162
Steiner, Rudolf 142–5
Sufism 90
superheroes 119, 158, 159, 172–82
    Doctor Manhattan 180–82
    Man of Steel (film) 177–8
    Magneto 178–80, 182
    Superman 161, 176–80
Suprematist art 169
Surrealism 131–42
Swift, Jonathan, *Gulliver's Travels* (book)
    163–5
Sylvester, Alfred 61–9

Takis, *Electro-magnetic i 203*
Tennyson, Alfred 27–8
Teorema (film) 45
Times of India 61
theosophy 60, 89–90, 93, 122, 131
Thomson, Mungo
    Levitating Mass 234
    Levitating Pentagon 234
Thousand and One Nights 24, 56, 120
Tibet 103, 129, 138, 225
Tissandier, Albert, *Ascension du 26
    Septembre 51*
transcendental meditation 111, 115–19

Urquhart, Jane, *Changing Heaven*
    (book) 82–6

Varo, Remedios 131–6, 142
    Bankers in Action 132
    Capillary Locomotion 133

Wallace, Alfred Russel 92, 94, 109
Walters, Larry 262
Watchmen (film) 241
weighing scales 28–9, 64, 99, 103–9
Weizmann, Chaim 250–51
Wells, Herbert George 241
Wilde, Oscar, *Salome* (play) 77–8
Wilson, Maurice 128–9
witchcraft 40–45, 91, 107
Woolf, Tom, *The Right Stuff* (book) 186

Yeager, Chuck 187, 189
yoga 90, 102

Zedong, Mao 30
Zionism 248–9